Microsoft® Windows
Multimedia
Programmer's Workbook

Written, edited, and produced by
Microsoft Corporation

Distributed by Microsoft Press

MICROSOFT®
WINDOWS™

PROGRAMMER'S
REFERENCE
LIBRARY

PUBLISHED BY
Microsoft Press
A Division of Microsoft Corporation
One Microsoft Way, Redmond, Washington 98052-6399

Library of Congress Cataloging-in-Publication Data

Microsoft Windows multimedia programmer's workbook / Microsoft
    Corporation.
        p.   cm. -- (Microsoft Windows multimedia programmer's
    reference library)
      Includes index.
      ISBN 1-55615-390-2
      1. Computer animation.   2. Computer sound processing.
    3. Microsoft Windows (Computer program)   I. Microsoft.   II. Series.
    TR897.5.M536 1991
    006.6'76 -- dc20   91-13144
                                                  CIP

Printed and bound in the United States of America.

  2 3 4 5 6 7 8 9 MLML 6 5 4 3 2

Distributed to the book trade in Canada by Macmillan of Canada, a division of Canada Publishing Corporation.

Distributed to the book trade outside the United States and Canada by Penguin Books Ltd.

Penguin Books Ltd., Harmondsworth, Middlesex, England
Penguin Books Australia Ltd., Ringwood, Victoria, Australia
Penguin Books N.Z. Ltd., 182-190 Wairau Road, Auckland 10, New Zealand

British Cataloging-in-Publication Data available.

Document Number: MM20348-0691

Contents

Chapter 1   Introduction to Windows with Multimedia

Chapter 2   The Media Control Interface (MCI)

Chapter 3　Introduction to Audio

Chapter 4　High-Level Audio Services

Chapter 5   Low-Level Audio Services

Chapter 6   The Multimedia Movie Player

Chapter 7   Using the Movie Player Functions

Chapter 8   Special Video Topics

Chapter 9   Timer and Joystick Services

Chapter 10   Multimedia File I/O Services

Appendix Writing Screen Savers

Glossary

Index

About This Workbook

This workbook contains information you can use to write applications for Microsoft® Windows™ graphical environment with Multimedia Extensions 1.0, or Windows with Multimedia. It describes the architecture of Windows with Multimedia, as well as the different functions for creating applications that use multimedia features.

This introduction contains background information you should review, including the following:

- The basics you should already know about writing Windows applications

- The organization of this workbook

- A description of the sample applications provided with the Multimedia Development Kit (MDK)

- Typographical and notational conventions used in this workbook

- A description of the other documentation provided with the MDK

What You Should Know

This workbook assumes you are familiar with writing applications for Microsoft Windows, version 3.0 or later, using the C programming language. For more information on programming for Windows, see the *Guide to Programming* (provided with the Microsoft Windows Software Development Kit) or one of the books listed in the section "Further Information," at the end of this introduction.

Some chapters in this workbook assume additional knowledge on your part. The introductions to these chapters list these assumptions.

Contents of this Workbook

This workbook provides information that experienced Windows 3.0 programmers can use to include multimedia features in their applications. The workbook includes the following information:

- Chapter 1 introduces the development environment for writing multimedia applications.

- Chapter 2 describes the Media Control Interface (MCI). MCI is an extensible software interface that provides high-level, device-independent capabilities for controlling media such as audio and animation resources, audio/visual peripherals, and external devices like videodisc players.

- Chapters 3 through 5 describe the audio functions of the Multimedia extensions, including waveform audio, MIDI, and compact-disc audio.

- Chapters 6 and 7 describe the animation functions of the Multimedia extensions.

- Chapter 8 describes the enhanced multimedia video services. Chapter 9 describes high-resolution timer services and joystick input services.

- Chapter 10 describes the multimedia file I/O services.

- The Appendix describes how to write screen savers for Windows with Multimedia. The Glossary defines terms used in this workbook and in the *Programmer's Reference*.

You should read Chapters 1 and 2 for a general overview of the Multimedia extensions. After reading these chapters, refer to those chapters that discuss the particular multimedia features you want to include in your applications.

Sample Applications

Each chapter includes sample C code illustrating important concepts discussed in the chapter. The Multimedia Development Kit also includes, on disc, complete program examples that illustrate the use of the Multimedia extensions. The Setup program (described in *Getting Started*) installs these sample programs on your system. Compile and run these examples to see how the functions work in actual programs, or use the examples as the basis for writing your own multimedia applications.

The following table lists the sample applications provided with the MDK. Each program is installed in a subdirectory of the \MWINDEV\MMSAMPLE directory (note that the subdirectory names match the program names).

Program	Function	Demonstrates
BOUNCER	Screen saver for Windows with Multimedia	Screen-saver functions, high-level sound playback
JOYTOY	Joystick toy shoots holes in your desktop	Joystick functions, high-level sound playback
LOWPASS	Low-pass filter for waveform-audio files	Multimedia file I/O functions
MCITEST	Interactively sends command strings to MCI devices	MCI command-string interface
MIDIMON	Displays a textual listing of MIDI input messages	MIDI recording functions, low-level callback functions
MMPLAY	Plays multimedia movies	Multimedia animation functions
REVERSE	Plays a waveform-audio file in reverse	Multimedia file I/O functions, waveform-audio functions

Document Conventions

The following document conventions are used throughout this workbook:

Type Style	Used For
bold	A specific term intended to be used literally; for example, language key words, function names, and macro names. You must type these terms exactly as shown.
italic	Placeholders for information you must provide. For example, the following syntax for the **sndPlaySound** function indicates you must substitute values for the *lpszSound* and *wFlags* parameters, separated by a comma: **WORD sndPlaySound**(*lpszSound, wFlags*) Italic is also used for terms defined in text and the Glossary.
ALL CAPITALS	Directory names, filenames, and acronyms.
`Monospace`	Code examples.
Vertical ellipsis . . .	Indicates a portion of the program is omitted in a program example.
Horizontal ellipsis ...	For a given function, there are several functions that have the same form but different prefixes; for example, **...GetNumDevs** substitutes for the **auxGetNumDevs**, **midiInGetNumDevs**, **midiOutGetNumDevs**, **waveInGetNumDevs**, and **waveOutGetNumDevs** functions, all of which have similar syntax and functionality. Also indicates a single statement is omitted in a program example.

Other MDK Manuals

This workbook explains how to use the functions, messages, and data structures of the Multimedia extensions. Other MDK documentation describes additional aspects of multimedia software development. The MDK includes the following manuals:

- The *Getting Started* guide is intended for both multimedia application programmers and multimedia authors. It describes the MDK and other software required to develop multimedia applications. It also explains how to install the MDK software.

- The *Programmer's Reference* is a definitive summary of the application programming interface (API) for the Multimedia extensions. It describes the functions, messages, data structures, file formats, and commands within the extensions. You can use the Setup program to install an online version of the *Programmer's Reference*.

- The *Data Preparation Tools User's Guide* describes the data-preparation tools provided with the MDK. These tools allow authors to edit media elements, such as bitmaps and waveforms, and to convert data files.

- The *Multimedia Authoring Guide* describes the authoring process for multimedia titles. It describes how to acquire and prepare data for multimedia titles.

- The *Multimedia Viewer Developer's Guide* describes how to build titles for the Multimedia Viewer software.

Unless otherwise noted, the manuals cross-referenced in this workbook are those included in the MDK.

Further Reading

For additional information on programming with Windows, see the following books:

Petzold, Charles. *Programming Windows*, Second Edition. Redmond: Microsoft Press, 1990.

Norton, Peter and Paul L. Yao. *Peter Norton's Windows 3.0 Power Programming Techniques*. New York: Bantam Books, 1990.

Chapter 1
Introduction to Windows with Multimedia

Windows with Multimedia is a superset of the Windows 3.0 programming environment. The Multimedia extensions provide application developers with high-level and low-level services for developing multimedia applications using the extended capabilities of a multimedia personal computer.

This chapter covers the following topics:

- An introduction to the features of Windows with Multimedia

- The architecture of Windows with Multimedia

- The design philosophy and implementation of the Multimedia extensions

- Basic information about developing and debugging applications using the Multimedia extensions

Before reading this chapter, you should install Windows with Multimedia, the Microsoft Windows 3.0 Software Development Kit, and the Microsoft Windows Multimedia Development Kit on your computer. See the *Getting Started* manual for installation instructions.

About Windows with Multimedia

Windows with Multimedia consists of Windows 3.0 plus the Multimedia extensions. The Multimedia extensions enhance Windows 3.0 by providing the following services for multimedia applications:

- A Media Control Interface (MCI) for controlling media devices.

  - Extensible string-based and message-based interfaces for communicating with MCI device drivers.

  - MCI device drivers for playing and recording waveform audio, playing MIDI (Musical Instrument Digital Interface) files, playing compact disc audio from a CD-ROM disc drive, and controlling Pioneer videodisc players.

- Low-level API support for multimedia-related services.

  - Low-level support for playing and recording audio with waveform and MIDI audio devices.

  - Low-level support for getting input from analog joysticks, and for precision timer services.

- Multimedia file I/O services providing buffered and unbuffered file I/O, and support for standard IBM/Microsoft Resource Interchange File Format (RIFF) files. The services are extensible with custom I/O procedures that can be shared among applications.

- Device drivers designed for multimedia applications.

  - Enhanced high-resolution video display drivers for Video 7 and Paradise VGA cards providing 256 colors, improved performance, and new features.

  - A high-resolution VGA video display driver that displays color bitmaps as gray-scale images. The driver supports 16 shades of gray.

  - A high-resolution VGA video display driver that allows the use of a custom 16-color palette as well as the standard palatte.

  - A low-resolution VGA video display driver that provides 320-by-200 resolution with 256 colors.

  - A device driver providing support for drawing to and manipulating in-memory DIBs with Windows GDI functions.

- Control Panel applets that let users change display drivers, set up a screen saver, install multimedia device drivers, assign waveform sounds to system alerts, configure the MIDI Mapper, and calibrate joysticks.

- A MIDI Mapper supporting standard MIDI patch services. This allows MIDI files to be authored independently of end-user MIDI synthesizer setups.

Architecture of the Multimedia Extensions

Although the Multimedia extensions are made up of a number of files, the architecture can be viewed as consisting of just a few software modules. Any one of these modules can be represented by a single file, or by a collection of files. The following illustration shows the relationship between Windows and modules of the Multimedia extensions.

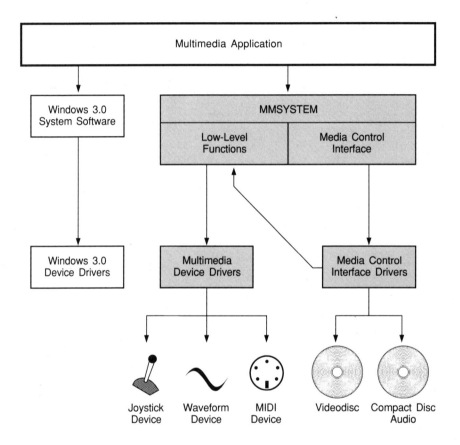

The relationship between Windows and the Multimedia extensions.

This illustration is a simplified view of the relationship between Windows 3.0 and the Multimedia extensions. The connections between modules indicate control flow. The dependencies on Windows 3.0 are not shown—almost every module of the Multimedia extensions uses Windows system software.

The following software modules make up the Multimedia extensions:

- The MMSYSTEM library providing the Media Control Interface services and low-level multimedia support functions.

- Multimedia device drivers providing communication between the low-level MMSYSTEM functions and multimedia devices such as waveform, MIDI, joystick, and timer hardware.

- Drivers for the Media Control Interface providing high-level control of media devices.

Multimedia Extensions Design Philosophy

The architecture of the Multimedia extensions is designed around the concepts of *extensibility* and *device-independence*. Extensibility allows the software architecture to easily accommodate advances in technology without changes to the architecture itself. Device-independence allows multimedia applications to be easily developed that will run on a wide range of hardware providing different levels of multimedia support.

Three design elements of the system software provide extensibility and device-independence:

- A translation layer (MMSYSTEM) that isolates applications from device drivers and centralizes device-independent code.

- Run-time linking that allows the MMSYSTEM translation layer to link to the drivers it needs.

- A well-defined and consistent driver interface that minimizes special-case code and makes the installation and upgrade process easier.

In the following illustration, you can see how the translation layer translates a Multimedia extensions function call into a call to an audio device driver.

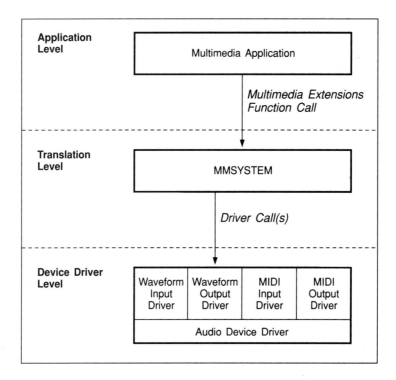

Relationship between an application and multimedia device drivers.

Some function calls might result in multiple driver calls, or they might be handled by MMSYSTEM without causing any driver calls.

Building a Multimedia Application

Before beginning to write your multimedia application, you must be familiar with programming in the Windows 3.0 environment. Then you can take advantage of the multimedia capabilities offered by the Multimedia extensions.

Including Header Files

When using the Multimedia extensions, you must include one or more of the following header files in all source modules that call a Multimedia extensions function. These header files depend on declarations made in the WINDOWS.H header file. If you include any of the following header files, you must first include WINDOWS.H:

- MMSYSTEM.H (for system functions)

- MMP.H (for movie-playback functions)

The header files provide function prototypes as well as definitions of data types and constants.

Linking with Multimedia Libraries

You must also link to at least one of the following import libraries when linking an application that uses Multimedia extension functions:

- MMSYSTEM.LIB (for system functions)

- MMP.LIB (for movie-playback functions)

Debugging a Multimedia Application

The Multimedia Development Kit includes the following services and tools to aid in debugging applications that use the Multimedia extensions:

- A debugging version of the Multimedia Extensions 1.0 software that displays commands sent to MCI and performs error checking unavailable in the retail version.

- A Multimedia extensions function, **OutputDebugStr** that can send messages to a debugging monitor.

These services supplement the debugging services and tools provided with the Windows Software Development Kit. See the *Tools* manual provided with the Windows SDK for information about using the SDK debugging tools.

The Debugging Version of the Multimedia Extensions

The Multimedia Development Kit provides both retail and debugging versions of the Multimedia extensions. The debugging version provides the following services:

- Detects invalid waveform and MIDI device handles.

- Displays a string representation of commands sent to MCI.

- Contains symbolic information that can be used with Microsoft CodeView for Windows (**CVW**) and the Microsoft Windows 80386 Debugger (**WDEB386**).

If the debugging version detects an invalid waveform or MIDI device handle, it reports the error on the debugging monitor and calls the **FatalExit** function with an exit code of 0x1000. If the error occurs while you are running **CVW**, the fatal exit is reported in the **CVW** command window. If the error occurs while you are running **WDEB386**, the fatal exit is reported on the debugging monitor. In either case, the debugger (**CVW** or **WDEB386**) prompts with an "Abort, Break, or Ignore" message allowing you to terminate Windows, enter the debugger, or continue from the point of the fatal exit. See the chapters on **CVW** and **WDEB386** in the Windows SDK *Tools* manual for more information on debugging fatal exits.

The debugging version displays commands sent to MCI on the debugging monitor. All commands, whether sent with command strings or with command messages, are displayed in command-string format. See the *Programmer's Reference* for information on MCI command strings. The MCI debugging output can be disabled—for more information, see "Controlling Debugging Output," later in this chapter.

The debugging version includes symbolic information not provided in the retail version. This information makes it easier to determine the cause of certain errors such as general protection (GP) faults. If you're using the debugging version with **CVW** or **WDEB386**, you can determine what part of the Multimedia extensions code was executing when a failure occured. See the Windows SDK *Tools* manual for information on using **CVW** and **WDEB386**.

Installing the Debugging Version of the Multimedia Extensions

The MDK includes two batch files to switch between the retail and debugging versions of the Multimedia extensions:

Batch File	Description
MMN2D.BAT	Installs the debugging version.
MMD2N.BAT	Installs the retail version.

Note The batch files MMN2D.BAT and MMD2N.BAT install the debugging and retail versions of Windows as well as the Multimedia extensions.

The OutputDebugStr Function

The **OutputDebugStr** function is similar to the **OutputDebugString** function provided by Windows, with the addition of the following enhancements:

- You can call **OutputDebugStr** at interrupt time, so you can use it in low-level callback functions.

- You can control the destination of output from **OutputDebugStr** with entries in the SYSTEM.INI file. You can turn the output off, or direct it to either the COM1 port or to a secondary monochrome display adapter.

Note Output from **OutputDebugStr** is available only in the debugging version of the Multimedia extensions. You don't need remove calls to **OutputDebugStr** from your application to run with the retail version of the Multimedia extensions.

Controlling Debugging Output

To control the MCI debugging output and the output from **OutputDebugStr**, set the MCI and DebugOutput keynames in the [mmsystem] section of SYSTEM.INI to the values shown in the following table:

Setting	Description
DebugOutput=0	**OutputDebugStr** and MCI debugging output is not displayed.
DebugOutput=1	**OutputDebugStr** and MCI debugging output is sent to the COM1 port.
DebugOutput=2	**OutputDebugStr** and MCI debugging output is sent to a secondary monochrome display adapter.
MCI=0	MCI debugging output is disabled.
MCI=1	Normal MCI debugging output is enabled. Normal MCI debugging output reports a string representation of each MCI command.
MCI=2	Extended MCI debugging output is enabled. Extended MCI debugging output reports the length of time that a command took to complete along with a string representation of the command.

If debugging output is directed to a secondary monochrome display adapter where **CVW** is running, the debugging output appears in the **CVW** command window.

Note Fatal-exit reports are always directed to the AUX device (usually assigned to COM1), and cannot be disabled. Only MCI debugging output and output from **OutputDebugStr** can be disabled and directed to either COM1 or a secondary monochrome display adapter.

Chapter 2
The Media Control Interface (MCI)

The Media Control Interface (MCI) provides applications with device-independent capabilities for controlling devices such as audio and visual peripherals. Your application can use MCI to control standard multimedia devices for audio playback, audio recording, and animation playback. MCI can also control optional devices such as videodisc players.

This chapter contains an introduction to MCI and provides background information you need to use it. Topics discussed in this chapter include the following:

- General information on MCI devices

- Using the MCI command-message interface

- Sending and using MCI commands

- Using callback functions with MCI commands

- Obtaining MCI system information

- Using the MCI command-string interface

Chapter 4, "High-Level Audio Services," and Chapter 6, "The Multimedia Movie Player," both contain specific details and programming examples on how to use MCI to control specific MCI devices.

MCI Architecture

The MMSYSTEM module contains the Media Control Interface, which coordinates activities and communicates with MCI device drivers. Some MCI device drivers, such as those for videodisc players and movie playback services, control the target device directly. Other MCI device drivers, such as those for MIDI services and waveform services, use MMSYSTEM functions to indirectly control the target devices. Finally, some MCI device drivers, such as the MCI Movie Player, provide a high-level interface to other Windows DLLs. The following illustration shows this interaction:

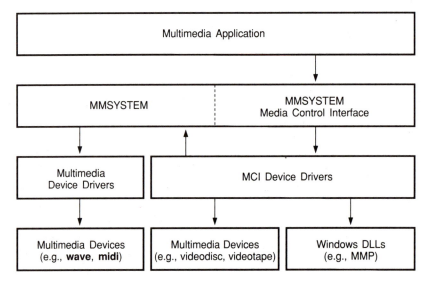

The relationship between an application and MCI.

About MCI Devices

Your application identifies an MCI device by specifying an MCI *device type*. A device type indicates the physical type of device. The following table lists the MCI device types you can use.

Device Type	Description
cdaudio	CD audio player
dat	Digital audio tape player
digitalvideo	Digital video in a window (not GDI based)
mmmovie	Multimedia Movie Player
other	Undefined MCI device
overlay	Overlay device (analog video in a window)
scanner	Image scanner
sequencer	MIDI sequencer
vcr	Videotape recorder or player
videodisc	Videodisc player
waveaudio	Audio device that plays digitized waveform files

The system software includes device drivers for the device types that are
fundamental to many multimedia presentations. The system software includes the
following MCI device drivers:

Device Type	Device Driver	Description
cdaudio	MCICDA.DRV	An MCI device driver for playing compact disc audio.
mmmovie	MCIMMP.DRV	An MCI device driver for playing Multimedia Movie files.
sequencer	MCISEQ.DRV	An MCI device driver for playing MIDI audio.
videodisc	MCIPIONR.DRV	An MCI device driver for playing the Pioneer LD-V4200 videodisc player.
waveaudio	MCIWAVE.DRV	An MCI device driver for playing and recording waveform audio.

The [mci] section of the SYSTEM.INI file contains a list of the installed device
types. If you have a particular device type installed more than once, the device-
type names used in the SYSTEM.INI file will have integers appended to them.

These integers create unique names for each MCI device-type entry. For example, if you installed two occurrences of the "cdaudio" device-type, their unique names would be "cdaudio" and "cdaudio1".

MCI classifies device drivers as *compound* and *simple*. Compound device drivers use a *device element*—a media element associated with a device—during operation. For most compound drivers, the device element is the source or destination data file. For file elements, the element name refers to a file and its path.

Simple device drivers don't require a device element for playback. Compact disc audio is an example of a simple device driver.

Function Prefixes

All MCI functions begin with the **mci** prefix.

MCI Data Types

The MMSYSTEM.H file defines new data types and function prototypes for MCI functions. You must include this header file in any source module that uses MCI. The following list shows the common MCI data structures defined in the MMSYSTEM.H file for MCI commands (additional data structures for extended commands are listed in the audio and animation MCI chapters):

MCI_BREAK_PARMS
A data structure for the parameters of the MCI_BREAK command message.

MCI_GENERIC_PARMS
A data structure for the parameters of a command message that does not have message-specific parameters.

MCI_GETDEVCAPS_PARMS
A data structure for the parameters of the MCI_GETDEVCAPS command message.

MCI_INFO_PARMS
A data structure for the parameters of the MCI_INFO command message.

MCI_LOAD_PARMS
A data structure for the parameters of the MCI_LOAD command message.

MCI_OPEN_PARMS
A data structure for the parameters of the MCI_OPEN command message.

MCI_PLAY_PARMS
A data structure for the parameters of the MCI_PLAY command message.

MCI_RECORD_PARMS
A data structure for the parameters of the MCI_RECORD command message.

MCI_SAVE_PARMS
A data structure for the parameters of the MCI_SAVE command message.

MCI_SEEK_PARMS
A data structure for the parameters of the MCI_SEEK command message.

MCI_SET_PARMS
A data structure for the parameters of the MCI_SET command message.

MCI_STATUS_PARMS
A data structure for the parameters of the MCI_STATUS command message.

MCI_SYSINFO_PARMS
A data structure for the parameters of the MCI_SYSINFO command message.

Each of these data structures has a corresponding far pointer data type defined for it. The names of these data types are a combination of the data structure names and a LP prefix. For example, LPMCI_OPEN_PARMS is the far pointer data type for MCI_OPEN_PARMS.

Sending MCI Commands

There are two MCI interfaces you can use to communicate with MCI devices: command-message functions and command-string functions. You can use either set of functions to access all MCI device capabilities. The difference between the two interfaces is in their basic command structure and the method in which they pass information to devices.

The command-message interface uses messages to control MCI devices. A bit-vector of flags and a pointer to a data structure is sent with each message. The flags and information data structure let an application send information to a device and receive returned data. MCI passes device messages and information directly to the device.

The command-string interface uses text commands to control MCI commands. Text strings contain all the information needed to execute a command. MCI parses the text string and translates it into the message, flags, and data structure that is then sent to the command-message interface. Because of this process, this interface is slightly slower than the command-message interface.

Choosing Between Functions

Each interface has unique properties you can use in your application. The command-message interface is more versatile if your application controls an MCI device directly. If this is the case, your application can directly and easily manipulate and decode data used by this interface. For example, your application can play an audio or video segment when a user successfully completes a task. The MCI examples in the audio and animation chapters of this workbook use the command-message interface to control MCI devices.

The command-string interface should be selected if your application uses a text-based interface to let the user control an MCI device. In such an application, the user can easily read and create the necessary command strings. For example, your application might read a user-written script that controls MCI devices. The MCI commands in the script can be sent directly to MCI without intermediate processing by your application.

Using the Command-Message Interface

The Multimedia extensions provide the following functions you can use when sending MCI command messages:

---

mciSendCommand
Sends a command message to an MCI device.

mciGetDeviceID
Returns the device ID assigned when the device was opened.

mciGetErrorString
Returns the error string corresponding to an error number.

Sending Command Messages

You use **mciSendCommand** to send command messages to MCI devices. This function has the following syntax:

DWORD mciSendCommand*(wDeviceID, wMessage, dwParam1, dwParam2)*

The WORD *wDeviceID* identifies the MCI device that receives the message *wMessage* and associated data *dwParam1* and *dwParam2*. The *dwParam1* DWORD specifies the flags for the message and the *dwParam2* DWORD specifies a pointer to the message data structure.

MCI command messages use the flags in *dwParam1* for two purposes: to request options, and to indicate which fields of the corresponding data structure contain data. If data is associated with a flag, remember to assign the data to the appropriate data field of the data structure as well as set the *dwParam1* flag. If you don't need to use the data structure to send any information to the device, you can use NULL for the pointer to the data structure.

MCI creates a device identifier when you open a device using the MCI_OPEN message. (When sending an open message, you can set *wDeviceID* to NULL.) After the device is open, obtain the device identifier from the **wDeviceID** field of the MCI_OPEN_PARMS data structure. Retain this value for use with subsequent MCI commands. You can also determine *wDeviceID* by calling **mciGetDeviceID**. (The argument for **mciGetDeviceID** is the device name, which can be the device element name, the device alias, or the device type used to register the device.)

You can use MCI_ALL_DEVICE_ID as *wDeviceID* for any message that does not return information. When you specify MCI_ALL_DEVICE_ID, all devices opened by the current task receive the command. For example, sending MCI_CLOSE with this ID closes all open devices, and sending MCI_PLAY1 with it starts playback of all devices opened by the task. While this ID is convenient to send a message to all your devices, don't rely on it to synchronize devices; the timing between messages can vary.

The **mciSendCommand** function returns zero if successful. If the function fails, the low-order word of the return value contains an error code. You can send this error code to **mciGetErrorString** to get a text description of it.

About MCI Commands

Your application controls MCI devices by sending commands to devices. MCI commands can be divided into the following categories:

■ Commands directly interpreted by MCI.

■ Commands supported by all MCI devices.

■ Commands that are optional (if a device uses an optional command, it must respond to all flags for that command that apply to the device type).

■ Commands specific to a device type or class; for example, videodisc players or digital audio tape recorders (these commands contain both unique commands and extensions to commands supported by other devices).

The following list summarizes the command messages that are handled directly by the system rather than being passed on to MCI devices:

Message	Description
MCI_SYSINFO	Returns information on MCI devices.
MCI_BREAK	Sets a break key for a specified MCI device.
MCI_SOUND	Plays system sounds identified in the [Sounds] section of the WIN.INI file.

The following list contains command messages supported by all MCI devices:

Message	Description
MCI_CLOSE	Closes an MCI device.
MCI_GETDEVCAPS	Obtains the capabilities of an MCI device.
MCI_INFO	Obtains information from an MCI device.
MCI_OPEN	Initializes an MCI device.
MCI_STATUS	Returns status information from an MCI device.

The following list summarizes the optional command messages (if a device supports a particular command message, it must respond to all flags that apply to that device type):

Message	Description
MCI_LOAD	Loads data from a disk file.
MCI_PAUSE	Pauses playing or recording.
MCI_PLAY	Starts transmitting output data.
MCI_RECORD	Starts recording input data.
MCI_RESUME	Resumes playing or recording.
MCI_SAVE	Saves data to a disk file.
MCI_SEEK	Seeks forward or backward.
MCI_SET	Sets device information.
MCI_STATUS	Returns status information from an MCI device. (Additional flags for this command supplement those for the command in the previous table.)
MCI_STOP	Stops playing or recording.

MCI devices can have additional command messages or extend the definition of the command messages presented in the previous lists. You can find examples of extended messages in the audio and animation chapters of this workbook. The *Programmer's Reference* contains a complete description of each command message.

Opening a Device

Before using a device, you must initialize it using the MCI_OPEN command message. The variations of this command make it one of the most complex of all MCI commands.

Obtaining the Device ID

MCI always needs a pointer to the data structure corresponding to the MCI_OPEN command message. Most devices use the MCI_OPEN_PARMS data structure. However, some devices use a device-specific data structure that defines the same data fields as MCI_OPEN_PARMS, as well as additional device-specific data fields. The MCI_OPEN_PARMS data structure has the following fields:

```
typedef struct {
    DWORD  dwCallback;        /* callback for MCI_NOTIFY */
    WORD   wDeviceID;         /* device ID returned to user */
    WORD   wReserved0;        /* reserved */
    LPSTR  lpstrDeviceType;   /* device type */
    LPSTR  lpstrElementName;  /* device element */
    LPSTR  lpstrAlias;        /* optional device alias */
} MCI_OPEN_PARMS;
```

MCI uses the **wDeviceID** field of this structure to return the device ID to your application. You should check the return value from **mciSendCommand** before using the device ID to be sure that it is valid. A non-zero return value indicates that an error occurred during the open process.

Other fields used in opening a device correspond to the following flags for the command.

Flag	Description
MCI_OPEN_ALIAS	Specifies that the **lpstrAlias** field of the data structure contains a pointer to a device alias.
MCI_OPEN_ELEMENT	Specifies that the **lpstrElementName** field of the data structure contains a pointer to the element name.
MCI_OPEN_SHAREABLE	Specifies that the device or element was opened as shareable.
MCI_OPEN_TYPE	Specifies that the **lpstrDeviceType** field of the data structure contains a pointer to the device-type identifier.
MCI_OPEN_TYPE_ID	Specifies that the **lpstrDeviceType** field of the data structure contains an integer device-type identifier.

Opening Simple Devices

Simple devices don't require a device element. Typically, this means a device does not have a file associated with it. For example, CD audio and videodisc players operate on the installed disc; the device does not need any application-supplied information on the contents of the media it is to operate.

To open a simple device, your application can use just the **wDeviceID** and **lpstrDeviceType** fields of the data structure. Set the **wDeviceID** field to NULL for the initial open. Set the **lpstrDeviceType** field to point to the null-terminated string specifying either the device type used in your SYSTEM.INI file or the filename of the device driver. If you specify the filename of the device driver, do not include the path to the file. You can optionally exclude the .DRV extension. When sending this data structure to MCI, tell MCI that the **lpstrDeviceType** field contains data by also sending it the MCI_OPEN_TYPE flag in *dwParam1*.

Opening Compound Devices

Compound devices use the **lpstrElementName** field for the device element and the **lpstrDeviceType** field for the device type. The MCI_OPEN_ELEMENT and MCI_OPEN_TYPE flags tell MCI that the fields in the data structure contain valid information. Depending on your application, there are three ways you can open a compound device:

■ Specify only the device type

■ Specify both the device type and the device element

■ Specify only the device element

To determine the capabilities of a device, you can open a device by specifying just the device type. You can specify the device type either by using the device type from the SYSTEM.INI file or by using the filename of the device driver. If you specify the filename of the device driver, don't include the path to the file. You can optionally exclude the .DRV extension. When opened this way, most compound devices will only let you determine their capabilities and close them.

To associate a device element with a particular device, you must specify both the device type (or filename) and element name. This combination lets your application specify the MCI device it needs.

To associate a default MCI device with a device element, you can specify NULL for the device type. In this case, MCI uses the extension of the device-element name to select the default device from the list in the [mci extensions] section of your WIN.INI file. The entries in the [mci extensions] section have the following form:

file extension=device type

MCI implicitly uses the *device type* if the extension is found. The following fragment shows a typical [mci extensions] section:

```
[mci extensions]
wav=waveaudio
mid=sequencer
rmi=sequencer
mmm=animation
```

Using the Shareable Flag

If your application opens a device or device element without the MCI_OPEN_SHAREABLE flag, no other application can access it simultaneously. If your application opens a device or device element as shareable, other applications can also access it by also opening it as shareable. The shared device or device element gives each application the ability to change the operating parameters or state of the device or device element.

If you make a device or device element shareable, your application should not make any assumptions about the state of a device. When working with shared devices, your application might need to compensate for changes made by other applications using the same services.

If a device can service only one application or task, it will fail an open that uses the MCI_OPEN_SHAREABLE flag.

Using the Device Type Constant

Your application can identify the device type by an integer rather than by string name. The following list contains the constants you can use to identify device types (if you use a constant to identify the device type, you must use the MCI_OPEN_TYPE_ID flag combined with the MCI_OPEN_TYPE flag):

Device Type	Constant
animation	MCI_DEVTYPE_ANIMATION
cdaudio	MCI_DEVTYPE_CD_AUDIO
dat	MCI_DEVTYPE_DAT
digitalvideo	MCI_DEVTYPE_DIGITAL_VIDEO
other	MCI_DEVTYPE_OTHER
overlay	MCI_DEVTYPE_OVERLAY
scanner	MCI_DEVTYPE_SCANNER
sequencer	MCI_DEVTYPE_SEQUENCER
vcr	MCI_DEVTYPE_VIDEOTAPE
videodisc	MCI_DEVTYPE_VIDEODISC
waveaudio	MCI_DEVTYPE_WAVEFORM_AUDIO

When the MCI_OPEN_TYPE_ID flag is combined with the MCI_OPEN_TYPE flag, MCI interprets the low-order word of the **lpstrDeviceType** field as the device-type constant. MCI uses the high-order word of this field to distinguish between multiple occurrences of a device type in your SYSTEM.INI file.

For example, if your SYSTEM.INI file lists "waveaudio1" and "waveaudio2", and your application sets the low-order word of **lpstrDeviceType** to the "waveaudio" constant and the high-order word to 2, MCI would address the device identified by "waveaudio2". MCI would address "waveaudio1" if your application set the high-order word to 0 or 1 (setting the high-order word to 0 tells MCI to use an unnumbered device or the lowest-numbered device).

Closing a Device

The MCI_CLOSE command message releases access to a device or device element. MCI frees a device when all tasks using a device have closed it. To help MCI manage devices, your application should explicitly close each device or device element when it finishes with it.

Using the Wait and Notify Flags

By default, MCI commands return immediately to the application, even if it takes several minutes to complete the action initiated by the command. For example, after a VCR device receives a rewind command, control returns to the sending application before the tape has finished rewinding. You can use either of the following flags to modify this default action:

Flag	Description
MCI_NOTIFY	Directs the device to return control immediately and post the MM_MCINOTIFY message when the requested action is complete.
MCI_WAIT	Directs the device to wait until the requested action is complete before returning control to the application.

Using the Notify Flag

The MCI_NOTIFY flag directs MCI to post the MM_MCINOTIFY message when the device completes an action. Your application specifies the handle to the destination window for the message in the low-order word of the **dwCallBack** field of the data structure sent with the command message. Every data structure associated with a command message contains this field. MCI can have only one notification message active for each device.

When MCI posts the MM_MCINOTIFY message, it sets the low-order word of *lParam* parameter of the window procedure to the ID of the device initiating the callback. The *wParam* parameter of the window procedure contains a constant specifying the status of the callback. MCI uses the following constants:

- MCI_NOTIFY_SUCCESSFUL

- MCI_NOTIFY_SUPERSEDED

- MCI_NOTIFY_ABORTED

- MCI_NOTIFY_FAILURE

When writing the window procedure, you can use these constants to select the appropriate action for the window procedure. These constants have the following definitions:

- MCI_NOTIFY_SUCCESSFUL indicates the conditions required for initiating the callback are satisfied and the command completed without interruption.

- MCI_NOTIFY_SUPERSEDED indicates MCI had a notification pending and it received another notify request. When MCI sends this constant, it resets the callback conditions to correspond to the notify request of the new command.

- MCI_NOTIFY_ABORTED indicates that your application sent a new command that prevented the callback conditions set by a previous command from being satisfied. For example, the stop command cancels a notification pending for the "play to 500" command. If your application interrupts a command and also requests notification, MCI will send only this message and not inform the window procedure of the notify command being superseded.

- MCI_NOTIFY_FAILURE indicates a device error occurred while a device was executing the MCI command. For example, MCI posts this message when a hardware error occurs during a play command.

Using the Wait Flag and Break Command Message

When a command message uses the MCI_WAIT flag, MCI returns control to the calling application when the target device completes the command. The user can cancel a wait operation by pressing a break key. If possible, MCI does not interrupt the command associated with the wait flag. For example, breaking the command "play to 500 wait" cancels the wait operation without interrupting the play operation.

By default, MCI defines the break key as CTRL+BREAK. Your application can redefine this key using the MCI_BREAK command message. This message uses the MCI_BREAK_PARMS data structure. MCI_BREAK has the following flags:

Flag	Description
MCI_BREAK_KEY	Specifies the virtual-key code to be used for the break key.
MCI_BREAK_HWND	Indicates a window handle that must be the current window to enable break detection for a particular MCI device (usually the main window of the application).
MCI_BREAK_OFF	Disables any existing break key for a particular device.

To set the break key, set the **nVirtKey** field of the data structure to the virtual-key code. MCI sets the key when you send this value using the MCI_BREAK_KEY flag.

If you want the break key active only when a particular window has the focus, you can combine the MCI_BREAK_HWND flag with the MCI_BREAK_KEY flag. Specify the window by putting its window handle in the **hwndBreak** field of the data structure.

Obtaining MCI System Information

The MCI_SYSINFO message obtains system information about MCI devices. MCI handles this message without relaying it to any MCI device. MCI returns the system information in the MCI_SYSINFO_PARMS data structure. The MCI_SYSINFO_PARMS data structure has the following fields:

```
typedef struct {
    DWORD   dwCallback;     /* callback for MCI_NOTIFY */
    LPSTR   lpstrReturn;    /* pointer to buffer for return information */
    DWORD   dwRetSize;      /* size of buffer */
    DWORD   dwNumber;       /* index number */
    WORD    wDeviceType;    /* device type */
    WORD    wReserved0;     /* reserved */
} MCI_SYSINFO_PARMS;
```

The MCI_SYSINFO command message has the following flags.

Flag	Description
MCI_SYSINFO_QUANTITY	Specifies that MCI will return the number of devices of a given type listed in the [mci] section of SYSTEM.INI. When used with the MCI_SYSINFO_OPEN flag, the number of open devices will be returned.
MCI_SYSINFO_NAME	Specifies that MCI will return the name of a device that satisfies the query. When used with the MCI_SYSINFO_OPEN flag, only the names of open devices will be returned.
MCI_SYSINFO_OPEN	Specifies that MCI will return the number or names of open devices.
MCI_SYSINFO_INSTALLNAME	Specifies that MCI will return the name listed in the SYSTEM.INI file used to install the device.

You use the MCI_SYSINFO_QUANTITY flag to determine the number of devices for a particular type listed in the [mci] section of the SYSTEM.INI file. For this flag, set the **wDeviceType** field of the data structure to the device type. When requesting the number of devices, set the *wDeviceID* parameter to NULL. MCI returns the number of devices as a DWORD in the **lpstrReturn** field of the data structure. If you combine the MCI_SYSINFO_QUANTITY flag with the MCI_SYSINFO_OPEN flag, MCI returns the number of devices opened by the task of that type.

Once you have the number of devices, you can enumerate the names of the devices using the MCI_SYSINFO_NAME flag. To get information using this flag, you must create a buffer for the return name. In the data structure, specify a pointer to the buffer, the size of the buffer, the index number corresponding to the device (1 is the first device), and the device type. This information is entered in the **lpstrReturn**, **dwRetSize**, **dwNumber**, and **wDeviceType** fields. MCI returns the device name in the buffer. When requesting a name of a particular device, set the *wDeviceID* parameter to NULL. To restrict the names to open devices, use the MCI_SYSINFO_OPEN flag with MCI_SYSINFO_NAME.

To obtain information on all devices in the system, you can assign MCI_ALL_DEVICE_ID to the *wDeviceID* parameter. When you use this identifier, MCI ignores the contents of the **wDeviceType** field and returns information on all MCI devices listed in the SYSTEM.INI file. When you use the MCI_SYSINFO_OPEN flag with the MCI_ALL_DEVICE_ID identifier, MCI returns information on the devices opened by the task.

You can obtain the installation name of an open device with the MCI_SYSINFO_INSTALLNAME flag. To get the installation name you must create a buffer for the return name. In the data structure, specify a pointer to the buffer and the size of the buffer in the **lpstrReturn** and **dwRetSize** fields. MCI places the device that corresponds to the *wDeviceID* parameter name in the buffer.

Using the Command-String Interface

This section discusses the command-string interface. See the *Programmer's Reference* for a description of the use of the string commands passed to the command-string interface. The following functions can be used with MCI command strings:

---

mciSendString
Sends a command string to an MCI device driver. This function also has parameters for callback functions and return strings.

mciGetErrorString
Returns the error string corresponding to an error number.

mciExecute
Sends a command string to an MCI device driver.

Sending Command Strings Using mciSendString

You use the **mciSendString** function to send command strings to a device. It has the following syntax:

WORD FAR PASCAL mciSendString(*lpstrCommand, lpstrRtnString, wRtnLength, hCallback*)

The far pointer *lpstrCommand* points to the a null-terminated string that specifies the MCI control command. The string has the following form:

command   device_name   arguments

The second parameter, *lpstrRtnString*, points to an application-supplied buffer for a return string. The third parameter, *wRtnLength*, specifies the size of this buffer. If an MCI command returns a value or a string, MCI copies it into *lpstrRtnString* as a null-terminated string (integers are converted to strings). If the length of the return string exceeds the size of the buffer, MCI returns an error. You can assign NULL to *lpstrRtnString* if you don't want the return string, or for commands that don't supply return information.

The last parameter, *hCallback*, is a handle to the window that receives the MM_MCINOTIFY message. MCI ignores this parameter unless the command contains the **notify** flag. This parameter must contain a valid window handle if the notify flag is used.

The following statement passes the "play to 500" command string to a videodisc device driver:

```
dwErrorCode = mciSendString ("play videodisc1 to 500", NULL, 0, 0L);
```

The **mciSendString** function returns zero if successful. If the function fails, it returns an error code. If there is an error, you can get a description of it by passing the error code to **mciGetErrorString**.

The MCITEST application contains examples of using **mciSendString** and **mciGetErrorString**. You can use this application to experiment with MCI devices and command strings.

Sending Command Strings Using mciExecute

Like **mciSendString**, **mciExecute** also sends command strings to MCI. The **mciExecute** function relies on MMSYSTEM to display error messages and it cannot get return information; thus, it uses fewer parameters than **mciSendString**. It has the following syntax:

BOOL FAR PASCAL mciExecute(*lpstrCommand*)

MMSYSTEM displays error messages in a message box. The name of the destination device appears as the message-box title.

Chapter 3
Introduction to Audio

The Multimedia extensions provide two levels of audio services. Before you can use either level, you must understand what each level offers and how it fits into the audio architecture.

This chapter covers the following topics:

- The different types and levels of audio services

- An overview of the audio architecture

- Audio file formats used by the Multimedia extensions

- Books and specifications providing additional information about audio

This chapter assumes you have a basic knowledge of digital audio and MIDI. For more information on these subjects, see "Further Reading" at the end of this chapter for a list of related books and specifications.

About Audio Services

Multimedia extensions provide several different types and levels of audio services. You should become familiar with these types and levels so you can choose the services appropriate for your application.

Types of Audio Services

Different types of audio services require different formats for the audio information and different technologies to reproduce audio. The Multimedia extensions offer the following types of audio services:

- *Waveform audio services* provide playback and recording support for digital audio hardware. Waveform audio is useful for reproducing non-musical audio material such as sound effects and voice-over narration. Waveform audio has moderate storage space and data transfer rate requirements—as low as 11K per second of audio.

- *MIDI audio services* provide support for MIDI file and MIDI event playback through internal or external synthesizers and MIDI event recording. MIDI audio is useful with music-related applications such as music composition and MIDI sequencer programs. Because it requires less storage space and a lower data transfer rate than waveform audio, you might want to use MIDI audio services to provide introductory and background music in your applications.

- *Compact disc audio services* provide support for playback of Red Book audio information on compact discs with the CD-ROM drive on multimedia computers. Compact disc audio offers the highest quality reproduction of musical material, but has the highest storage space requirements—176K per second of audio. You cannot read from the CD-ROM drive while playing compact disc audio.

Levels of Audio Services

The different levels of audio services let you choose services appropriate to the requirements of your application and to your programming ability. The Multimedia extensions offer two levels of audio services:

- *High-level audio services* allow you to play and record audio files with as little as one function call. Compared to low-level audio services, high-level services are easier to use and require less programming. High-level services also meet the audio requirements of most applications.

- *Low-level audio services* allow you to communicate directly with audio device drivers to manage playback and recording. Low-level audio services require more programming than high-level services, but give you more control over audio playback and recording.

Choosing the Appropriate Services

The easiest way of playing and recording audio is to use high-level audio services. If the high-level audio services don't meet the audio needs of your application, you can use low-level audio services to write your own routines to manage audio playback and recording.

Multimedia Extensions Audio Architecture

The Multimedia extensions provide audio services through high-level audio functions, Media Control Interface (MCI) device drivers, low-level audio functions, the MIDI Mapper, and low-level audio device drivers. The following illustration shows the relationship between an application and the elements of the Multimedia extensions that provide audio support:

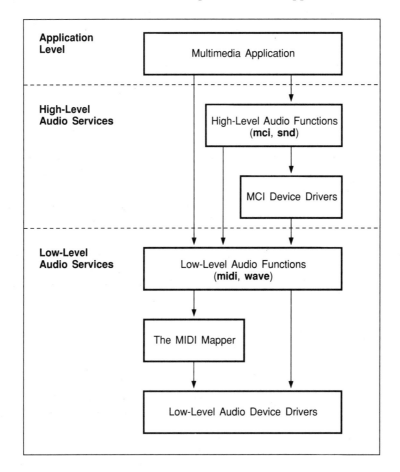

The relationship between an application and the Multimedia extensions.

For details on the overall architecture of the Multimedia extensions, see Chapter 1, "Introduction to Windows with Multimedia."

High-Level Audio Functions

MCI functions, along with MCI device drivers, provide high-level audio support for MIDI, waveform, and compact disc audio devices. MCI drivers can play disk-resident (hard disk and CD-ROM) audio files in the background while an application runs in the foreground. In addition to MCI, the Multimedia extensions provide high-level audio support with two special-purpose functions that play waveform sounds: **MessageBeep** and **sndPlaySound**. You can also use these functions to play waveform sounds associated with system alerts and sounds identified by entries in the WIN.INI file.

High-level audio functions should meet the audio requirements of most applications. For information on using MCI and the **MessageBeep** and **sndPlaySound** functions, see Chapter 4, "High-Level Audio Services."

Low-Level Audio Functions

Low-level audio functions provide a device-independent interface to audio hardware in multimedia computers. These functions supply low-level audio services by letting applications communicate directly with the audio device drivers. MCI drivers and the **MessageBeep** and **sndPlaySound** functions use these low-level functions to provide high-level audio services.

Low-level audio functions are provided for applications, such as audio tools programs, that have special-purpose audio requirements. For example, a MIDI sequencer application would use low-level audio functions to record and play MIDI data. For information on using low-level audio services, see Chapter 5, "Low-Level Audio Services."

The MIDI Mapper

The MIDI Mapper provides *standard patch services* for device-independent playback of MIDI files. Standard patch services ensure different MIDI snythesizers use the same instrument sounds to reproduce the music in a MIDI file.

The MIDI Mapper translates and redirects messages sent to it by low-level MIDI output functions. Because the high-level MIDI services use low-level MIDI output functions, the MIDI Mapper can be used with high-level MIDI services, as well as low-level MIDI services. For information on the architecture of the MIDI Mapper and how to use the Mapper with high-level audio services, see Chapter 4, "High-Level Audio Services." For information on using the Mapper with low-level audio services, see Chapter 5, "Low-Level Audio Services."

MIDI files must follow certain authoring guidelines to use the standard patch services provided by the MIDI Mapper. For details on these authoring guidelines, see Chapter 4, "High-Level Audio Services."

Audio File Formats

The Multimedia extensions support a tagged file structure called the Resource Interchange File Format (RIFF). There are two RIFF file formats currently defined for audio files:

RIFF File Format	File Extension	Description
RMID	.RMI	MIDI audio file
WAVE	.WAV	Waveform audio file

The WAVE file format supports a number of different digital audio data formats. All multimedia computers support PCM (pulse code modulated) data formats of 8-bit mono at sample rates of 11.025 kHz and 22.05 kHz.

In addition to RMID files, the MCI MIDI sequencer plays standard MIDI files in the format defined by the International MIDI Association in the "Standard MIDI Files 1.0" specification. See "Further Reading" at the end of this chapter for information on how to obtain this specification. RMID files are standard MIDI files with a RIFF header.

For more information on RIFF files and the RMID and WAVE file formats, see the file formats chapter in the *Programmer's Reference*.

Using RIFF Files

The multimedia file I/O services include functions for working with RIFF files. For information on using these functions, see Chapter 10, "Multimedia File I/O Services."

Further Reading

For more information on digital audio, digital-signal processing, and computer music, see the following books:

Boom, Michael. *Music Through MIDI*. Redmond: Microsoft Press, 1987.

Chamberlin, Hal. *Musical Applications of Microprocessors*. Hasbrouk Heights: Hayden Book Company, Inc., 1985.

Pohlmann, Ken. *Principles of Digital Audio*. Indianapolis: Howard W. Sams & Co., 1985.

Roads, Curtis, and John Strawn. *Foundations of Computer Music*. Cambridge: The MIT Press, 1985.

Strawn, John F. *Digital Audio Engineering, An Anthology*. Los Altos: William Kaufmann, Inc., 1985.

Strawn, John F. *Digital Audio Signal Processing, An Anthology*. Los Altos: William Kaufmann, Inc., 1985.

For information on MIDI and standard MIDI files, see the following MIDI specifications:

MIDI 1.0 Detailed Specification

Standard MIDI Files 1.0

The specifications listed above are available from the International MIDI Association at the following address:

International MIDI Association
5316 West 57th Street
Los Angeles, CA 90056

Chapter 4
High-Level Audio Services

This chapter explains how to use the high-level audio services of the Multimedia extensions to add sound to applications. For an overview of the audio services, see Chapter 3, "Introduction to Audio."

This chapter covers the following topics:

- Playing waveform sounds

- Using the Media Control Interface (MCI) to play and record audio

- Using the MIDI Mapper for device-independent MIDI file playback

- Authoring MIDI files

This chapter assumes you have a basic knowledge of digital audio and MIDI. If you need additional information on these subjects, see "Further Reading" at the end of Chapter 3, "Introduction to Audio."

Function Prefixes

High-level audio function names begin with the following prefixes:

Prefix	Description
snd	System alert sound functions
mci	Media Control Interface functions

Playing Waveform Sounds

One basic use of sound is associating a sound with a user action or with a warning or alert message. These sounds tend to be short in duration and are often played repeatedly. The Multimedia extensions provide two functions to play waveform sounds:

MessageBeep
  Plays the sound that corresponds to a given system-alert level.

sndPlaySound
  Plays the sound that corresponds to the given filename or WIN.INI entry.

These functions provide the following methods of playing waveform sounds:

- Playing WAVE files stored on a hard disk or CD-ROM

- Playing in-memory WAVE resources

- Playing WAVE files specified by entries in the WIN.INI file

- Playing WAVE files associated with system-alert levels

Restrictions in Playing Waveform Sounds

There are some restrictions to using **sndPlaySound** and **MessageBeep** to play waveform sounds:

- The entire sound must fit in available physical memory.

- The sound must be in a data format playable by one of the installed waveform audio device drivers.

Use **sndPlaySound** and **MessageBeep** to play WAVE files that are relatively small in size—up to about 100K. For larger sound files, use the Media Control Interface (MCI) services. For information on using MCI, see "Playing and Recording Audio Using MCI," later in this chapter.

Using the sndPlaySound Function

The **sndPlaySound** function has the following syntax:

WORD sndPlaySound(*lpszSound, wFlags*)

The parameter *lpszSound* is an LPSTR and points to a null-terminated string containing the name of the sound to be played. This name can be a keyname in the [sounds] section of the WIN.INI file or it can be the filename of a WAVE file. Optionally, *lpszSound* can be a far pointer to an in-memory image of a WAVE file. See the following section, "Playing WAVE Resources," for details on using in-memory WAVE file images.

The *wFlags* parameter specifies optional flags that affect how the sound is played. If the SND_SYNC flag is specified, the sound is played synchronously—**sndPlaySound** doesn't return until playback is complete. If the SND_ASYNC flag is specified, the sound is played asynchronously—**sndPlaySound** returns as soon as the sound begins playing. If neither of these flags is specified, the sound is played synchronously.

Playing WAVE Files

As an example, the following statement plays the C:\SOUNDS\BELLS.WAV file:

```
sndPlaySound("C:\\SOUNDS\\BELLS.WAV", SND_SYNC);
```

If the specified file does not exist, or will not fit into the available physical memory, **sndPlaySound** plays the default system sound specified by the SystemDefault entry in the [sounds] section of the WIN.INI file. If there is no SystemDefault entry, **sndPlaySound** fails without producing any sound. If you don't want the default system sound to play, specify the SND_NODEFAULT flag, as shown in the following example:

```
sndPlaySound("C:\\SOUNDS\\BELLS.WAV", SND_SYNC | SND_NODEFAULT);
```

Looping Sounds

If you specify the SND_LOOP and SND_ASYNC flags for the *wFlags* parameter, the sound will continue to play repeatedly; for example:

```
sndPlaySound("C:\\SOUNDS\\BELLS.WAV", SND_LOOP | SND_ASYNC);
```

If you want to loop a sound, you must play it asynchronously. You cannot use the SND_SYNC flag with the SND_LOOP flag. A looped sound will continue to play until **sndPlaySound** is called to play another sound. To stop playing a sound (looped or asynchronous) without playing another sound, use the following statement:

```
sndPlaySound(NULL, 0);
```

Playing WAVE Resources

You can also build WAVE files into an application as resources and use **sndPlaySound** to play these sounds by specifying the SND_MEMORY flag. The SND_MEMORY flag indicates the *lpszSound* parameter is a pointer to an in-memory image of the WAVE file. To include a WAVE file as a resource in an application, add the following entry to the application's resource script (.RC) file:

```
soundName WAVE c:\sounds\bells.wav
```

The name "soundName" is a placeholder for a name that you create to refer to this WAVE resource. WAVE resources are loaded and accessed just like other user-defined Windows resources. The function in the following example plays a specified WAVE resource.

```
/* Plays a specified WAVE resource */
BOOL PlayResource(LPSTR lpName)
{
    HANDLE hResInfo, hRes;
    LPSTR lpRes;
    BOOL bRtn;

    /* Find the WAVE resource */
    hResInfo = FindResource(hInst, lpName, "WAVE");
    if (!hResInfo) return FALSE;

    /* Load the WAVE resource */
    hRes = LoadResource(hInst, hResInfo);
    if (!hRes) return FALSE;

    /* Lock the WAVE resource and play it */
    lpRes = LockResource(hRes);
    if (lpRes) {
        bRtn = sndPlaySound(lpRes, SND_MEMORY | SND_SYNC | SND_NODEFAULT);
        UnlockResource(hRes);
    }
    else
        bRtn = 0;

    /* Free the WAVE resource and return success or failure */
    FreeResource(hRes);
    return bRtn;
}
```

To play a WAVE resource using this function, pass the function a far pointer to a string containing the name of the resource, as shown in the following example:

```
PlayResource("soundName");
```

Playing Sounds Specified in WIN.INI

The **sndPlaySound** function will also play waveform sounds referred to by a key-name in the [sounds] section of WIN.INI. This allows users to assign their own sounds to system alerts and warnings, or to user actions, such as a mouse button click. For example, the [sounds] section of WIN.INI might look like this:

```
[sounds]
SystemDefault=C:\SOUNDS\BUMMER.WAV
SystemAsterisk=C:\SOUNDS\WHALES.WAV
SystemExclamation=C:\SOUNDS\LASER.WAV
SystemHand=C:\SOUNDS\OHOH.WAV
SystemQuestion=C:\SOUNDS\JIBERISH.WAV
SystemStart=C:\SOUNDS\CHORD.WAV
MouseClick=C:\SOUNDS\CLICK.WAV
```

To play a sound identified by a WIN.INI entry, call **sndPlaySound** with the *lpszSound* parameter pointing to a string containing the name of the entry that identifies the sound. For example, to play the sound associated with the "MouseClick" entry in the [sounds] section of WIN.INI, and wait for the sound to complete before returning, use the following statement:

```
sndPlaySound("MouseClick", SND_SYNC);
```

If the specified WIN.INI entry or the waveform file it identifies does not exist, or if the sound will not fit into the available physical memory, **sndPlaySound** plays the default system sound specified by the SystemDefault entry. If there is no SystemDefault entry, **sndPlaySound** fails without producing any sound. If you don't want the default system sound to play, specify the SND_NODEFAULT flag when you call **sndPlaySound,** as in the following example:

```
sndPlaySound("MouseClick", SND_SYNC | SND_NODEFAULT);
```

Note The **sndPlaySound** function always searches the [sounds] section of WIN.INI for a keyname matching *lpszSound* before attempting to load a file with this name.

Playing System Alert Sounds

If you are familiar with programming for the Windows environment, you should recognize the **MessageBeep** function. Windows with Multimedia replaces the Windows **MessageBeep** function that produced a beep on the computer speaker with a function that uses the waveform hardware to produce a variety of user-selectable sounds. The **MessageBeep** function has the following syntax:

void MessageBeep*(wAlert)*

The syntax of **MessageBeep** remains the same, except its previously unused parameter is now used. The *wAlert* parameter is a WORD and specifies the alert level. Valid flags for *wAlert* are the same as those passed to **MessageBox**: MB_ICONASTERISK, MB_ICONEXCLAMATION, MB_ICONHAND, and MB_ICONQUESTION.

When you call the **MessageBeep** function, it searches the [sounds] section of the WIN.INI file for the WAVE file that corresponds to the specified alert level. The following table identifies the WIN.INI entries for system-alert sounds:

WIN.INI Entry	Description
SystemDefault	Identifies the sound produced when **MessageBeep** is called with *wAlert* set to an invalid alert level or when the requested alert sound can't be found. This is called the default system sound.
SystemAsterisk	Identifies the sound produced when **MessageBeep** is called with *wAlert* set to MB_ICONASTERISK.
SystemExclamation	Identifies the sound produced when **MessageBeep** is called with *wAlert* set to MB_ICONEXCLAMATION.
SystemHand	Identifies the sound produced when **MessageBeep** is called with *wAlert* set to MB_ICONHAND.
SystemQuestion	Identifies the sound produced when **MessageBeep** is called with *wAlert* set to MB_ICONQUESTION.

If **MessageBeep** is called with *wAlert* set to zero, it plays the default system sound. If *wAlert* is set to –1, it uses the computer speaker to produce a standard beep sound. If **MessageBeep** can't play the requested sound, it plays the default system sound. If it can't play the default system sound, then it produces a beep sound using the computer speaker.

The Sounds applet of the Control Panel allows users to set these WIN.INI entries to customize their environment for system-alert sounds. It also allows users to disable these alert sounds.

Playing and Recording Audio Using MCI

The Media Control Interface (MCI) provides a high-level interface for controlling both internal and external media devices. MCI provides support for playing waveform, MIDI, and compact disc audio and for recording waveform audio. MCI is the easiest way for multimedia applications to play and record audio.

MCI uses device drivers to interpret and execute high-level MCI commands. MCI device drivers can stream digital audio and MIDI data directly from a storage device to the appropriate device driver, allowing applications to play files too large to fit in available physical memory. This data streaming takes place in the background while an application is running. The application is responsible only for setting up MCI and telling it to start playing or recording.

Before reading this section, you should become acquainted with MCI by reading Chapter 2, "The Media Control Interface (MCI)." MCI provides two types of interfaces: a command-message interface and a command-string interface. This section explains how to use the command-message interface for waveform, MIDI, and compact disc audio devices. See the MCI chapter for information about the command-string interface.

MCI Audio Data Types

The MMSYSTEM.H header file defines data types and function prototypes for MCI. You must include this header file in any source module that uses MCI functions.

The following list contains data types for parameter blocks used with extended MCI commands related to audio. For a complete list of all MCI data types, see the chapter on data types in the *Programmer's Reference*.

MCI_SEQ_SET_PARMS
A data structure for specifying a parameter block for the MCI_SET command for MIDI sequencer devices.

MCI_SOUND_PARMS
A data structure for specifying a parameter block for the MCI_SOUND command.

MCI_WAVE_OPEN_PARMS
A data structure for specifying a parameter block for the MCI_OPEN command for waveform audio devices.

MCI_WAVE_SET_PARMS
A data structure for specifying a parameter block for the MCI_SET command for waveform audio devices.

MCI Audio Commands

MCI provides a standard set of commands applying to all types of media devices. Some of these commands can be extended to accomodate unique features of a particular type of device. For a complete reference to MCI command messages, see the message-directory chapter in the *Programmer's Reference*.

The following table lists common audio playback and recording tasks along with the corresponding MCI command message to perform each task:

Audio Task	MCI Command
Play sounds	
Play a waveform sound	MCI_SOUND
Open and close audio devices	
Open an audio device	MCI_OPEN
Close an audio device	MCI_CLOSE
Control playback and recording	
Play all or part of audio selection, resume playback from pause	MCI_PLAY
Stop playback	MCI_STOP
Pause playback	MCI_PAUSE
Change current location	MCI_SEEK
Cue a device so playback or recording begins with minimum delay	MCI_CUE
Begin recording on a waveform audio device	MCI_RECORD
Save a recorded waveform audio file	MCI_SAVE
Query and set audio devices	
Query device information such as the product name and the name of the device element currently associated with the device (returns information in string format)	MCI_INFO
Query device capabilities such as the device type, number of inputs and outputs (if the device can record)	MCI_GETDEVCAPS
Query device status such as current playback position, media length, media format, time format, record level, CD audio track, MIDI sequencer tempo	MCI_STATUS
Set device parameters such as time format, waveform data format, MIDI sequencer tempo	MCI_SET

Using the MCI_SOUND Command

Use the MCI_SOUND command to play a sound stored as a WAVE file. MCI_SOUND uses the MCI_SOUND_PARMS parameter block to specify the filename of the WAVE file or the name of an alias defined in the [Sounds] section of WIN.INI. MMSYSTEM.H defines MCI_SOUND_PARMS as follows:

```
typedef struct {
    DWORD   dwCallback;           /* callback for MCI_NOTIFY flag */
    LPSTR   lpstrSoundName;       /* filename of WAVE file to play */
} MCI_SOUND_PARMS;
```

The following function plays the sound identified by the *lpszSoundName* parameter:

```
/* Plays a given sound using MCI_SOUND. Returns as soon as playback
 * begins. Returns 0L on success; otherwise, it returns an MCI error code.
 */
DWORD playWAVESound(LPSTR lpszSoundName)
{
    DWORD dwReturn;
    MCI_SOUND_PARMS mciSoundParms;

    /* Play the given sound. Because there is no device to close,
     * don't notify a window or wait for command completion.
     */
    mciSoundParms.lpstrSoundName = lpszSoundName;
    if (dwReturn = mciSendCommand(NULL, MCI_SOUND, MCI_SOUND_NAME,
                            (DWORD)(LPVOID) &mciSoundParms))
    {
        /* Error playing sound, return error code.
         */
        return (dwReturn);
    }

    return (0L);
}
```

The sound played by MCI_SOUND must fit in available physical memory and be in a data format playable by one of the installed waveform audio device drivers.

Opening MCI Audio Devices

Unlike MCI_SOUND, many MCI commands require that an audio device be opened before it can be accessed. Use the MCI_OPEN command along with the MCI_OPEN_PARMS parameter block to open an audio device and obtain an MCI device ID. Subsequent commands use this device ID to identify the device to receive the command. MMSYSTEM.H defines the MCI_OPEN_PARMS parameter block as follows:

```
typedef struct {
    DWORD   dwCallback;          /* callback for MCI_NOTIFY flag */
    WORD    wDeviceID;           /* device ID returned to user */
    WORD    wReserved0;          /* reserved */
    LPSTR   lpstrDeviceType;     /* device type */
    LPSTR   lpstrElementName;    /* device element */
    LPSTR   lpstrAlias;          /* optional device alias (reserved) */
} MCI_OPEN_PARMS;
```

The MCI device ID is returned in the **wDeviceID** field. You should always check the return value of **mciSendCommand** after sending an MCI_OPEN command before using this device ID. A non-zero return value indicates that there was an error in opening the device and the returned device ID will not be valid.

Extended Parameter Block for Waveform Devices

For waveform audio devices, you can use an extended parameter block, MCI_WAVE_OPEN_PARMS. This structure has a **dwBufferSeconds** field to specify the number of seconds of buffering used by the MCI waveform device driver. If you use this field, you must specify the MCI_WAVE_OPEN_BUFFER flag for the *dwParam1* parameter of **mciSendCommand** to validate the field. MMSYSTEM.H defines the MCI_WAVE_OPEN_PARMS parameter block as follows:

```
typedef struct {
    DWORD   dwCallback;          /* callback for MCI_NOTIFY flag */
    WORD    wDeviceID;           /* device ID returned to user */
    WORD    wReserved0;          /* reserved */
    LPSTR   lpstrDeviceType;     /* device type */
    LPSTR   lpstrElementName;    /* device element */
    LPSTR   lpstrAlias;          /* optional device alias (reserved) */
    DWORD   dwBufferSeconds;     /* buffer size in seconds */
} MCI_WAVE_OPEN_PARMS;
```

Unless you want to specify the number of seconds of buffering for the driver to use, you can use the MCI_WAVE_OPEN_PARMS parameter block when you open waveform audio devices.

When you open a simple device, such as a compact disc audio device, you must specify the device type in the **lpstrDeviceType** field. When you open a compound device, such as a waveform or MIDI sequencer device, the device type is optional.

Use the **lpstrDeviceType** field of the MCI_OPEN_PARMS structure to specify the device type. MCI lets you use a string or a constant for this field. The following table shows the strings and constants for MCI audio device types:

Device Type	String	Constant
Compact disc	"cdaudio"	MCI_DEVTYPE_CD_AUDIO
Waveform	"waveaudio"	MCI_DEVTYPE_WAVEFORM_AUDIO
MIDI sequencer	"sequencer"	MCI_DEVTYPE_SEQUENCER

Using a string is the default convention for specifying device types. If you use a constant to specify the device type, you must specify the MCI_OPEN_TYPE_ID flag in addition to the MCI_OPEN_TYPE flag.

Opening Waveform and MIDI Sequencer Devices

Waveform and MIDI sequencer devices are compound devices. Compound devices require an associated device element—a WAVE or MIDI file. There are three ways to open compound devices:

- Specify only the device type.

- Specify only the device element and let MCI select the device type from the file extension of the device element.

- Specify both the device type and the device element.

Use the first approach, specifying only the device type, when opening a device to query its capabilities with the MCI_GETDEVCAPS command and when you plan to use the device to play more than one device element.

If you don't specify a device type when you open a compound device, MCI will choose an appropriate device type by looking at the file extension of the device element and at entries in the [mci extensions] section of WIN.INI. The following code fragment uses this technique to open a MIDI sequencer device to play a MIDI file named CHOPIN.RMI:

```
WORD wDeviceID;
MCI_OPEN_PARMS mciOpenParms;
    .
    .
    .
/* Open the device by specifying only the device element
 */
mciOpenParms.lpstrElementName = "CHOPIN.RMI";
if (mciSendCommand(0,                                    // device ID
                   MCI_OPEN,                             // command
                   MCI_OPEN_ELEMENT,                     // flags
                   (DWORD)(LPVOID) &mciOpenParms))       // parameter block
    /* Error, unable to open device
     */
    ...
else
    /* Device opened successfully, get the device ID
     */
    wDeviceID = mciOpenParms.wDeviceID;
```

Instead of letting MCI choose the device type, you can specify the type when you open the device. The following code fragment uses this technique to open a waveform audio device to play the C:\SOUNDS\BELLS.WAV file. This example uses a string to specify the device type. For an example using a constant to specify the device type, see "Opening Compact Disc Devices," later in this chapter.

```
WORD wDeviceID;
MCI_OPEN_PARMS mciOpenParms;
   .
   .
   .
/* Open the device by specifying both the device element and the device type
 */
mciOpenParms.lpstrDeviceType = "waveaudio";
mciOpenParms.lpstrElementName = "C:\\SOUNDS\\BELLS.WAV";
if (mciSendCommand(0,                                     // device ID
               MCI_OPEN,                                  // command
               MCI_OPEN_ELEMENT | MCI_OPEN_TYPE,          // flags
               (DWORD)(LPVOID) &mciOpenParms))            // parameter block
    /* Error, unable to open device
     */
    ...
else
    /* Device opened successfully, get the device ID
     */
    wDeviceID = mciOpenParms.wDeviceID;
```

Using the MIDI Mapper with the MCI Sequencer

The MIDI Mapper is the default output device for the MCI MIDI sequencer. It provides standard patch services for device-independent playback of MIDI files. Applications that use the MCI sequencer to play MIDI files should use the MIDI Mapper. For details on the MIDI Mapper, see "The MIDI Mapper," later in this chapter. For information on authoring device-independent MIDI files, see "Authoring MIDI Files," also later in this chapter.

When you open the MCI MIDI sequencer, MCI attempts to select the MIDI Mapper as the output device. If the Mapper is unavailable because it's already in use, MCI selects another MIDI output device.

Note   The MIDI Mapper currently supports only one client at a time. This might change in future versions of the Multimedia extensions.

After opening the sequencer, you should check to see if the MIDI Mapper was available and selected as the output device. The following code fragment uses the MCI_STATUS command to verify that the MIDI Mapper is the output device for the MCI sequencer:

```
WORD wDeviceID;
DWORD dwReturn;
MCI_STATUS_PARMS mciStatusParms;
    .
    .
    .
/* Make sure the opened device is the MIDI Mapper
 */
mciStatusParms.dwItem = MCI_SEQ_STATUS_PORT;
if (dwReturn = mciSendCommand(wDeviceID, MCI_STATUS, MCI_STATUS_ITEM,
                             (DWORD)(LPVOID) &mciStatusParms))
{
    /* Error sending MCI_STATUS command */
    ...
    return;
}
if (LOWORD(mciStatusParms.dwReturn) == MIDIMAPPER)
    /* The MIDI Mapper is the output device */
    ...

else
    /* The MIDI Mapper is not the output device */
    ...
```

MCI also provides a command to explicitly select the MIDI Mapper as the output device for the sequencer. The following code fragment uses the MCI_SET command to select the MIDI Mapper as the output device for the MCI sequencer:

```
WORD wDeviceID;
DWORD dwReturn;
MCI_SEQ_SET_PARMS mciSeqSetParms;
    .
    .
    .
/* Set the MIDI Mapper as the output port for the open device
 */
mciSeqSetParms.dwPort = MIDIMAPPER;
if (dwReturn = mciSendCommand(wDeviceID, MCI_SET, MCI_SEQ_SET_PORT,
                             (DWORD)(LPVOID) &mciSeqSetParms))
{
    /* Error, unable to set Mapper as output port */
    ...
}
```

Before querying the sequencer or setting an output port, you must successfully open the sequencer. Both of the previous examples assume that the *wDeviceID* parameter contains a valid device ID for the sequencer.

Opening Compact Disc Devices

Because a compact disc audio device is a simple device, you need only specify the device type when opening it by using either a string or a constant ID. The following code fragment opens a compact disc device using a constant ID to specify the device type:

```
WORD wDeviceID;
MCI_OPEN_PARMS mciOpenParms;
 .
 .
 .
/* Open the device by specifying a device ID constant
 */
mciOpenParms.lpstrDeviceType = (LPSTR) MCI_DEVTYPE_CD_AUDIO;
if (mciSendCommand(0,                                    // device ID
                MCI_OPEN,                                // command
                MCI_OPEN_TYPE | MCI_OPEN_TYPE_ID,        // flags
                (DWORD)(LPVOID) &mciOpenParms))          // parameter block
    /* Error, unable to open device
     */
    ...
else
    /* Device opened successfully, get the device ID
     */
    wDeviceID = mciOpenParms.wDeviceID;
```

Handling MCI Errors

You should always check the return value of the **mciSendCommand** function. If it indicates an error, you can use **mciGetErrorString** to get a textual description of the error. You can also interpret the error code yourself—MMSYSTEM.H defines constants for MCI error return codes.

Note To interpret an **mciSendCommand** error return value yourself, mask the high-order word—the low-order word contains the error code. However, if you pass the error return to **mciGetErrorString**, you must pass the entire DWORD value.

The following function takes the MCI error code specified by *dwError*, passes it to **mciGetErrorString**, and displays the resulting textual error description using **MessageBox**.

```
/* Uses mciGetErrorString to get a textual description of an MCI error.
 * Displays the error description using MessageBox.
 */
void showError(DWORD dwError)
{
    char szErrorBuf[MAXERRORLENGTH];

    MessageBeep(MB_ICONEXCLAMATION);
    if(mciGetErrorString(dwError, (LPSTR) szErrorBuf, MAXERRORLENGTH))
        MessageBox(hMainWnd, szErrorBuf, "MCI Error", MB_ICONEXCLAMATION);
    else
        MessageBox(hMainWnd, "Unknown Error", "MCI Error",
                MB_ICONEXCLAMATION);
}
```

Starting Playback

Once you successfully open an MCI audio device, you can use the MCI_PLAY command along with the MCI_PLAY_PARMS parameter block to begin playback. MMSYSTEM.H defines the MCI_PLAY_PARMS parameter block as follows:

```
typedef struct {
    DWORD   dwCallback;         /* callback for MCI_NOTIFY flag */
    DWORD   dwFrom;             /* playback begin position */
    DWORD   dwTo;               /* playback end position */
} MCI_PLAY_PARMS;
```

Playback begins at the current position in the device element. When a device element is opened, the current position is set to the beginning of the media. After a device element is played, the current position is at the end of the media. You can use the MCI_SEEK command to change the current position, as explained in "Changing the Current Position," later in this chapter.

You can also set beginning and ending positions for playback by specifying the MCI_FROM and MCI_TO flags with the MCI_PLAY command. If you specify one of these flags, you must fill in the corresponding **dwFrom** or **dwTo** field in the MCI_PLAY_PARMS structure with the desired beginning or ending time. If you are using a time format other than the default time format (milliseconds), you must set the time format before specifying a beginning or ending time with MCI_PLAY.

Example of Playing a WAVE File

The following function opens a waveform device and plays the WAVE file specified by the *lpszWAVEFileName* parameter:

```
/* Plays a given WAVE file using MCI_OPEN, MCI_PLAY. Returns when playback
 * begins. Returns 0L on success, otherwise returns an MCI error code.
 */
DWORD playWAVEFile(HWND hWndNotify, LPSTR lpszWAVEFileName)
{
    WORD wDeviceID;
    DWORD dwReturn;
    MCI_OPEN_PARMS mciOpenParms;
    MCI_PLAY_PARMS mciPlayParms;

    /* Open the device by specifying the device type and device element.
     * MCI will choose a device capable of playing the given file.
     */
    mciOpenParms.lpstrDeviceType = "waveaudio";
    mciOpenParms.lpstrElementName = lpszWAVEFileName;
    if (dwReturn = mciSendCommand(0, MCI_OPEN,
                                MCI_OPEN_TYPE | MCI_OPEN_ELEMENT,
                                (DWORD)(LPVOID) &mciOpenParms))
    {
        /* Failed to open device; don't close it, just return error
         */
        return (dwReturn);
    }

    /* Device opened successfully, get the device ID
     */
    wDeviceID = mciOpenParms.wDeviceID;

    /* Begin playback. The window procedure function for the parent window
     * will be notified with an MM_MCINOTIFY message when playback is
     * complete. At this time, the window procedure closes the device.
     */
    mciPlayParms.dwCallback = (DWORD) hWndNotify;
    if (dwReturn = mciSendCommand(wDeviceID, MCI_PLAY, MCI_NOTIFY,
                                (DWORD)(LPVOID) &mciPlayParms))
    {
        mciSendCommand(wDeviceID, MCI_CLOSE, 0, NULL);
        return (dwReturn);
    }

    return (0L);
}
```

Example of Playing a MIDI File

The following function opens a MIDI sequencer device, verifies that the MIDI Mapper was selected as the output port, plays the MIDI file specified by the *lpszMIDIFileName* parameter, and closes the device after playback is complete:

```
/* Plays a given MIDI file using MCI_OPEN, MCI_PLAY. Returns as soon as
 * playback begins. The window procedure function for the given window
 * will be notified when playback is complete. Returns 0L on success;
 * otherwise, it returns an MCI error code.
 */
DWORD playMIDIFile(HWND hWndNotify, LPSTR lpszMIDIFileName)
{
    WORD wDeviceID;
    DWORD dwReturn;
    MCI_OPEN_PARMS mciOpenParms;
    MCI_PLAY_PARMS mciPlayParms;
    MCI_STATUS_PARMS mciStatusParms;
    MCI_SEQ_SET_PARMS mciSeqSetParms;

    /* Open the device by specifying the device type and device element.
     * MCI will attempt to choose the MIDI Mapper as the output port.
     */
    mciOpenParms.lpstrDeviceType = "sequencer";
    mciOpenParms.lpstrElementName = lpszMIDIFileName;
    if (dwReturn = mciSendCommand(NULL, MCI_OPEN,
                                 MCI_OPEN_TYPE | MCI_OPEN_ELEMENT,
                                 (DWORD)(LPVOID) &mciOpenParms))
    {
        /* Failed to open device; don't close it, just return error.
         */
        return (dwReturn);
    }

    /* Device opened successfully, get the device ID.
     */
    wDeviceID = mciOpenParms.wDeviceID;

    /* See if the output port is the MIDI Mapper.
     */
    mciStatusParms.dwItem = MCI_SEQ_STATUS_PORT;
    if (dwReturn = mciSendCommand(wDeviceID, MCI_STATUS, MCI_STATUS_ITEM,
                                 (DWORD)(LPVOID) &mciStatusParms))
    {
        mciSendCommand(wDeviceID, MCI_CLOSE, 0, NULL);
        return (dwReturn);
    }
```

```
/* The output port is not the MIDI Mapper,
 * ask if user wants to continue.
 */
if (LOWORD(mciStatusParms.dwReturn) != MIDIMAPPER)
{
    if (MessageBox(hMainWnd,
                "The MIDI Mapper is not available. Continue?",
                "", MB_YESNO) == IDNO)
    {
        /* User does not want to continue. Not an error,
         * just close the device and return.
         */
        mciSendCommand(wDeviceID, MCI_CLOSE, 0, NULL);
        return (0L);
    }
}

/* Begin playback. The window procedure function for the parent window
 * will be notified with an MM_MCINOTIFY message when playback is
 * complete. At this time, the window procedure closes the device.
 */
mciPlayParms.dwCallback = (DWORD) hWndNotify;
if (dwReturn = mciSendCommand(wDeviceID, MCI_PLAY, MCI_NOTIFY,
                            (DWORD)(LPVOID) &mciPlayParms))
{
    mciSendCommand(wDeviceID, MCI_CLOSE, 0, NULL);
    return (dwReturn);
}

return (0L);
}
```

Example of Playing a Compact Disc Track

The following function opens a compact disc device, plays the track specified by
the *wTrack* parameter, and closes the device after playback is complete:

```
/* Plays a given compact disc track using MCI_OPEN, MCI_PLAY. Returns as
 * soon as playback begins. The window procedure function for the given
 * window will be notified when playback is complete. Returns 0L on success;
 * otherwise, it returns an MCI error code.
 */
DWORD playCDTrack(HWND hWndNotify, BYTE bTrack)
{
    WORD wDeviceID;
    DWORD dwReturn;
    MCI_OPEN_PARMS mciOpenParms;
    MCI_SET_PARMS mciSetParms;
    MCI_PLAY_PARMS mciPlayParms;

    /* Open the compact disc device by specifying the device type.
     */
    mciOpenParms.lpstrDeviceType = "cdaudio";
    if (dwReturn = mciSendCommand(NULL, MCI_OPEN,
                                  MCI_OPEN_TYPE,
                                  (DWORD)(LPVOID) &mciOpenParms))
    {
        /* Failed to open device; don't close it, just return error.
         */
        return (dwReturn);
    }

    /* Device opened successfully, get the device ID.
     */
    wDeviceID = mciOpenParms.wDeviceID;

    /* Set the time format to track/minute/second/frame.
     */
    mciSetParms.dwTimeFormat = MCI_FORMAT_TMSF;
    if (dwReturn = mciSendCommand(wDeviceID, MCI_SET, MCI_SET_TIME_FORMAT,
                                  (DWORD)(LPVOID) &mciSetParms))
    {
        mciSendCommand(wDeviceID, MCI_CLOSE, 0, NULL);
        return (dwReturn);
    }
```

```
        /* Begin playback from the given track and play until the beginning of
         * the next track. The window procedure function for the parent window
         * will be notified with an MM_MCINOTIFY message when playback is
         * complete. Unless the play command fails, the window procedure
         * closes the device.
         */
        mciPlayParms.dwFrom = 0L;
        mciPlayParms.dwTo = 0L;
        mciPlayParms.dwFrom = MCI_MAKE_TMSF(bTrack, 0, 0, 0);
        mciPlayParms.dwTo = MCI_MAKE_TMSF(bTrack + 1, 0, 0, 0);
        mciPlayParms.dwCallback = (DWORD) hWndNotify;
        if (dwReturn = mciSendCommand(wDeviceID, MCI_PLAY,
                                MCI_FROM | MCI_TO | MCI_NOTIFY,
                                (DWORD)(LPVOID) &mciPlayParms))
        {
            mciSendCommand(wDeviceID, MCI_CLOSE, 0, NULL);
            return (dwReturn);
        }

        return (0L);
}
```

To specify a track-relative position with a compact disc device, you must use the track/minute/second/frame time format. See "Setting the Time Format," later in this chapter for details on setting time formats.

Changing the Current Position

To change the current position in a device element, use the MCI_SEEK command along with the MCI_TO flag and the MCI_SEEK_PARMS parameter block. MMSYSTEM.H defines the MCI_SEEK_PARMS parameter block as follows:

```
typedef struct {
    DWORD    dwCallback;        /* callback for MCI_NOTIFY flag */
    DWORD    dwTo;              /* seek position */
} MCI_SEEK_PARMS;
```

If you use the **dwTo** field to specify a seek position with MCI_SEEK, you should query the time format and set it if necessary.

In addition to specifying a position with the **dwTo** field, you can specify the MCI_SEEK_TO_START or MCI_SEEK_TO_END flags for the *dwParam1* parameter of **mciSendCommand** to seek to the starting and ending positions of the device element. If you use one of these flags, don't specify the MCI_TO flag.

Setting the Time Format

Use the MCI_SET command along with the MCI_SET_PARMS parameter block to set the time format for an open device. Set the **dwTimeFormat** field in the parameter block to one of the constants identified in the following table:

Time Format	Constant
Waveform Devices	
Milliseconds	MCI_FORMAT_MILLISECONDS
Samples	MCI_FORMAT_SAMPLES
Bytes	MCI_FORMAT_BYTES
Compact Disc Devices	
Milliseconds	MCI_FORMAT_MILLISECONDS
Minute/Second/Frame	MCI_FORMAT_MSF
Track/Minute/Second/Frame	MCI_FORMAT_TMSF
MIDI Sequencer Devices	
Milliseconds	MCI_FORMAT_MILLISECONDS
MIDI Song Pointer	MCI_SEQ_FORMAT_SONGPTR
SMPTE, 24 Frame	MCI_FORMAT_SMPTE_24
SMPTE, 25 Frame	MCI_FORMAT_SMPTE_25
SMPTE, 30 Frame	MCI_FORMAT_SMPTE_30
SMPTE, 30 Frame Drop	MCI_FORMAT_SMPTE_30DROP

As an example, the following code fragment sets the time format to milliseconds on the device specified by *wDeviceID*:

```
WORD wDeviceID;
MCI_SET_PARMS mciSetParms;
    .
    .
    .
/* Set time format to milliseconds
 */
mciSetParms.dwTimeFormat = MCI_FORMAT_MILLISECONDS;
if (mciSendCommand(wDeviceID, MCI_SET, MCI_SET_TIME_FORMAT,
              (DWORD)(LPVOID) &mciSetParms))
```

```
        /* Error, unable to set time format
         */
        ...
else
        /* Time format set successfully
         */
        ...
```

Using the Minute/Second/Frame Time Format

For the minute/second/frame time format specified with the MCI_FORMAT_MSF constant, the time is relative to the beginning of the media. The time is packed into a DWORD, as shown in the following illustration:

HIWORD		LOWORD	
HIBYTE (Unused)	**LOBYTE** Frames	**HIBYTE** Seconds	**LOBYTE** Minutes

DWORD packing for the minute/second/frame time format.

The MMSYSTEM.H header file defines the following macros to get and set elements of a minute/second/frame packed DWORD:

MCI_MSF_MINUTE
  Gets minute value in a minute/second/frame DWORD.

MCI_MSF_SECOND
  Gets second value in a minute/second/frame DWORD.

MCI_MSF_FRAME
  Gets frame value in a minute/second/frame DWORD.

MCI_MAKE_MSF
  Sets minute, second, and frame values in a minute/second/frame DWORD.

Note   The first few seconds of audio compact discs contain table of contents data. To play from the beginning of a disc using the minute/second/frame time format, use the MCI_STATUS command to get the position of the first track and play from that position.

Using the Track/Minute/Second/Frame Time Format

For the track/minute/second/frame time format specified with the MCI_FORMAT_TMSF constant, the time is relative to the beginning of the specified track. The time is packed into a DWORD, as shown in the following illustration:

HIWORD		LOWORD	
HIBYTE	**LOBYTE**	**HIBYTE**	**LOBYTE**
Frames	Seconds	Minutes	Track

DWORD packing for the track/minute/second/frame time format.

The MMSYSTEM.H header file defines the following macros to get and set elements of a track/minute/second/frame packed DWORD:

MCI_TMSF_TRACK
  Gets track value in a track/minute/second/frame DWORD.

MCI_TMSF_MINUTE
  Gets minute value in a track/minute/second/frame DWORD.

MCI_TMSF_SECOND
  Gets second value in a track/minute/second/frame DWORD.

MCI_TMSF_FRAME
  Gets frame value in a track/minute/second/frame DWORD.

MCI_MAKE_TMSF
  Sets track, minute, second, and frame values in a track/minute/second/frame DWORD.

Using the SMPTE Time Formats

SMPTE (Society of Motion Picture and Television Engineers) time formats are based on standard time formats developed for the motion picture and television industries. For SMPTE time formats, the time is packed into a DWORD, as shown in the following illustration:

HIWORD		**LOWORD**	
HIBYTE Frames	**LOBYTE** Seconds	**HIBYTE** Minutes	**LOBYTE** Hours

DWORD packing for SMPTE time format.

Closing MCI Audio Devices

After you finish using an MCI device, you must use the MCI_CLOSE command to close the device. If you are playing a compound device, such as a waveform or MIDI device, and want to play a different device element using the same device, close the device and reopen it using the new device element.

Note If you're playing multiple device elements with the same device, you'll get better performance if you open the device by explictly specifying its type and then open, play, and close the individual device elements separately. Don't close the device until you are through playing all of the device elements. Otherwise, the driver will be reloaded each time you open the device.

Getting Information About Devices and Media

Use the MCI_STATUS command along with the MCI_STATUS_PARMS parameter block to get information about the status of an open device and its associated device element. MMSYSTEM.H defines the MCI_STATUS_PARMS parameter block as:

```
typedef struct {
    DWORD   dwCallback;     /* callback for MCI_NOTIFY flag */
    DWORD   dwReturn;       /* status information is returned here */
    DWORD   dwItem;         /* identifies status item */
    DWORD   dwTrack;        /* track number */
} MCI_STATUS_PARMS;
```

Before using the MCI_STATUS command, you must identify the status item to query for by putting a constant in the **dwItem** field of the parameter block. The following list shows different status items you can query for and the corresponding constant for each item for different types of audio devices:

Status Item	Constant
All Audio Devices	
Length of the media	MCI_STATUS_LENGTH
Current position	MCI_STATUS_POSITION
Current mode	MCI_STATUS_MODE
Time format	MCI_STATUS_TIME_FORMAT
Ready state	MCI_STATUS_READY
Waveform Devices	
Block alignment	MCI_WAVE_STATUS_BLOCKALIGN
Format tag	MCI_WAVE_STATUS_FORMATTAG
Number of channels	MCI_WAVE_STATUS_CHANNELS
Sample rate	MCI_WAVE_STATUS_SAMPLESPERSEC
Average bytes per second	MCI_WAVE_STATUS_AVGBYTESPERSEC
Bits per sample	MCI_WAVE_STATUS_BITSPERSAMPLE
Record level	MCI_WAVE_STATUS_LEVEL

Status Item	Constant
Compact Disc Devices	
Number of tracks	MCI_STATUS_NUMBER_OF_TRACKS
Media present	MCI_STATUS_MEDIA_PRESENT
Current track	MCI_STATUS_CURRENT_TRACK
MIDI Sequencer Devices	
Tempo	MCI_SEQ_STATUS_TEMPO
Port	MCI_SEQ_STATUS_PORT
SMPTE offset	MCI_SEQ_STATUS_OFFSET
division type of file	MCI_SEQ_STATUS_DIVTYPE

Getting Track-Relative Information for Compact Disc Devices

For compact disc devices, you can get the starting position and length of a track by specifying the MCI_TRACK flag and setting the **dwTrack** field of MCI_STATUS_PARMS to the desired track number. To get the starting position of a track, set the **dwItem** field to MCI_STATUS_POSITION. To get the length of a track, set **dwItem** to MCI_STATUS_LENGTH. For example, the following function gets the total number of tracks on the disc and the starting position of each track. It then uses the **MessageBox** function to report the starting positions of the tracks.

```
/* Uses the MCI_STATUS command to get and display the starting times
 * for the tracks on a compact disc. Returns 0L on success; otherwise,
 * it returns an MCI error code.
 */
DWORD getCDTrackStartTimes(void)
{
    WORD wDeviceID;
    int i, iNumTracks;
    DWORD dwReturn;
    DWORD dwPosition;
    DWORD *pMem;
    char szTempString[64];
    char szTimeString[512] = "\0";        // big enough for 20 tracks
    MCI_OPEN_PARMS mciOpenParms;
    MCI_SET_PARMS mciSetParms;
    MCI_STATUS_PARMS mciStatusParms;
```

```
/* Open the compact disc device by specifying the device type.
 */
mciOpenParms.lpstrDeviceType = "cdaudio";
if (dwReturn = mciSendCommand(NULL, MCI_OPEN,
                                MCI_OPEN_TYPE,
                                (DWORD)(LPVOID) &mciOpenParms))
{
    /* Failed to open device; don't have to close it, just return error.
     */
    return (dwReturn);
}

/* Device opened successfully, get the device ID.
 */
wDeviceID = mciOpenParms.wDeviceID;

/* Set the time format to minute/second/frame format.
 */
mciSetParms.dwTimeFormat = MCI_FORMAT_MSF;
if (dwReturn = mciSendCommand(wDeviceID, MCI_SET, MCI_SET_TIME_FORMAT,
                                (DWORD)(LPVOID) &mciSetParms))
{
    mciSendCommand(wDeviceID, MCI_CLOSE, 0, NULL);
    return (dwReturn);
}

/* Get the number of tracks; limit to number we can display (20).
 */
mciStatusParms.dwItem = MCI_STATUS_NUMBER_OF_TRACKS;
if (dwReturn = mciSendCommand(wDeviceID, MCI_STATUS, MCI_STATUS_ITEM,
                                (DWORD)(LPVOID) &mciStatusParms))
{
    mciSendCommand(wDeviceID, MCI_CLOSE, 0, NULL);
    return (dwReturn);
}
iNumTracks = mciStatusParms.dwReturn;
iNumTracks = min(iNumTracks, 20);

/* Allocate memory to hold starting positions.
 */
pMem = (DWORD *)LocalAlloc(LPTR, iNumTracks * sizeof(DWORD));
if (pMem == NULL)
{
    mciSendCommand(wDeviceID, MCI_CLOSE, 0, NULL);
    return (-1);
}
```

```
/* For each track, get and save the starting position and
 * build a string containing starting positions.
 */
for(i=1; i<=iNumTracks; i++)
{
    mciStatusParms.dwItem = MCI_STATUS_POSITION;
    mciStatusParms.dwTrack = i;
    if (dwReturn = mciSendCommand(wDeviceID, MCI_STATUS,
                                  MCI_STATUS_ITEM | MCI_TRACK,
                                  (DWORD)(LPVOID) &mciStatusParms))
    {
        mciSendCommand(wDeviceID, MCI_CLOSE, 0, NULL);
        return (dwReturn);
    }

    pMem[i-1] = mciStatusParms.dwReturn;

    wsprintf(szTempString, "Track %2d - %02d:%02d:%02d\n",
             i,
             MCI_MSF_MINUTE(pMem[i-1]),
             MCI_MSF_SECOND(pMem[i-1]),
             MCI_MSF_FRAME(pMem[i-1]));

    lstrcat(szTimeString, szTempString);
}

/* Use MessageBox to display starting times.
 */
MessageBox(hMainWnd, szTimeString, "Track Starting Position",
           MB_ICONINFORMATION);

/* Free memory and close the device.
 */
LocalFree((HANDLE) pMem);
if (dwReturn = mciSendCommand(wDeviceID, MCI_CLOSE, 0, NULL))
{
    return (dwReturn);
}

return (0L);
}
```

Recording with Waveform Audio Devices

MCI supports recording with waveform audio devices. You can insert recorded information into an existing file or record into a new file. To record to an existing file, open a waveform device and device element as you would normally. To record into a new file, specify a zero-length filename for the device element when you open the device.

When MCI creates a new file for recording, the waveform data format is set to a default format specified by the device driver. To use a format other than the default format, you can use MCI_SET to change the format.

To begin recording, use the MCI_RECORD command along with the MCI_RECORD_PARMS parameter block. MMSYSTEM.H defines the MCI_RECORD_PARMS parameter block as follows:

```
typedef struct {
    DWORD   dwCallback;          /* callback for MCI_NOTIFY flag */
    DWORD   dwFrom;              /* record begin position */
    DWORD   dwTo;                /* record end position */
} MCI_RECORD_PARMS;
```

If you record to an existing file, you can use the MCI_TO and MCI_FROM flags to specify beginning and ending insertion points for recording. For example, if you record to an existing file 20 seconds long, and you begin recording at 5 seconds and end recording at 10 seconds, you will have a recording 25 seconds long, as shown in the following illustration:

5 Seconds **Original**	5 Seconds **New**	15 Seconds **Original**

Recording waveform audio to an existing file.

If you don't specify an ending position, recording continues until you send an MCI_STOP command, or until the driver runs out of free disk space. If you record to a new file, you can't use the MCI_FROM flag to specify a beginning position—recording always starts at the beginning of a new file. However, you can specify an end position to terminate recording when recording to a new file.

Note   MCI does not support deleting or recording over portions of a recorded waveform. Applications such as waveform editors should be implemented using low-level audio functions.

Saving a Recorded File

When recording is complete, use the MCI_SAVE command along with the MCI_SAVE_PARMS parameter block to save the recording before closing the device. MMSYSTEM.H defines the MCI_SAVE_PARMS parameter block as follows:

```
typedef struct {
    DWORD   dwCallback;     /* callback for MCI_NOTIFY flag */
    LPSTR   lpfilename;     /* filename for saved file */
} MCI_SAVE_PARMS;
```

If you close the device without saving, the recorded data is lost.

Checking Input Levels

To get the level of the input signal before recording on a waveform input device, use the MCI_STATUS command. Specify the MCI_STATUS_ITEM flag and set **dwItem** in MCI_STATUS_PARMS to MCI_WAVE_STATUS_LEVEL. The average input signal level is returned in the **dwReturn** field of the MCI_STATUS_PARMS parameter block. The left-channel value is in the high-order word and the right- or mono-channel value is in the low-order word, as shown in the following illustration:

HIWORD	LOWORD
Left-Channel Level	Right- or Mono-Channel Level

DWORD packing for waveform input levels.

The input level is represented as an unsigned value. For 8-bit samples, this value ranges from 0 through 127 (0x7F). For 16-bit samples, it ranges from 0 through 32,767 (0x7FFF).

Example of Recording with a Waveform Audio Device

The following function opens a waveform audio device with a new file, records for the specified time, plays the recording, and prompts the user to see if the recording should be saved as a file:

```
/* Uses the MCI_OPEN, MCI_RECORD, MCI_SAVE commands to record and
 * save a waveform audio file. Returns 0L on success; otherwise,
 * it returns an MCI error code.
 */
DWORD recordWAVEFile(DWORD dwMilliSeconds)
{
    WORD wDeviceID;
    DWORD dwReturn;
    MCI_OPEN_PARMS mciOpenParms;
    MCI_RECORD_PARMS mciRecordParms;
    MCI_SAVE_PARMS mciSaveParms;
    MCI_PLAY_PARMS mciPlayParms;

    /* Open a waveform device with a new file for recording.
     */
    mciOpenParms.lpstrDeviceType = "waveaudio";
    mciOpenParms.lpstrElementName = "";
    if (dwReturn = mciSendCommand(0, MCI_OPEN,
                                MCI_OPEN_ELEMENT | MCI_OPEN_TYPE,
                                (DWORD)(LPVOID) &mciOpenParms))
    {
        /* Failed to open device; don't close it, just return error.
         */
        return (dwReturn);
    }

    /* Device opened successfully, get the device ID.
     */
    wDeviceID = mciOpenParms.wDeviceID;

    /* Begin recording and record for the specified number of milliseconds.
     * Wait for recording to complete before continuing. Assume the
     * default time format for the waveform device (milliseconds).
     */
    mciRecordParms.dwTo = dwMilliSeconds;
    if (dwReturn = mciSendCommand(wDeviceID, MCI_RECORD, MCI_TO | MCI_WAIT,
                                (DWORD)(LPVOID) &mciRecordParms))
    {
        mciSendCommand(wDeviceID, MCI_CLOSE, 0, NULL);
        return (dwReturn);
    }
```

```
/* Play the recording and query user to save the file.
 */
mciPlayParms.dwFrom = 0L;
if (dwReturn = mciSendCommand(wDeviceID, MCI_PLAY,
                             MCI_FROM | MCI_WAIT,
                             (DWORD)(LPVOID) &mciPlayParms))
{
    mciSendCommand(wDeviceID, MCI_CLOSE, 0, NULL);
    return (dwReturn);
}
if (MessageBox(hMainWnd, "Do you want to save this recording?",
               "", MB_YESNO) == IDNO)
{
    mciSendCommand(wDeviceID, MCI_CLOSE, 0, NULL);
    return (0L);
}

/* Save the recording to a file named "tempfile.wav". Wait for
 * the operation to complete before continuing.
 */
mciSaveParms.lpfilename = "tempfile.wav";
if (dwReturn = mciSendCommand(wDeviceID, MCI_SAVE,
                             MCI_SAVE_FILE | MCI_WAIT,
                             (DWORD)(LPVOID) &mciSaveParms))
{
    mciSendCommand(wDeviceID, MCI_CLOSE, 0, NULL);
    return (dwReturn);
}

return (0L);
}
```

Using the MCI MIDI Sequencer

The MCI MIDI sequencer plays standard MIDI files and RIFF MIDI files (RMID files). Standard MIDI files conform to the "Standard MIDI Files 1.0" specification. See Chapter 3, "Introduction to Audio," for information on this specification. Because RMID files are standard MIDI files with a RIFF header, information on standard MIDI files also applies to RMID files.

There are currently three variations of standard MIDI files. The MCI sequencer plays only two of these: Format 0 and Format 1 MIDI files.

Querying for Sequence Division Types

The *division type* of a MIDI sequence refers to the technique used to represent the time between MIDI events in the sequence. Use the MCI_STATUS command and set the **dwItem** field of the MCI_STATUS_PARMS parameter block to MCI_SEQ_STATUS_DIVTYPE to determine the division type of a sequence.

If the MCI_STATUS command is successful, the **dwReturn** field of the MCI_STATUS_PARMS parameter block contains one of the following values to indicate the division type:

Value	Division Type
MCI_SEQ_DIV_PPQN	PPQN (parts-per-quarter note)
MCI_SEQ_DIV_SMPTE_24	SMPTE, 24 fps (frames per second)
MCI_SEQ_DIV_SMPTE_25	SMPTE, 25 fps
MCI_SEQ_DIV_SMPTE_30	SMPTE, 30 fps
MCI_SEQ_DIV_SMPTE_30DROP	SMPTE, 30 fps drop frame

You must know the division type of a sequence to change or query its tempo. You can't change the division type of a sequence using the MCI sequencer.

Querying and Setting the Tempo

Use the MCI_STATUS command and set the **dwItem** field of the
MCI_STATUS_PARMS parameter block to MCI_SEQ_STATUS_TEMPO
to get the tempo of a sequence. If the MCI_STATUS command is successful,
the **dwReturn** field of the MCI_STATUS_PARMS parameter block
contains the current tempo.

To change tempo, use the MCI_SET command with the MCI_SEQ_SET_PARMS
parameter block. Specify the MCI_SEQ_SET_TEMPO flag and set the **dwTempo**
field of the parameter block to the desired tempo. MMSYSTEM.H defines the
MCI_SEQ_SET_PARMS parameter block as follows:

```
typedef struct {
    DWORD    dwCallback;       /* callback for MCI_NOTIFY flag */
    DWORD    dwTimeFormat;     /* time format */
    DWORD    dwAudio;          /* audio channel (not used by sequencer) */
    DWORD    dwTempo;          /* tempo */
    DWORD    dwPort;           /* output port */
    DWORD    dwSlave;          /* slave sync type */
    DWORD    dwMaster;         /* master sync type */
    DWORD    dwOffset;         /* SMPTE offset */
} MCI_SEQ_SET_PARMS;
```

Tempo Representation and Division Type

The way tempo is represented depends on the division type of the sequence. If the
division type is PPQN, the tempo is represented in beats per minute. If the division
type is one of the SMPTE division types, the tempo is represented in frames per
second. See the previous section, "Querying for Sequence Division Types," for
information on determining the division type of a sequence.

Changing Sequencer Synchronization

To change the synchronization mode of a sequencer device, use the
MCI_SET command along with the MCI_SEQ_SET_MASTER and
MCI_SEQ_SET_SLAVE flags. Two fields in the MCI_SEQ_SET_PARMS
parameter block, **dwMaster** and **dwSlave**, are used to specify the master
and slave synchronization modes.

The master synchronization mode controls synchronization information sent by the sequencer to an output port. The slave synchronization mode controls where the sequencer gets its timing information to play a MIDI file. The following table shows the different modes for master and slave synchronization and the corresponding constant for the **dwMaster** and **dwSlave** fields:

Synchronization Mode	Constant
Master	
MIDI Sync—Send timing information to output port using MIDI timing clock messages	MCI_SEQ_MIDI
SMPTE Sync—Send timing information to output port using MIDI quarter frame messages	MCI_SEQ_SMPTE
No Sync—Send no timing information	MCI_SEQ_NONE
Slave	
File Sync—Get timing information from MIDI file	MCI_SEQ_FILE
MIDI Sync—Get timing information from input port using MIDI timing clock messages	MCI_SEQ_MIDI
SMPTE Sync—Get timing information from input port using MIDI quarter frame messages	MCI_SEQ_SMPTE
No Sync—Get timing information from MCI commands only and ignore timing information such as tempo changes that are in the MIDI file	MCI_SEQ_NONE

Note Currently, for master synchronization, the MCI MIDI sequencer supports only the "no synchronization" mode (MCI_SEQ_NONE). For slave synchronization, it only supports the file synchronization mode (MCI_SEQ_FILE) and the "no synchronization" mode (MCI_SEQ_NONE).

The MIDI Mapper

The MIDI Mapper's standard patch services provide device-independent MIDI file playback for applications. You don't need to understand exactly how the MIDI Mapper works to use these services. The MIDI Mapper can be used with the MCI MIDI sequencer or with low-level MIDI output services of the Multimedia extensions.

To learn more about the MIDI Mapper or about authoring standard MIDI files for Windows with Multimedia, read this section to become familiar with how the MIDI Mapper works. For specific information on how to use the MIDI Mapper, see "Using the MIDI Mapper with the MCI Sequencer," earlier in this chapter, or see Chapter 5, "Low-Level Audio Services."

MIDI Notational Conventions

Unless stated otherwise, all references to MIDI channel numbers use the logical channel numbers 1 through 16. These logical channel numbers correspond to the physical channel numbers 0 through 15 that are actually part of the MIDI message. All references to MIDI program-change and key values use the physical values 0 through 127. All numbers are decimal unless preceded by a "0x" prefix, in which case they are hexadecimal.

In the discussion of the MIDI Mapper, the term *source* refers to the input side of the Mapper. The term *destination* refers to the output side of the Mapper. For example, a source channel is the MIDI channel of a message sent to the Mapper, a destination channel is the MIDI channel of a message sent from the Mapper to an output device.

The MIDI Mapper and the Multimedia Extensions

The MIDI Mapper is part of the system software. The following illustration shows how the MIDI Mapper relates to other elements of the audio services:

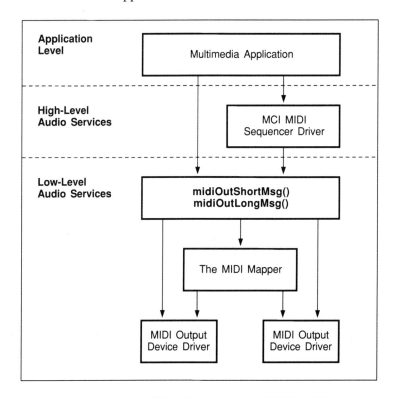

The relationship of the MIDI Mapper to the Multimedia extensions.

From the viewpoint of an application, the MIDI Mapper looks like another MIDI output device. The MIDI Mapper receives messages sent to it by the low-level MIDI output functions **midiOutShortMsg** and **midiOutLongMsg**. The Mapper modifies these messages and redirects them to a MIDI output device according to the current MIDI setup map. The current MIDI setup map is selected by the user using the MIDI Control Panel. Only the user can select the current setup map; applications cannot change the current setup map.

The MIDI Mapper Architecture

The MIDI Mapper uses a MIDI setup map to determine how to translate and redirect messages it receives. A MIDI setup map consists of the following types of maps:

- Channel map

- Patch map

- Key map

The following illustration shows how channel, patch, and key maps comprise a MIDI setup map:

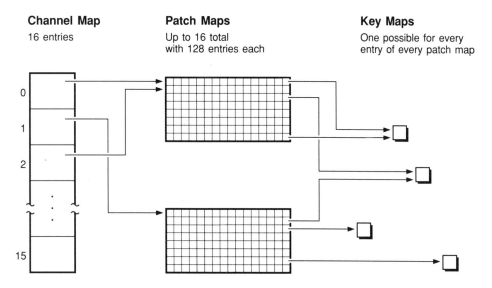

The MIDI Mapper architecture.

The Channel Map

The channel map affects all MIDI channel messages. MIDI channel messages include note-on, note-off, polyphonic-key-aftertouch, control-change, program-change, channel-aftertouch, and pitch-bend-change messages. The MIDI Mapper uses a single channel map with an entry for each of the 16 MIDI channels. Each channel map entry specifies the following:

■ A destination channel for the MIDI message

■ A destination output device for the MIDI message

■ An optional patch map specifying other possible modifications for the MIDI message

The destination channel is set to one of the 16 MIDI channels. MIDI messages are modified to reflect each new channel assignment. For example, if the destination channel entry for MIDI channel 4 is set to 6, all MIDI messages sent to channel 4 will be mapped to channel 6, as shown in the following illustration:

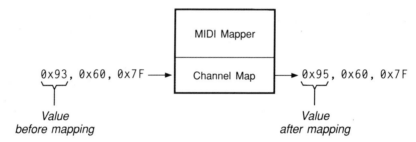

Channel mapping.

In this example, the MIDI status byte 0x93 is mapped to 0x95. The low nibble of a MIDI status byte specifies the channel number. Source channels are set to either active or inactive. Messages sent to inactive source channels are ignored, allowing the channel to be muted or turned off.

The destination output device is set to one of the available MIDI output devices. A MIDI output device can be an internal synthesizer or a physical MIDI output port attached to an external MIDI synthesizer.

MIDI system messages are MIDI messages from 0xF0 to 0xFF. There is no channel associated with MIDI system messages, so they can't be mapped. MIDI system messages are sent to all MIDI output devices listed in a channel map.

Patch Maps

Each channel map entry can have an associated patch map. Patch maps affect MIDI program-change and volume-controller messages. Program-change messages tell a synthesizer to change the instrument sound for a specified channel. Volume-controller messages set the volume for a channel.

A patch map has a translation table with an entry for each of the 128 program-change values. Each patch map specifies the following:

- A destination program-change value

- A volume scalar

- An optional key map

When program-change messages are received by the MIDI Mapper, the destination program-change value is substituted for the program-change value in the message. For example, if the destination program-change value for program-change 16 is 18, the Mapper modifies the MIDI program-change message, as shown in the following illustration:

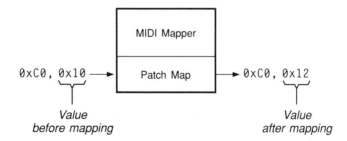

Patch mapping.

The Volume Scalar

The purpose of the volume scalar is to allow adjustments between the relative output levels of different patches on a synthesizer. For example, if the bass patch on a synthesizer is too loud compared to its piano patch, you can change the setup map to scale the bass volume down or the piano volume up.

The volume scalar specifies a percentage value for changing all MIDI main-volume controller messages that follow an associated program-change message. For example, if the volume scalar value is 50%, then the Mapper modifies MIDI main-volume controller messages, as shown in the following illustration:

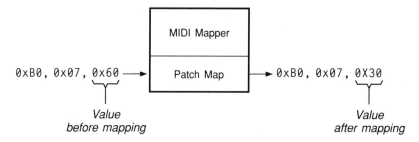

Volume scaling.

Key Maps

Each entry in the patch map translation table can have an associated key map. Key maps affect note-on, note-off, and polyphonic-key-aftertouch messages. A key map has a translation table with an entry for each of the 128 MIDI key values. For example, if the entry for key value 60 is 72, then the Mapper modifies MIDI note-on messages, as shown in the following illustration:

```
                        ┌─────────────────┐
                        │   MIDI Mapper    │
                        ├─────────────────┤
0x90, 0x3C, 0x7F ─────→ │     Key Map      │ ──→ 0x90, 0x48, 0X7F
                        └─────────────────┘
        ‿                                            ‿
      Value                                        Value
 before mapping                                after mapping
```

Key mapping.

Key maps are useful with synthesizers having key-based percussion instruments where a particular percussion sound is assigned to each key. Key maps are usually assigned to the first patch in the patch maps on the percussion channels (10 and 16).

Summary of Maps and MIDI Messages

The following table contains a list of status bytes for MIDI messages and shows which types of maps affect each message:

MIDI Status	Description	Map Types
0x80–0x8F	Note-off	Channel maps, key maps
0x90–0x9F	Note-on	Channel maps, key maps
0xA0–0xAF	Polyphonic-key-aftertouch	Channel maps, key maps
0xB0–0xBF	Control-change	Channel maps, patch maps[1]
0xC0–0xCF	Program-change	Channel maps, patch maps
0xD0–0xDF	Channel-aftertouch	Channel maps
0xE0–0xEF	Pitch-bend-change	Channel maps
0xF0–0xFF	System	Not mapped[2]

1. Patch maps affect only controller 7 (main volume).

2. System messages are sent to all devices listed in a channel map.

Authoring MIDI Files

The "MIDI 1.0 Detailed Specification" does not define any standard patch assignments for synthesizers. Therefore, when you create a MIDI file, it won't be reproduced correctly unless it is played back on the same MIDI synthesizer setup used to create it. For example, if you create a piano concerto for your Yamaha DX7 and try to play it back on a Roland LAPC-1, it might be played with a flute instead of a piano.

To enable MIDI files to be a viable format for representing music in multimedia computing, the Multimedia extensions provide MIDI authoring guidelines. These guidelines include a list of standard patch assignments and standard key assignments for percussion instruments. Using the MIDI Mapper, MIDI files authored to these guidelines can be played on any multimedia computer with internal or external MIDI synthesizers.

About Base-Level and Extended Synthesizers

Although it is difficult to clearly quantify distinctions between synthesizers, it is important to have some guidelines so you can create MIDI files that will play on all multimedia computers. The terms used to distinguish synthesizers for the purpose of authoring MIDI files are *base-level synthesizer* and *extended synthesizer*.

The distinctions between base-level and extended synthesizers are made solely on the number of instruments and notes the synthesizer can play, not on the quality or the cost of the synthesizer. The following table shows the minimum capabilities of base-level and extended synthesizers:

Synthesizer	Melodic Instruments		Percussive Instruments	
	Number	**Polyphony**	**Number**	**Polyphony**
Base-Level	3 instruments	6 notes	3 instruments	3 notes
Extended	9 instruments	16 notes	8 instruments	16 notes

Polyphony is the number of notes the synthesizer can play simultaneously. The polyphony expressed above applies to each group of instruments—melodic and percussive. For example, a base-level synthesizer is capable of playing six notes distributed among three melodic instruments and three notes distributed among three percussive instruments. The melodic instruments are each on different MIDI channels, and the percussive instruments are key-based—all on a single MIDI channel.

All multimedia computers provide at least a base-level synthesizer. Users can enhance their computer by adding internal or external synthesizers, which can be either base-level or extended synthesizers. When a user adds a synthesizer, the user must configure the MIDI Mapper to use the new device, or the instrument sounds will not be correct when playing MIDI files. The MIDI Control Panel applet allows a user to configure the MIDI Mapper as needed.

Authoring Guidelines for MIDI Files

Follow these guidelines to author device-independent MIDI files for Windows with Multimedia:

- Author for both base-level and extended synthesizer setups.

- Use MIDI channels 13 through 16 for base-level synthesizer data (reserve channel 16 for key-based percussion instruments).

- Use MIDI channels 1 through 10 for extended synthesizer data (reserve channel 10 for key-based percussion instruments).

- Prioritize MIDI data by putting crucial data in the lower-numbered channels.

- Limit the polyphony of non-percussive channels to a total of 6 notes for base-level data and 16 notes for extended data.

- Limit the polyphony of percussive channels to a total of 3 notes for base-level data and 16 notes for extended data.

- Use the standard MIDI patch assignments and key assignments.

- Always send a program-change message to a channel to select a patch before sending other messages to that channel. For the two percussion channels (10 and 16), select program number 0.

- Always follow a MIDI program-change message with a MIDI main-volume-controller message (controller number 7) to set the relative volume of the patch.

- Use a value of 80 (0x50) for the main volume controller for normal listening levels. For quieter or louder levels, you can use lower or higher values.

The following illustration summarizes the use of the 16 MIDI channels in a standard MIDI file authored for Windows with Multimedia:

Channel	Description	Polyphony
1	Extended Melodic Tracks	
2		
3		
4		
5		16 Notes
6		
7		
8		
9		
10	Extended Percussion Track	16 Notes
11	Unused Tracks	
12		
13	Base-Level Melodic Tracks	
14		6 Notes
15		
16	Base-Level Percussion Track	3 Notes

Prioritizing MIDI Data

Synthesizers don't always fall cleanly into the base-level and extended designations defined earlier. It's up to the end-user to determine how to use synthesizers capable of more than the base-level requirements, but not fully meeting the extended requirements. For this reason, it's important to prioritize the melodic data by putting the most critical data in lower-numbered channels. For example, a user may have a synthesizer capable of playing six melodic instruments with 12-note polyphony. The user can use this device as an extended synthesizer by setting up the MIDI Mapper to play only the first six melodic channels and ignore any information on channels seven, eight, and nine.

Standard MIDI Patch Assignments

The standard MIDI patch assignments for authoring MIDI files for use with the Multimedia extensions are based on the MIDI Manufacturers Association (MMA) General MIDI Mode specification. The following illustration shows the standard MIDI patch assignments.

Piano	Chromatic Percussion	Organ	Guitar
0 Acoustic Grand Piano	8 Celesta	16 Hammond Organ	24 Acoustic Guitar (nylon)
1 Bright Acoustic Piano	9 Glockenspiel	17 Percussive Organ	25 Acoustic Guitar (steel)
2 Electric Grand Piano	10 Music box	18 Rock Organ	26 Electric Guitar (jazz)
3 Honky-tonk Piano	10 Vibraphone	19 Church Organ	27 Electric Guitar (clean)
4 Rhodes Piano	12 Marimba	20 Reed Organ	28 Electric Guitar (muted)
5 Chorused Piano	13 Xylophone	21 Accordion	29 Overdriven Guitar
6 Harpsichord	14 Tubular Bells	22 Harmonica	30 Distortion Guitar
7 Clavinet	15 Dulcimer	23 Tango Accordion	31 Guitar Harmonics

Bass	Strings	Ensemble	Brass
32 Acoustic Bass	40 Violin	48 String Ensemble 1	56 Trumpet
33 Electric Bass (finger)	41 Viola	49 String Ensemble 2	57 Trombone
34 Electric Bass (pick)	42 Cello	50 SynthStrings 1	58 Tuba
35 Fretless Bass	43 Contrabass	51 SynthStrings 2	59 Muted Trumpet
36 Slap Bass 1	44 Tremolo Strings	52 Choir Aahs	60 French Horn
37 Slap Bass 2	45 Pizzicato Strings	53 Voice Oohs	61 Brass Section
38 Synth Bass 1	46 Orchestral Harp	54 Synth Voice	62 Synth Brass 1
39 Synth Bass 2	47 Timpani	55 Orchestra Hit	63 Synth Brass 2

Reed	Pipe	Synth Lead	Synth Pad
64 Soprano Sax	72 Piccolo	80 Lead 1 (square)	88 Pad 1 (new age)
65 Alto Sax	73 Flute	81 Lead 2 (sawtooth)	89 Pad 2 (warm)
66 Tenor Sax	74 Recorder	82 Lead 3 (caliope lead)	90 Pad 3 (polysynth)
67 Baritone Sax	75 Pan Flute	83 Lead 4 (chiff lead)	91 Pad 4 (choir)
68 Oboe	76 Bottle Blow	84 Lead 5 (charang)	92 Pad 5 (bowed)
69 English Horn	77 Shakuhachi	85 Lead 6 (voice)	93 Pad 6 (metallic)
70 Bassoon	78 Whistle	86 Lead 7 (fifths)	94 Pad 7 (halo)
71 Clarinet	79 Ocarina	87 Lead 8 (brass + lead)	95 Pad 8 (sweep)

Synth Effects	Ethnic	Percussive	Sound Effects
96 FX 1 (rain)	104 Sitar	112 Tinkle Bell	120 Guitar Fret Noise
97 FX 2 (soundtrack)	105 Banjo	113 Agogo	121 Breath Noise
98 FX 3 (crystal)	106 Shamisen	114 Steel Drums	122 Seashore
99 FX 4 (atmosphere)	107 Koto	115 Woodblock	123 Bird Tweet
100 FX 5 (brightness)	108 Kalimba	116 Taiko Drum	124 Telephone Ring
101 FX 6 (goblins)	109 Bagpipe	117 Melodic Tom	125 Helicopter
102 FX 7 (echoes)	110 Fiddle	118 Synth Drum	126 Applause
103 FX 8 (sci-fi)	111 Shanai	119 Reverse Cymbal	127 Gunshot

Standard MIDI Key Assignments

The standard MIDI key assignments for percussion instruments are based on the MIDI Manufacturers Association (MMA) General MIDI Mode specification. The following illustration shows the standard key assignments for MIDI files authored for Windows with Multimedia:

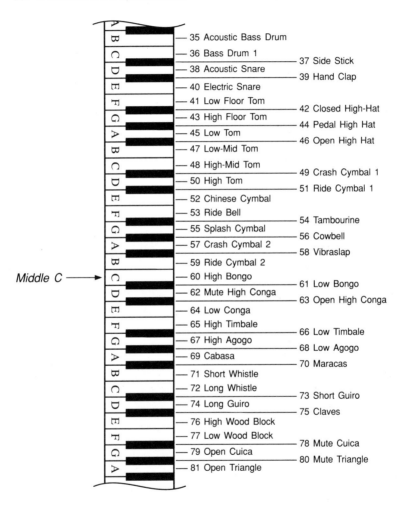

Standard MIDI key assignments for key-based percussion instruments.

Chapter 5
Low-Level Audio Services

This chapter explains how to use the low-level audio services of the Multimedia extensions to manage playback and recording of waveform and MIDI audio. For an overview of the audio services, see Chapter 3, "Introduction to Audio."

This chapter covers the following topics:

- Using low-level audio services

- Playing waveform audio

- Recording waveform audio

- Playing MIDI audio

- Recording MIDI audio

- Using auxiliary audio devices

You should have a basic knowledge of digital audio and MIDI before reading this chapter. If you need additional information on these subjects, see "Further Reading" at the end of Chapter 3, "Introduction to Audio."

Function Prefixes

Low-level audio function names begin with the following prefixes:

Prefix	Description
aux	Auxiliary audio functions
midi	MIDI audio functions
wave	Waveform audio functions

Using Low-Level Audio Services

Low-level audio services control different types of audio devices, including waveform, MIDI, and auxiliary audio devices. Many of the concepts of using low-level services apply to more than one type of device. This section presents general information on using low-level audio services. It covers the following topics:

- Querying audio devices

- Opening and closing device drivers

- Allocating and preparing audio data blocks

- Managing audio data blocks

- Using the MMTIME data structure

- Handling errors

Subsequent sections in this chapter discuss using specific types of audio devices.

Querying Audio Devices

Before playing or recording audio, you must determine the capabilities of the audio hardware present in the system. Audio capability can vary from one multimedia computer to the next; applications should not make assumptions about the audio hardware present in a given system.

Getting the Number of Devices

The Multimedia extensions provide the following functions to determine how many devices of a certain type are available in a given system:

---

auxGetNumDevs
  Retrieves the number of auxiliary audio devices present in the system.

midiInGetNumDevs
  Retrieves the number of MIDI input devices present in the system.

midiOutGetNumDevs
  Retrieves the number of MIDI output devices present in the system.

waveInGetNumDevs
  Retrieves the number of waveform input devices present in the system.

waveOutGetNumDevs
  Retrieves the number of waveform output devices present in the system.

Audio devices are identified by a device identifier (device ID). The device ID is determined implicitly from the number of devices present in a given system. Device IDs range from 0 to 1 less than the number of devices present. For example, if there are 2 MIDI output devices in a system, valid device IDs are 0 and 1.

Getting the Capabilities of a Device

Once you determine how many devices of a certain type are present in a system, you can inquire about the capabilities of each device. The Multimedia extensions provide the following functions to determine the capabilities of audio devices:

auxGetDevCaps
Retrieves the capabilities of a given auxiliary audio device.

midiInGetDevCaps
Retrieves the capabilities of a given MIDI input device.

midiOutGetDevCaps
Retrieves the capabilities of a given MIDI output device.

waveInGetDevCaps
Retrieves the capabilities of a given waveform input device.

waveOutGetDevCaps
Retrieves the capabilities of a given waveform output device.

Device-Capability Data Structures   Each of these functions takes a far pointer to a data structure the function fills with information on the capabilities of a specified device. The following are the data structures that correspond to each of the device-inquiry functions:

Function	Data Structure
auxGetDevCaps	AUXCAPS
midiInGetDevCaps	MIDIINCAPS
midiOutGetDevCaps	MIDIOUTCAPS
waveInGetDevCaps	WAVEINCAPS
waveOutGetDevCaps	WAVEOUTCAPS

All of the device capabilities data structures have the following fields:

Field	Description
wMid	Specifies a manufacturer ID for the author of the device driver.
wPid	Specifies a product ID for the device.
szPname	Specifies an array of characters containing the name of the device in a null-terminated string.
vDriverVersion	Specifies the version number of the device driver.

Microsoft will assign manufacturer IDs and product IDs specified by the **wMid** and **wPid** fields. The MMSYSTEM.H file contains constants for currently defined IDs.

The **szPname** field points to a null-terminated string containing the product name. You should use the product name to identify devices to users.

The **vDriverVersion** field specifies a version number for the device driver. The high-order of this field is the major version number; the low-order byte is the minor version number.

Opening and Closing Device Drivers

After getting the capabilities of an audio device, you must open the device before you can use it. Audio devices aren't guaranteed to be shareable, so a particular device might not be available when you request it. If this happens, you should notify the user and allow the user to try to open the device again. When you open an audio device, you should close the device as soon as you finish using it.

The Multimedia extensions provide the following functions to open and close different types of audio devices:

---

midiInOpen
Opens a specified MIDI input device for recording.

midiInClose
Closes a specified MIDI input device.

midiOutOpen
Opens a MIDI output device for playback.

midiOutClose
Closes a specified MIDI output device.

waveInOpen
Opens a waveform input device for recording.

waveInClose
Closes a specified waveform input device.

waveOutOpen
Opens a waveform output device for playback.

waveOutClose
Closes a specified waveform output device.

These functions are discussed in detail later in this chapter.

About Device Handles

Each function that opens an audio device takes as parameters a device ID, a pointer to a memory location, and some parameters unique to each type of device. The memory location is filled with a device handle. Use this device handle to identify the open audio device when calling other audio functions.

The distinction between audio-device IDs and audio-device handles is subtle, but very important. Don't confuse the two in your application. The differences between device IDs and device handles are as follows:

- Device IDs are determined implicitly from the number of devices present in a system, which is obtained by using the **…GetNumDevs** functions.

- Device handles are returned when device drivers are opened by using the **…Open** functions.

- The only functions that take device IDs as parameters are the **…GetDevCaps**, **…Open**, and **…Volume** functions. All other functions take device handles.

There are no functions for opening and closing auxiliary audio devices. Auxiliary audio devices don't need to be opened and closed like MIDI and waveform devices because there is no continuous data transfer associated with them. All auxiliary audio functions take device IDs to identify devices.

Allocating and Preparing Audio Data Blocks

Some low-level audio functions require applications to allocate data blocks to pass to the device drivers for playback or recording purposes. Each of these functions uses a data structure (or header) to describe its data block. The following table identifies these functions and their associated header structures (the MMSYSTEM.H file defines the data structures for these headers):

Function	Header	Purpose
waveOutWrite	WAVEHDR	Waveform playback
waveInAddBuffer	WAVEHDR	Waveform recording
midiOutLongMsg	MIDIHDR	MIDI system-exclusive playback
midiInAddBuffer	MIDIHDR	MIDI system-exclusive recording

Before you use one of the functions listed above to pass a data block to a device driver, you must allocate memory for the data block according to the guidelines discussed in the following sections of this chapter.

Allocating Memory for Audio Data Blocks

Before preparing a data block, you must allocate memory for the data block and the header structure that describes the data block.

▶ **To allocate memory:**

1. Use **GlobalAlloc** with the GMEM_MOVEABLE and GMEM_SHARE flags to get a handle to the memory block.

2. Pass this handle to **GlobalLock** to get a pointer to the memory block.

To free a data block, use **GlobalUnlock** and **GlobalFree**.

Preparing Audio Data Blocks

Before you pass an audio data block to a device driver, you must prepare the data block by passing it to a **...PrepareHeader** function. When the device driver is finished with the data block and returns it, you must clean up this preparation by passing the data block to an **...UnprepareHeader** function before any allocated memory can be freed.

The Multimedia extensions provide the following functions for preparing and cleaning up audio data blocks:

midiInPrepareHeader
Prepares a MIDI input data block.

midiInUnprepareHeader
Cleans up the preparation on a MIDI input data block.

midiOutPrepareHeader
Prepares a MIDI output data block.

midiOutUnprepareHeader
Cleans up the preparation on a MIDI output data block.

waveInPrepareHeader
Prepares a waveform input data block.

waveInUnprepareHeader

Cleans up the preparation on a waveform input data block.

waveOutPrepareHeader

Prepares a waveform output data block.

waveOutUnprepareHeader

Cleans up the preparation on a waveform output data block.

Managing Audio Data Blocks

Unless the audio data is small enough to be contained in a single data block, applications must continually supply the device driver with data blocks until playback or recording is complete. This is true for waveform input and output, and for MIDI system-exclusive input and output. Regular MIDI channel messages don't require data blocks for input or output.

Even if a single data block is used, applications must be able to determine when a device driver is finished with the data block so the application can free the memory associated with the data block and header structure. There are three ways to determine when a device driver is finished with a data block:

- By specifying a window to receive a message sent by the driver when it is finished with a data block.

- By specifying a callback function to receive a message sent by the driver when it is finished with a data block.

- By polling a bit in the **dwFlags** field of the WAVEHDR or MIDIHDR data structure sent with each data block.

If an application doesn't get a data block to the device driver when needed, there can be an audible gap in playback or a loss of incoming recorded information. This requires at least a double-buffering scheme—staying at least one data block ahead of the device driver.

Note   To get time stamped MIDI input data, you must use a callback function.

Using a Window to Process Driver Messages

The easiest type of callback to use to process driver messages is a window callback. To use a window callback, specify the CALLBACK_WINDOW flag in the *dwFlags* parameter and a window handle in the low-order word of the *dwCallback* parameter of the **...Open** function. Driver messages will be sent to the window-procedure function for the window identified by the handle in *dwCallback*.

Messages sent to the window function are specific to the audio device type used. For details on these messages, see the sections later in this chapter on using window messages for each specific audio device type.

Using a Callback Function to Process Driver Messages

You can also write your own low-level callback function to process messages sent by the device driver. To use a low-level callback function, specify the CALLBACK_FUNCTION flag in the *dwFlags* parameter and the address of the callback in the *dwCallback* parameter of the **...Open** function.

Messages sent to a callback function are similar to messages sent to a window, except they have two DWORD parameters instead of a WORD and a DWORD parameter. For details on these messages, see the sections on using low-level callbacks for each specific audio device type.

Writing Low-Level Callback Functions Callback functions for the low-level audio services are accessed at interrupt time, and therefore must be carefully written to adhere to the following set of rules:

- The callback function must reside in a dynamic-link library (DLL) and be exported in the module-definition file for the DLL.

- The code and data segments for the callback functions must be specified as FIXED in the module-definition file for the DLL.

- Any data the callback function accesses must be handled in one of the following ways:

  - Declared in the FIXED data segment of the callback DLL.

  - Allocated with **GlobalAlloc** using the GMEM_MOVEABLE and GMEM_SHARE flags, and locked using **GlobalLock** and **GlobalPageLock**.

  - Allocated with **LocalAlloc** from a FIXED local heap.

- The callback cannot make any Windows or Multimedia extensions calls except **PostMessage**, **timeGetTime**, **timeGetSystemTime**, **timeSetEvent**, **timeKillEvent**, **midiOutShortMsg**, **midiOutLongMsg**, and **OutputDebugStr**.

Note Since low-level callback functions must reside in a DLL, you don't need to use **MakeProcInstance** to get a procedure instance address for the callback.

Passing Instance Data to Callbacks

To pass instance data from an application to a low-level callback residing in a DLL, use one of the following techniques:

- Pass the instance data using the *dwInstance* parameter of the function that opens the device driver.

- Pass the instance data using the **dwUser** field of the WAVEHDR and MIDIHDR data structures that identify an audio data block being sent to a device driver.

If you need more than 32 bits of instance data, pass a pointer to a data structure containing the additional information. Be sure to follow the memory-allocation guidelines listed in "Using a Callback Function to Process Driver Messages," earlier in this chapter.

Managing Data Blocks by Polling

In addition to using a callback, you can poll the **dwFlags** field of a WAVEHDR or MIDIHDR structure to determine when an audio device is finished with a data block. There are times when it's better to poll **dwFlags** rather than waiting for a window to receive messages from the drivers. For example, after you call **waveOutReset** to release pending data blocks, you can immediately poll to be sure that the data blocks are indeed done before proceeding to call **waveOutUnprepareHeader** and free the memory for the data block.

MMSYSTEM.H defines two flags for testing the **dwFlags** field: WHDR_DONE for a WAVEHDR structure, and MHDR_DONE for a MIDIHDR structure. For example, to test a MIDIHDR structure, use the following technique:

```
if(lpMidiHdr->dwFlags & MHDR_DONE)
    /* Driver is finished with the data block */
else
    /* Driver is not finished with the data block */
```

Using the MMTIME Structure

The Multimedia extensions use a structure called MMTIME to represent time. Low-level audio functions that use MMTIME include **waveInGetPosition** and **waveOutGetPosition**. The **timeGetSystemTime** function also uses MMTIME to represent system time.

The MMTIME structure is defined in the MMSYSTEM.H header file as follows:

```
typedef struct mmtime_tag {
    WORD  wType;                    // Contents of the union
    union {
        DWORD ms;                   // Milliseconds (wType = TIME_MS)
        DWORD sample;               // Samples (wType = TIME_SAMPLES)
        DWORD cb;                   // Byte count (wType = TIME_BYTES)

        struct {                    // SMPTE (wType = TIME_SMPTE)
            BYTE hour;              // Hours
            BYTE min;               // Minutes
            BYTE sec;               // Seconds
            BYTE frame;            // Frames
            BYTE fps;               // Frames per second
            BYTE dummy;            // Pad byte
        } smpte;

        struct {                    // MIDI (wType = TIME_MIDI)
            DWORD songptrpos;       // Song pointer position
        } midi;
    } u;
} MMTIME;
```

Setting the Time Format

MMTIME can represent time in one or more different formats including milliseconds, samples, SMPTE, and MIDI song-pointer formats. The **wType** field specifies the format used to represent time. Before calling a function that uses the MMTIME structure, you must set the **wType** field to indicate your requested time format. Be sure to check **wType** after the call to see if the requested time format is supported. If the requested time format is not supported, the time is specified in an alternate time format selected by the device driver and the **wType** field is changed to indicate the selected time format. MMSYSTEM.H defines the following flags for the **wType** field of the MMTIME structure:

Flag	Description
TIME_MS	Milliseconds
TIME_SAMPLES	Number of waveform audio samples
TIME_BYTES	Number of waveform audio bytes
TIME_SMPTE	SMPTE time
TIME_MIDI	MIDI song-position pointer

For details on using MMTIME with the **waveOutGetPosition** function, see "Getting the Current Playback Position," later in this chapter.

Getting the System Time

Use the **timeGetSystemTime** or **timeGetTime** functions to get the system time. System time is defined as the time (in milliseconds) since Windows was started. For more information on **timeGetSystemTime** and **timeGetTime**, see Chapter 9, "Timer and Joystick Services."

Handling Errors with Audio Functions

Low-level audio functions return a non-zero error code. The Multimedia extensions provide a set of functions that convert these error codes into a textual description of the error. The application must still look at the error value itself to determine how to proceed, but textual descriptions of errors can be used in dialog boxes describing errors to users.

The following functions can be used to get textual descriptions of low-level audio errors:

midiInGetErrorText
  Retrieves a textual description of a specified MIDI input error.

midiOutGetErrorText
  Retrieves a textual description of a specified MIDI output error.

waveInGetErrorText
  Retrieves a textual description of a specified waveform input error.

waveOutGetErrorText
  Retrieves a textual description of a specified waveform output error.

The only low-level audio functions that don't return error codes are the **...GetNumDevs** functions. These functions return a value of 0 if no devices are present in a system, or if any errors are encountered by the function.

Playing Waveform Audio

If your application plays waveform audio, you should use the Media Control Interface (MCI) to control waveform output devices. If the MCI waveform playback services don't meet the needs of your application, you can manage waveform playback by using the low-level waveform services.

Waveform Output Data Types

The MMSYSTEM.H header file defines data types and function prototypes for all of the audio functions. You must include this header file in any source module that uses these functions. MMSYSTEM.H defines the following data types for the waveform output functions.

HWAVEOUT

A handle to an open waveform output device.

WAVEOUTCAPS

A data structure used to inquire about the capabilities of a particular waveform output device.

WAVEFORMAT

A data structure that specifies the data formats supported by a particular waveform output device. This data structure is also used for waveform input devices.

WAVEHDR

A data structure that is a header for a block of waveform output data. This data structure is also used for waveform input devices.

Querying Waveform Output Devices

Before playing a waveform, you should call the **waveOutGetDevCaps** function to determine the waveform output capabilities of the playback device, as described earlier in this chapter. This function takes a pointer to a WAVEOUTCAPS structure, which it fills with information about the capabilities of a given device. This information includes the manufacturer and product IDs, a product name for the device, and the version number of the device driver.

In addition, the WAVEOUTCAPS structure provides information on the standard waveform formats and features supported by the device driver. The MMSYSTEM.H header file defines WAVEOUTCAPS as follows:

```
typedef struct waveoutcaps_tag {
  WORD   wMid;                      /* manufacturer ID */
  WORD   wPid;                      /* product ID */
  VERSION vDriverVersion;           /* driver version */
  char   szPname[MAXPNAMELEN];      /* product name */
  DWORD  dwFormats;                 /* supported standard formats */
  WORD   wChannels;                 /* number of channels */
  DWORD  dwSupport;                 /* supported features */
} WAVEOUTCAPS;
```

Determining Standard Format Support

The **dwFormats** field of the WAVEOUTCAPS structure specifies the standard waveform formats supported by a device. The MMSYSTEM.H header file defines the following standard waveform format identifiers for the **dwFormats** field:

Format Identifier	Waveform Format
WAVE_FORMAT_1M08	8-bit mono at 11.025 kHz
WAVE_FORMAT_1S08	8-bit stereo at 11.025 kHz
WAVE_FORMAT_1M16	16-bit mono at 11.025 kHz
WAVE_FORMAT_1S16	16-bit stereo at 11.025 kHz
WAVE_FORMAT_2M08	8-bit mono at 22.05 kHz
WAVE_FORMAT_2S08	8-bit stereo at 22.05 kHz
WAVE_FORMAT_2M16	16-bit mono at 22.05 kHz
WAVE_FORMAT_2S16	16-bit stereo at 22.05 kHz
WAVE_FORMAT_4M08	8-bit mono at 44.1 kHz
WAVE_FORMAT_4S08	8-bit stereo at 44.1 kHz
WAVE_FORMAT_4M16	16-bit mono at 44.1 kHz
WAVE_FORMAT_4S16	16-bit stereo at 44.1 kHz

The **dwFormats** field is a logical OR of the flags listed above. For example, to determine if a device supports a waveform format of 16-bit stereo at 44.1 kHz, use this technique:

```
if(waveOutCaps.dwFormats & WAVE_FORMAT_4S16)
    /* Format is supported */
else
    /* Format is not supported */
```

This information on standard-format support also applies to the WAVEINCAPS structure used with waveform input devices. For information on the WAVEINCAPS structure, see "Querying Waveform Input Devices," later in this chapter.

To determine if a specific format is supported by a device (as opposed to all standard formats supported by a device), use the **waveOutOpen** function with the WAVE_FORMAT_QUERY flag as shown in the next section.

Determining Non-Standard Format Support

Waveform devices can support non-standard formats not listed in the preceding table. To see if a particular format (standard or non-standard) is supported by a device, you can call **waveOutOpen** with the WAVE_FORMAT_QUERY flag. The WAVE_FORMAT_QUERY flag tells **waveOutOpen** to check if the requested format is supported. The wave device is not actually opened. The requested format is specified by the structure pointed to by the *lpFormat* parameter passed to **waveOutOpen**. For information about setting up this structure, see "Specifying Waveform Data Formats," later in this chapter. The following code fragment uses this technique to determine if a given waveform device supports a given format:

```
/* Determines if the given waveform output device supports a given wave-
 * form format. Returns 0 if the format is supported, WAVEERR_BADFORMAT
 * if the format is not supported, and one of the MMSYSERR_ error codes if
 * there are other errors encountered in opening the given waveform device.
 */
WORD IsFormatSupported(LPPCMWAVEFORMAT lpPCMWaveFormat, WORD wDeviceID)
{
    return (waveOutOpen(
            NULL,                             // ptr can be NULL for query
            wDeviceID,                        // the device ID
            (LPWAVEFORMAT)lpPCMWaveFormat,    // defines requested format
            NULL,                             // no callback
            NULL,                             // no instance data
            WAVE_FORMAT_QUERY));              // query only, don't open device
}
```

This technique to determine non-standard format support also applies to waveform input devices. The only difference is that the **waveInOpen** function is used in place of **waveOutOpen** to query for format support.

Note   To determine if a particular waveform-data format is supported by any of the waveform devices in a system, use the technique illustrated in the previous example, but specify the WAVE_MAPPER constant for the *wDeviceID* parameter. See "Selecting a Waveform Output Device," later in this chapter, for more information on using the WAVE_MAPPER constant.

Determining Capabilities of Waveform Output Devices

Waveform output devices vary in the capabilities they support. The **dwSupport** field of the WAVEOUTCAPS structure indicates whether a given device supports capabilities such as volume and pitch changes. MMSYSTEM.H defines the following flags for the **dwSupport** field:

Flag	Description
WAVECAPS_PITCH	Pitch-change support
WAVECAPS_PLAYBACKRATE	Playback-rate-change support
WAVECAPS_VOLUME	Volume-control support
WAVECAPS_LRVOLUME	Individual volume-control support for both left and right channels

The **dwSupport** field is a logical OR of the flags listed in the preceding table. For example, to determine if a device supports volume changes, use this technique:

```
if(waveOutCaps.dwSupport & WAVECAPS_VOLUME)
    /* Volume changes are supported */
else
    /* Volume changes are not supported */
```

For more information on playback volume levels, see "Changing Waveform Playback Volume," later in this chapter. For more information on pitch and playback rates, see "Changing Pitch and Playback Rates," also later in this chapter.

Opening Waveform Output Devices

Use **waveOutOpen** to open a waveform output device for playback. This function opens the device associated with the specified device ID and returns a handle to the open device by writing the handle to a specified memory location. The syntax of the **waveOutOpen** function is as follows:

WORD waveOutOpen(*lphWaveOut, wDeviceID, lpFormat, dwCallback, dwInstance, dwFlags)*

The *lphWaveOut* parameter is an LPHWAVEOUT and specifies a far pointer to a memory location the function fills with a handle to the open waveform output device. Use this handle to identify the waveform device when calling other waveform-output functions.

The *wDeviceID* parameter is a WORD and identifies the waveform output device to open. See "Getting the Number of Devices," earlier in this chapter, for details on device IDs. If you specify the WAVE_MAPPER constant, the function finds a waveform output device capable of playing the given format and attempts to open it.

The *lpFormat* parameter is an LPWAVEFORMAT and specifies a far pointer to a WAVEFORMAT data structure. This data structure contains information on the format of the waveform data that will be sent to the waveform device. The following section explains how to use this data structure. You can free the WAVEFORMAT data structure immediately after passing it to the **waveOutOpen** function.

The *dwCallback* parameter is a DWORD and specifies either a window handle or the address of a low-level callback function. The callback can be used to monitor the progress of the playback of waveform data so an application can determine when to send additional data blocks or when to free data blocks that have been sent. You must specify the appropriate flag in the *dwFlags* parameter to indicate which type of callback you want. If no callback is desired, this parameter is NULL.

The *dwInstance* parameter is a DWORD and specifies instance data sent to the callback function each time it is called.

The *dwFlags* parameter is a DWORD and specifies one or more flags for opening a waveform device. Use the WAVE_FORMAT_QUERY flag to specify that you don't want to actually open a device, but just query whether the device supports the specified format. For information on using WAVE_FORMAT_QUERY, see "Determining Non-Standard Format Support," earlier in this chapter. If you specify a window or low-level callback in the *dwCallback* parameter, you must specify either the CALLBACK_WINDOW or the CALLBACK_FUNCTION flag to indicate the type of callback you are using.

Selecting a Waveform Output Device

Some multimedia computers have multiple waveform output devices. Unless you know you want to open a specific waveform output device in a system, you should use the WAVE_MAPPER constant for the device ID when you open a device. The **waveOutOpen** function chooses the device in the system best capable of playing the given data format.

Specifying Waveform Data Formats

When you call **waveOutOpen** to open a device driver for playback or to query if the driver supports a particular data format, use the *lpFormat* parameter to specify a pointer to a structure containing the requested waveform data format.

The WAVEFORMAT Structure

The WAVEFORMAT structure specifies format information common to all types of waveform data formats. Currently, the only format supported is PCM, but in the future, other types such as ADPCM might be supported. The MMSYSTEM.H file defines the WAVEFORMAT structure as follows:

```
typedef struct waveformat_tag {
    WORD    wFormatTag;        /* format type */
    WORD    nChannels;         /* number of channels */
    DWORD   nSamplesPerSec;    /* number of samples per second */
    DWORD   nAvgBytesPerSec;   /* average data rate */
    WORD    nBlockAlign;       /* block alignment */
} WAVEFORMAT;
```

The **wFormatTag** field specifies the format type for the data. Currently, the only flag defined for this field is WAVE_FORMAT_PCM for PCM waveform data.

The **nChannels** field specifies the number of discrete channels in the format. Use a value of 1 for mono data and 2 for stereo data.

The **nSamplesPerSec** field specifies the sample rate.

The **nAvgBytesPerSec** field specifies the average data rate in bytes per second. For example, 16-bit stereo at 44.1 kHz has an average data rate of 176400 bytes per second (2 channels × 2 bytes per sample per channel × 44100 samples per second).

The **nBlockAlign** field specifies the minimum atomic unit of data that can be passed to a driver. For PCM data, the block alignment is the number of bytes used by a single sample, including data for both channels if the data is stereo. For example, the block alignment for 16-bit stereo PCM is 4 bytes (2 channels × 2 bytes per sample).

The PCMWAVEFORMAT Structure

In addition to the general information in the WAVEFORMAT structure, specific information is needed to completely describe a waveform data format. For PCM waveform data, the PCMWAVEFORMAT structure includes a WAVEFORMAT structure along with an additional field containing PCM-specific information as follows.

```
typedef struct pcmwaveformat_tag {
    WAVEFORMAT  wf;                     /* general format information */
    WORD        wBitsPerSample;         /* number of bits per sample */
} PCMWAVEFORMAT;
```

The **wf** field specifies general format information. The **wBitsPerSample** field specifies the number of bits per sample for PCM data.

Using the PCMWAVEFORMAT Structure

Use the PCMWAVEFORMAT structure to specify the format for PCM audio data. The following code fragment shows how to set up a PCMWAVEFORMAT structure for 11.025 kHz 8-bit mono and for 44.1 kHz 16-bit stereo. After setting up PCMWAVEFORMAT, the example calls the **IsFormatSupported** function to verify that the waveform output device supports the format. The source for **IsFormatSupported** is given in an example in "Determining Non-Standard Format Support," earlier in this chapter.

```
WORD wReturn;
PCMWAVEFORMAT pcmWaveFormat;

/* Set up PCMWAVEFORMAT for 11 kHz 8-bit mono
 */
pcmWaveFormat.wf.wFormatTag = WAVE_FORMAT_PCM;
pcmWaveFormat.wf.nChannels = 1;
pcmWaveFormat.wf.nSamplesPerSec = 11025L;
pcmWaveFormat.wf.nAvgBytesPerSec = 11025L;
pcmWaveFormat.wf.nBlockAlign = 1;
pcmWaveFormat.wBitsPerSample = 8;

/* See if format is supported by any device in system
 */
wReturn = IsFormatSupported(&pcmWaveFormat, WAVE_MAPPER);

/* Report results
 */
if (wReturn == 0)
    MessageBox(hMainWnd, "11 kHz 8-bit mono is supported.",
      "", MB_ICONINFORMATION);
else if (wReturn == WAVERR_BADFORMAT)
    MessageBox(hMainWnd, "11 kHz 8-bit mono is NOT supported.",
      "", MB_ICONINFORMATION);
else
    MessageBox(hMainWnd, "Error opening waveform device.",
      "Error", MB_ICONEXCLAMATION);
```

```
/* Set up PCMWAVEFORMAT for 44.1 kHz 16-bit stereo
 */
pcmWaveFormat.wf.wFormatTag = WAVE_FORMAT_PCM;
pcmWaveFormat.wf.nChannels = 2;
pcmWaveFormat.wf.nSamplesPerSec = 44100L;
pcmWaveFormat.wf.nAvgBytesPerSec = 44100L;
pcmWaveFormat.wf.nBlockAlign = 4;
pcmWaveFormat.wBitsPerSample = 16;

/* See if format is supported by any device in the system
 */
wReturn = IsFormatSupported(&pcmWaveFormat, WAVE_MAPPER);

/* Report results
 */
If (wReturn == 0)
    MessageBox(hMainWnd, "44.1 kHz 16-bit stereo is supported.",
      "", MB_ICONINFORMATION);
else if (wReturn == WAVERR_BADFORMAT)
    MessageBox(hMainWnd, "44.1 kHz 16-bit stereo is NOT supported.",
      "", MB_ICONINFORMATION);
else
    MessageBox(hMainWnd, "Error opening waveform device.",
      "Error", MB_ICONEXCLAMATION);
```

Getting Format Information from a WAVE File

The easiest way to get waveform-format information from a WAVE file is by using the Multimedia file I/O services. To do this, use **mmioDescend** to locate the "fmt " chunk containing the format information and then **mmioRead** to read the format chunk directly into the proper format structure (chunks are the basic building blocks of RIFF files). The following code fragment illustrates this technique. For more information about Multimedia file I/O, see Chapter 10, "Multimedia File I/O Services."

```
void ReversePlay()
{
    HMMIO       hmmio;
    MMCKINFO    mmckinfoParent;
    MMCKINFO    mmckinfoSubchunk;
    DWORD       dwFmtSize;
    char        szFileName[ MAX_FILENAME_SIZE ];
    HANDLE      hFormat;
    WAVEFORMAT  *pFormat;
    .
    .
    .
```

```
/* Open the given file for reading using buffered I/O.
 */
...

/* Locate a "RIFF" chunk with a "WAVE" form type
 * to make sure it's a WAVE file.
 */
...

/* Now, find the format chunk (form type "fmt "). It should be
 * a subchunk of the "RIFF" parent chunk.
 */
mmckinfoSubchunk.ckid = mmioFOURCC('f', 'm', 't', ' ');
if (mmioDescend(hmmio, &mmckinfoSubchunk, &mmckinfoParent,
    MMIO_FINDCHUNK))
{
    MessageBox(hwndApp, "WAVE file is corrupted.",
                NULL, MB_OK | MB_ICONEXCLAMATION);
    mmioClose(hmmio, 0);
    return;
}

/* Get the size of the format chunk, allocate and lock memory for it.
 */
dwFmtSize = mmckinfoSubchunk.cksize;
hFormat = LocalAlloc(LMEM_MOVEABLE, LOWORD(dwFmtSize));
if (!hFormat)
{
    MessageBox(hwndApp, "Out of memory.",
                NULL, MB_OK | MB_ICONEXCLAMATION);
    mmioClose(hmmio, 0);
    return;
}
pFormat = (WAVEFORMAT *) LocalLock(hFormat);
if (!pFormat)
{
    MessageBox(hwndApp, "Failed to lock memory for format chunk.",
                NULL, MB_OK | MB_ICONEXCLAMATION);
    LocalFree(hFormat);
    mmioClose(hmmio, 0);
    return;
}
```

```
    /* Read the format chunk.
     */
    if (mmioRead(hmmio, pFormat, dwFmtSize) != dwFmtSize)
    {
        MessageBox(hwndApp, "Failed to read format chunk.",
                   NULL, MB_OK | MB_ICONEXCLAMATION);
        LocalUnlock(hFormat);
        LocalFree(hFormat);
        mmioClose(hmmio, 0);
        return;
    }

    /* Make sure it's a PCM file.
     */
    if (pFormat->wFormatTag != WAVE_FORMAT_PCM)
    {
        LocalUnlock(hFormat);
        LocalFree(hFormat);
        mmioClose(hmmio, 0);
        MessageBox(hwndApp, "The file is not a PCM file.",
                   NULL, MB_OK | MB_ICONEXCLAMATION);
        return;
    }

    /* Make sure the system has a waveform output
     * device capable of playing this format.
     */
    if (waveOutOpen(&hWaveOut, WAVE_MAPPER, (LPWAVEFORMAT)pFormat, NULL,
                    0L, WAVE_FORMAT_QUERY))
    {
        LocalUnlock(hFormat);
        LocalFree(hFormat);
        mmioClose(hmmio, 0);
        MessageBox(hwndApp, "The waveform device can't play this format.",
                   NULL, MB_OK | MB_ICONEXCLAMATION);
        return;
    }
    .
    .
    .
}
```

Writing Waveform Data

After successfully opening a waveform output device driver, you can begin waveform playback. The Multimedia extensions provide the following function for sending data blocks to waveform output devices:

---

waveOutWrite
   Writes a data block to a waveform output device.

Use the WAVEHDR data structure to specify the waveform data block you are sending using **waveOutWrite**. This structure contains a pointer to a locked data block, the length of the data block, and some assorted flags. The MMSYSTEM.H file defines the WAVEHDR data structure as follows:

```
typedef struct wavehdr_tag {
    LPSTR                   lpData;            /* pointer to data block */
    DWORD                   dwBufferLength;    /* length of data block */
    DWORD                   dwBytesRecorded;   /* number of bytes recorded */
    DWORD                   dwUser;            /* user instance data */
    DWORD                   dwFlags;           /* assorted flags */
    DWORD                   dwLoops;           /* loop control counter */
    struct wavehdr_tag far  *lpNext;           /* private to driver */
    DWORD                   reserved;          /* private to driver */
} WAVEHDR;
```

After you send a data block to an output device using **waveOutWrite**, you must wait until the device driver is finished with the data block before freeing it. If you are sending multiple data blocks, you must monitor the completion of data blocks to know when to send additional blocks. For details on different techniques for monitoring data block completion, see "Managing Audio Data Blocks," earlier in this chapter.

Example of Writing Waveform Data

The following code fragment illustrates the steps required to allocate and set up a WAVEHDR data structure, and write a block of data to a waveform output device.

```
/* Global variables--Must be visible to window-procedure function so it
 * can unlock and free the data block after it has been played.
 */
HANDLE      hData       = NULL;      // handle to waveform data memory
HPSTR       lpData      = NULL;      // pointer to waveform data memory

void ReversePlay()
{
    HWAVEOUT    hWaveOut;
    HWAVEHDR    hWaveHdr;
    LPWAVEHDR   lpWaveHdr;
    HMMIO       hmmio;
    MMCKINFO    mmckinfoParent;
    MMCKINFO    mmckinfoSubchunk;
    WORD        wResult;
    HANDLE      hFormat;
    WAVEFORMAT  *pFormat;
    DWORD       dwDataSize;
    WORD        wBlockSize;
     .
     .
     .

    /* Open a waveform device for output using window callback.
     */
    if (waveOutOpen((LPHWAVEOUT)&hWaveOut, WAVE_MAPPER,
                    (LPWAVEFORMAT)pFormat,
                    (LONG)hwndApp, 0L, CALLBACK_WINDOW))
    {
        MessageBox(hwndApp, "Failed to open waveform output device.",
                   NULL, MB_OK | MB_ICONEXCLAMATION);
        LocalUnlock(hFormat);
        LocalFree(hFormat);
        mmioClose(hmmio, 0);
        return;
    }
```

```
/* Allocate and lock memory for the waveform data. The memory for
 * waveform data must be globally allocated with GMEM_MOVEABLE and
 * GMEM_SHARE flags.
 */
hData = GlobalAlloc(GMEM_MOVEABLE | GMEM_SHARE, dwDataSize );
if (!hData)
{
    MessageBox(hwndApp, "Out of memory.",
                NULL, MB_OK | MB_ICONEXCLAMATION);
    mmioClose(hmmio, 0);
    return;
}
lpData = GlobalLock(hData);
if (!lpData)
{
    MessageBox(hwndApp, "Failed to lock memory for data chunk.",
                NULL, MB_OK | MB_ICONEXCLAMATION);
    GlobalFree(hData);
    mmioClose(hmmio, 0);
    return;
}


/* Read the waveform data subchunk.
 */
if(mmioRead(hmmio, (HPSTR) lpData, dwDataSize) != dwDataSize)
{
    MessageBox(hwndApp, "Failed to read data chunk.",
                NULL, MB_OK | MB_ICONEXCLAMATION);
    GlobalUnlock(hData);
    GlobalFree(hData);
    mmioClose(hmmio, 0);
    return;
}

/* Allocate and lock memory for the header. This memory must also be
 * globally allocated with GMEM_MOVEABLE and GMEM_SHARE flags.
 */
hWaveHdr = GlobalAlloc(GMEM_MOVEABLE | GMEM_SHARE,
                    (DWORD) sizeof(WAVEHDR));
if (!hWaveHdr)
{
    GlobalUnlock(hData);
    GlobalFree(hData);
    MessageBox(hwndApp, "Not enough memory for header.",
                NULL, MB_OK | MB_ICONEXCLAMATION);
    return;
}
```

```
lpWaveHdr = (LPWAVEHDR) GlobalLock(hWaveHdr);
if (!lpWaveHdr)
{
    GlobalUnlock(hData);
    GlobalFree(hData);
    MessageBox(hwndApp, "Failed to lock memory for header.",
            NULL, MB_OK | MB_ICONEXCLAMATION);
    return;
}

/* After allocation, the header must be set up and prepared for use.
 */
lpWaveHdr->lpData = lpData;
lpWaveHdr->dwBufferLength = dwDataSize;
lpWaveHdr->dwFlags = 0L;
lpWaveHdr->dwLoops = 0L;
waveOutPrepareHeader(hWaveOut, lpWaveHdr, sizeof(WAVEHDR));

/* Then the data block can be sent to the output device. The
 * waveOutWrite function returns immediately and waveform data
 * is sent to the output device in the background.
 */
wResult = waveOutWrite(hWaveOut, lpWaveHdr, sizeof(WAVEHDR));
if (wResult != 0)
{
    waveOutUnprepareHeader(hWaveOut, lpWaveHdr, sizeof(WAVEHDR));
    GlobalUnlock( hData);
    GlobalFree(hData);
    MessageBox(hwndApp, "Failed to write block to device",
            NULL, MB_OK | MB_ICONEXCLAMATION);
    return;
}
    .
    .
    .
}
```

PCM Waveform Data Format

The **lpData** field in the WAVEHDR structure points to the waveform data samples. For 8-bit PCM data, each sample is represented by a single unsigned data byte. For 16-bit PCM data, each sample is represented by a 16-bit signed value. The following table summarizes the maximum, minimum, and midpoint values for PCM waveform data.

Data Format	Maximum Value	Minimum Value	Midpoint Value
8-bit PCM	255 (0xFF)	0	128 (0x80)
16-bit PCM	32767 (0x7FFF)	−32768 (0x8000)	0

PCM Data Packing   The order of the data bytes varies between 8-bit and 16-bit, and mono and stereo formats. The following illustrations show the data packing for different PCM waveform data formats:

Sample 1	Sample 2	Sample 3	Sample 4
Channel 0	Channel 0	Channel 0	Channel 0

Data packing for 8-bit mono PCM.

Sample 1		Sample 2	
Channel 0 (left)	Channel 1 (right)	Channel 0 (left)	Channel 1 (right)

Data packing for 8-bit stereo PCM.

Sample 1		Sample 2	
Channel 0	Channel 0	Channel 0	Channel 0
Low-Order Byte	High-Order Byte	Low-Order Byte	High-Order Byte

Data packing for 16-bit mono PCM.

Sample 1			
Channel 0 (left) Low-Order Byte	Channel 0 (left) High-Order Byte	Channel 1 (right) Low-Order Byte	Channel 1 (right) High-Order Byte

Data packing for 16-bit stereo PCM.

Using Window Messages to Manage Waveform Playback

The following messages can be sent to a window-procedure function for managing waveform playback:

Message	Description
MM_WOM_CLOSE	Sent when the device is closed using **waveOutClose**.
MM_WOM_DONE	Sent when the device driver is finished with a data block sent using **waveOutWrite**.
MM_WOM_OPEN	Sent when the device is opened using **waveOutOpen**.

A *wParam* and *lParam* parameter is associated with each of these messages. The *wParam* parameter always specifies a handle to the open waveform device. For the MM_WOM_DONE message, *lParam* specifies a far pointer to a WAVEHDR structure identifying the completed data block. The *lParam* parameter is unused for the MM_WOM_CLOSE and MM_WOM_OPEN messages.

The most useful message is MM_WOM_DONE. When this message signals that playback of a data block is complete, you can clean up and free the data block. Unless you need to allocate memory or initialize variables, you probably don't need to process the MM_WOM_OPEN and MM_WOM_CLOSE messages.

Example of Processing MM_WOM_DONE

The following code fragment shows how to process the MM_WOM_DONE message. This fragment assumes the application does not play multiple data blocks, so it can close the output device after playing a single data block.

```
/* WndProc--Main window procedure function.
 */
LONG FAR PASCAL WndProc(HWND hWnd, unsigned msg, WORD wParam, LONG lParam)
{
    switch (msg)
    {
        .
        .
        .

        case MM_WOM_DONE:
            /* A waveform data block has been played and can now be freed.
             */
            waveOutUnprepareHeader((HWAVEOUT) wParam,
                            (LPWAVEHDR) lParam, sizeof(WAVEHDR) );
```

```
                    GlobalUnlock(hData);
                    GlobalFree(hData);
                    waveOutClose((HWAVEOUT) wParam);

                    break;
        }

        return DefWindowProc(hWnd,msg,wParam,lParam);
}
```

Using a Low-Level Callback to Manage Waveform Playback

The syntax of the low-level callback function for waveform output devices
is as follows:

void FAR PASCAL waveOutCallback(*hWaveOut, wMsg, dwInstance,
dwParam1, dwParam2*)

The following messages can be sent to the *wMsg* parameter of waveform output
callback functions:

Message	Description
WOM_CLOSE	Sent when the device is closed using **waveOutClose**.
WOM_OPEN	Sent when the device is opened using **waveOutOpen**.
WOM_DONE	Sent when the device driver is finished with a data block sent using **waveOutWrite**.

These messages are similar to the messages sent to window-procedure functions,
however, the parameters are different. A handle to the open waveform device is
passed as a parameter to the callback, along with the DWORD of instance data
that was passed using **waveOutOpen**.

**Message-
Dependent
Parameters**
The callback has two message-dependent parameters: *dwParam1* and
dwParam2. For the WOM_DONE message, *dwParam1* specifies a far pointer
to a WAVEHDR structure identifying the completed data block and *dwParam2*
is not used. For the WOM_OPEN and WOM_CLOSE messages, neither of the
parameters are used.

After the driver is finished with a data block, you can clean up and free the data
block, as described in "Allocating and Preparing Audio Data Blocks," earlier in
this chapter. Because of the restrictions of low-level audio callbacks, you can't do
this within the callback—you must do this work outside of the callback.

Getting the Current Playback Position

While a waveform is playing, you can monitor the current playback position within the waveform. The Multimedia extensions provide the following function for this purpose:

waveOutGetPosition
Retrieves the current playback position of a waveform output device.

This function takes three parameters: a handle to a waveform output device, a far pointer to an MMTIME structure, and a WORD specifying the size of the MMTIME structure.

For waveform devices, the preferred time format to represent the current position is in samples. Thus, the current position of a waveform device is specified as the number of samples for one channel from the beginning of the waveform.

To query the current position of a waveform device, set the **wType** field of the MMTIME structure to the constant TIME_SAMPLES and pass this structure to **waveOutGetPosition**.

Stopping, Pausing, and Restarting Playback

While a waveform is playing, you can stop or pause playback. Once playback has been paused, you can restart it. The Multimedia extensions provide the following functions for controlling waveform playback:

waveOutPause
Pauses playback on a waveform output device.

waveOutReset
Stops playback on a waveform output device and marks all pending data blocks as done.

waveOutRestart
Resumes playback on a paused waveform output device.

Use **waveOutPause** to pause a waveform device that is currently playing. To resume playback on a paused device, use **waveOutRestart**. These functions take a single parameter: the waveform output device handle returned by **waveOutOpen**. Pausing a waveform device might not be instantaneous—the driver can finish playing the current block before pausing playback.

Generally, as soon as the first waveform data block is sent using **waveOutWrite**, the waveform device begins playing. If you don't want the waveform to start playing immediately, call **waveOutPause** before calling **waveOutWrite**. Then, when you want to begin playing the waveform, call **waveOutRestart**.

To stop a waveform from playing, use **waveOutReset**. This function differs from **waveOutPause** in that it also marks all pending data blocks as being done. You can't restart a device that has been stopped with **waveOutReset** by using **waveOutRestart**—you must use **waveOutWrite** to send the first data block to resume playback on the device.

Closing Waveform Output Devices

After waveform playback is complete, call **waveOutClose** to close the waveform device. If **waveOutClose** is called while a waveform is playing, the close operation will fail and the function returns an error code indicating that the device was not closed. If you don't want to wait for playback to end before closing the device, call **waveOutReset** before closing. This terminates playback and allows the device to be closed. Be sure to clean up the preparation on all data blocks before closing the waveform output device.

Changing Waveform Playback Volume

The Multimedia extensions provide the following functions to query and set the volume level of waveform output devices:

waveOutGetVolume
  Gets the volume level of the specified waveform device.

waveOutSetVolume
  Sets the volume level of the specified waveform device.

Not all waveform devices support volume changes. Some devices support individual volume control on both the left and right channels. See "Determining Capabilities of Waveform Output Devices," earlier in this chapter, for information on how to determine the volume-control capabilities of waveform devices.

Note Unless your application is designed to be a master volume-control application providing the user with volume control for all audio devices in a system, you should open an audio device before changing its volume. You should also query the volume level before changing it and restore the volume level to its previous level as soon as possible.

Volume is specified in a DWORD; the upper 16 bits specify the relative volume of the right channel, and the lower 16 bits specify the relative volume of the left channel, as shown in the following illustration:

HIWORD	LOWORD
Right-Channel Volume	Left- or Mono-Channel Volume

DWORD packing for waveform volume levels.

For devices that don't support left- and right-channel volume control, the lower 16 bits specify the volume level, and the upper 16 bits are ignored. Volume-level values range from 0x0 (silence) to 0xFFFF (maximum volume) and are interpreted logarithmically. The perceived volume increase is the same when increasing the volume level from 0x5000 to 0x6000 as it is from 0x4000 to 0x5000.

When querying with **waveOutGetVolume**, the volume is returned in a DWORD location specified by a far pointer parameter.

Changing Pitch and Playback Rate

Some waveform output devices can vary the pitch and the playback rate of waveform data. Not all waveform devices support pitch and playback-rate changes. See "Determining Capabilities of Waveform Output Devices," earlier in this chapter, for information on how to determine if a particular waveform device supports pitch and playback rate changes.

The differences between changing pitch and playback rate are:

- Changing the playback rate is performed by the device-driver and does not require specialized hardware. The sample rate is not changed, but the driver interpolates by skipping or synthesizing samples. For example, if the playback rate is changed by a factor of two, the driver skips every other sample.

- Changing the pitch requires specialized hardware. The playback rate and sample rate are not changed.

The Multimedia extensions provide the following functions to query and set waveform pitch and playback rates:

---

waveOutGetPitch
Gets the pitch for the specified waveform output device.

waveOutGetPlaybackRate
Gets the playback rate for the specified waveform output device.

waveOutSetPitch
Sets the pitch for the specified waveform output device.

waveOutSetPlaybackRate
Sets the playback rate for the specified waveform output device.

Specifying Pitch and Playback Rate   The pitch and playback rates are changed by a factor specified with a fixed-point number packed into a DWORD. The upper 16 bits specify the integer part; the lower 16 bits specify the fractional part of the number. For example, the value 1.5 is represented as 0x00018000L. The value 0.75 is represented as 0x0000C000L. A value of 1.0 (0x00010000) means the pitch or playback rate is unchanged.

Recording Waveform Audio

If the MCI waveform-recording services don't meet the needs of your application, you can handle waveform recording using the low-level waveform services.

Waveform Input Data Types

The MMSYSTEM.H file defines data types and function prototypes for all of the audio functions. You must include this header file in any source module that uses these functions. MMSYSTEM.H defines the following data types for waveform-input functions:

HWAVEIN
A handle to an open waveform input device.

WAVEINCAPS
A data structure used to inquire about the capabilities of a particular waveform input device.

WAVEFORMAT
A data structure that specifies the data formats supported by a particular waveform output device. This data structure is also used for waveform output devices.

WAVEHDR
A data structure that is a header for a block of waveform output data. This data structure is also used for waveform output devices.

Querying Waveform Input Devices

Before recording a waveform, you should call the **waveInGetDevCaps** function to determine the waveform input capabilities of the system. This function takes a pointer to a WAVEINCAPS structure, which it fills with information on the capabilities of a given device. This information includes the manufacturer and product IDs, a product name for the device, and the version number of the device driver. In addition, the WAVEINCAPS structure provides information on the standard waveform formats that the device supports. MMSYSTEM.H defines WAVEINCAPS as follows.

```
typedef struct waveincaps_tag {
  WORD  wMid;                       /* manufacturer ID */
  WORD  wPid;                       /* product ID */
  VERSION vDriverVersion;           /* driver version */
  char  szPname[MAXPNAMELEN];       /* product name */
  DWORD  dwFormats;                 /* supported standard formats */
  WORD  wChannels;                  /* number of channels */
} WAVEINCAPS;
```

Opening Waveform Input Devices

Use **waveInOpen** to open a waveform input device for recording. This function opens the device associated with the specified device ID and returns a handle to the open device by writing the handle to a specified memory location. The syntax of the **waveInOpen** function is as follows:

WORD waveInOpen(*lphWaveIn, wDeviceID, lpFormat, dwCallback, dwInstance, dwFlags*)

The *lphWaveIn* parameter is an LPHWAVEIN and specifies a far pointer to a memory location the function fills with a handle to the open waveform input device. Use this handle to identify the device when calling other waveform input functions.

The *wDeviceID* parameter is a WORD and identifies the waveform input device to be opened. See "Getting the Number of Devices," earlier in this chapter, for details on device IDs. If you specify the WAVE_MAPPER constant, the function will find a waveform input device capable of recording in the given format and attempt to open it.

The *lpFormat* parameter is an LPWAVEFORMAT and specifies a far pointer to a WAVEFORMAT data structure. This data structure contains information on the format of the recorded waveform data that will be sent back to the application. For details on using this data structure, see "Specifying Waveform Data Formats," earlier in this chapter. You can free the WAVEFORMAT data structure immediately after passing it to **waveInOpen**.

The *dwCallback* parameter is a DWORD and specifies either a window handle or the address of a low-level callback function. The callback can be used to monitor the progress of waveform recording so an application can determine when data blocks have been filled with waveform data and when to send additional data blocks for recording. You must specify the appropriate flag in the *dwFlags* parameter to indicate which type of callback you want. If no callback is needed, this parameter is NULL.

The *dwInstance* parameter is a DWORD and specifies 32 bits of instance data sent to the callback function each time it is called.

The *dwFlags* parameter is a DWORD and specifies one or more flags for opening a waveform device. Use the WAVE_FORMAT_QUERY flag to specify that you don't want to actually open a device, but just query whether the device supports a given format. For information on using WAVE_FORMAT_QUERY, see "Determining Non-Standard Format Support," earlier in this chapter. If you are specifying a window or low-level callback in the *dwCallback* parameter, you must specify either the CALLBACK_WINDOW or the CALLBACK_FUNCTION flag to indicate the type of callback used.

Selecting a Waveform Input Device

Some multimedia computers will have multiple waveform input devices. Unless you know you want to open a specific waveform input device in a system, you should use the WAVE_MAPPER constant for the device ID when you open a device. The **waveOutOpen** function will choose the device in the system best able to record in the given data format.

Managing Waveform Recording

Once you open a waveform input device, you can begin recording waveform data. Waveform data is recorded into application-supplied buffers specified by a WAVEHDR data structure. This is the same data structure used for waveform playback described in "Writing Waveform Data," earlier in this chapter. Memory for the WAVEHDR structure and its accompanying data buffer must be allocated and prepared, as shown in "Allocating and Preparing Audio Data Blocks," earlier in this chapter.

The Multimedia extensions provide the following functions to manage waveform recording:

waveInAddBuffer
  Sends a buffer to the device driver so it can be filled with recorded waveform data.

waveInReset
  Stops waveform recording and marks all pending buffers as done.

waveInStart
Starts waveform recording.

waveInStop
Stops waveform recording.

Use the **waveInAddBuffer** function to send data buffers to the device driver. As the buffers are filled with recorded waveform data, the application is notified with either a window message or with a callback message, depending on the flag specified when the device was opened.

Use the **waveInStart** function to begin recording. Before beginning recording, you should send at least one buffer to the driver, or incoming data might be lost. To stop waveform recording, use **waveInStop**.

Before closing the device using **waveOutClose**, call **waveOutReset** to mark any pending data blocks as being done.

Using Window Messages to Manage Waveform Recording

The following messages can be sent to a window procedure function for managing waveform recording:

Message	Description
MM_WIM_CLOSE	Sent when the device is closed using **waveInClose**.
MM_WIM_DATA	Sent when the device driver is finished with a data buffer sent using **waveInAddBuffer**.
MM_WIM_OPEN	Sent when the device is opened using **waveInOpen**.

There is a *wParam* and *lParam* parameter associated with each of these messages. The *wParam* parameter always specifies a handle to the open waveform device. The *lParam* parameter is unused for the MM_WIM_CLOSE and MM_WIM_OPEN messages.

For the MM_WIM_DATA message, *lParam* specifies a far pointer to a WAVEHDR structure that identifies the data buffer. This data buffer might not be completely filled with waveform data—recording can stop before the buffer is filled. Use the **dwBytesRecorded** field of the WAVEHDR structure to determine the amount of valid data present in the buffer.

The most useful message is MM_WIM_DATA. Unless you need to allocate memory or initialize variables, you probably don't need to use the MM_WIM_OPEN and MM_WIM_CLOSE messages. When the device driver is finished with a data block, you can clean up and free the data block as described in "Allocating and Preparing Audio Data Blocks," earlier in this chapter.

Using a Low-Level Callback to Manage Waveform Recording

This syntax of the low-level callback function for waveform input devices is as follows:

void FAR PASCAL waveInCallback(*hWaveIn, wMsg, dwInstance, dwParam1, dwParam2*)

The following messages can be sent to the *wMsg* parameter of waveform input callback functions:

Message	Description
WIM_CLOSE	Sent when the device is closed using **waveInClose**.
WIM_OPEN	Sent when the device is opened using **waveInOpen**.
WIM_DONE	Sent when the device driver is finished with a data block sent using **waveInAddBuffer**.

These messages resemble messages sent to window-procedure functions, but their parameters are different. A handle to an open waveform device is passed as a parameter to the callback function, along with the DWORD of instance data that was passed using **waveInOpen**.

Message-Dependent Parameters

The callback has two message-dependent parameters: *dwParam1* and *dwParam2*. For the WIM_CLOSE and WIM_OPEN messages, these parameters are not used. For the WIM_DONE message, *dwParam1* specifies a far pointer to a WAVEHDR structure identifying the completed data block and *dwParam2* is not used.

After the driver is finished with a data block, you can clean up and free the data block. Because of the restrictions of low-level audio callback functions, you can't do this within the callback. You must set some semaphores and do this outside of the callback. See "Using a Callback Function to Process Driver Messages," earlier in this chapter, for details on the restrictions on using callback functions.

Playing MIDI Audio

To play MIDI files, you should use the MCI sequencer. If the MCI sequencer services don't meet the needs of your application, you can manage MIDI playback using the low-level MIDI services.

MIDI Output Data Types

The MMSYSTEM.H header file defines data types and function prototypes for all low-level audio functions. You must include this header file in any source module that uses these functions. MMSYSTEM.H defines the following data types for low-level MIDI output functions:

HMIDIOUT

A handle to a MIDI output device.

MIDIHDR

A data structure that is a header for a block of MIDI system-exclusive data. This data structure is used for input as well as output.

MIDIOUTCAPS

A data structure used to inquire about the capabilities of a particular MIDI output device.

Querying MIDI Output Devices

Before playing MIDI audio, you should call the **midiOutGetDevCaps** function to determine the capabilities of the MIDI output hardware present in the system. This function takes a pointer to a MIDIOUTCAPS structure that it fills with information on the capabilities of a given device. This information includes the manufacturer and product IDs, a product name for the device, and the version number of the device driver. In addition, the MIDIOUTCAPS structure provides information on the device technology, the number of voices and notes supported, the MIDI channels that the device responds to, and features supported by the driver.

The MMSYSTEM.H file defines the MIDIOUTCAPS structure as follows:

```
typedef struct midioutcaps_tag {
  WORD  wMid;                     /* manufacturer ID */
  WORD  wPid;                     /* product ID */
  VERSION vDriverVersion;         /* driver version */
  char  szPname[MAXPNAMELEN];     /* product name */
  WORD  wTechnology;              /* device technology */
  WORD  wVoices;                  /* total simultaneous instruments */
  WORD  wNotes;                   /* total simultaneous notes */
  WORD  wChannelMask;             /* channels device responds to */
  DWORD dwSupport;                /* features supported */
} MIDIOUTCAPS;
```

Determining the Technology of the Device

MIDI output devices can be either internal synthesizers or external MIDI output ports. The **wTechnology** field specifies the technology of the device. MMSYSTEM.H defines the following flags to identify device technology:

Flag	Description
MOD_MIDIPORT	The device is an external MIDI output port.
MOD_SQSYNTH	The device is an internal square-wave synthesizer.
MOD_FMSYNTH	The device is an internal FM synthesizer.
MOD_SYNTH	The device is an internal synthesizer (generic).
MOD_MAPPER	The device is the MIDI Mapper.

Determining Capabilities of Internal Synthesizers

If the device is an internal synthesizer, additional device information is available in the **wVoices**, **wNotes**, and **wChannelMask** fields. If the device is an external output port, these fields are unused.

The **wVoices** field specifies the number of voices the device supports. Each voice can have a different sound or timbre. Voices are differentiated by MIDI channel. For example, a four-voice synthesizer uses four MIDI channels. The **wNotes** field specifies the *polyphony* of the device—the maximum number of notes that can be played simultaneously. The **wChannelMask** field is a bit representation of the MIDI channels that the device responds to. For example, if the device responds to the first eight MIDI channels, **wChannelMask** is 0x00FF.

The **dwSupport** field of the MIDIOUTCAPS structure indicates if the device driver supports volume changes and patch caching. MMSYSTEM.H defines the following flags for the **dwSupport** field:

Flag	Description
MIDICAPS_VOLUME	Indicates the driver supports volume control.
MIDICAPS_LRVOLUME	Indicates the driver supports individual volume control the left and right channels.
MIDICAPS_CACHE	Indicates the driver supports patch caching.

Volume changes are only supported by internal synthesizer devices. External MIDI output ports don't support volume changes. For information on changing volume, see "Changing Internal MIDI Synthesizer Volume," later in this chapter.

Opening MIDI Output Devices

Use the **midiOutOpen** function to open a MIDI output device for playback. This function opens the device associated with the specified device ID and returns a handle to the open device by writing the handle to a specified memory location. The syntax of **midiOutOpen** is as follows:

WORD midiOutOpen(*lphMidiOut, wDeviceID, dwCallback, dwInstance, dwFlags*)

The *lphMidiOut* parameter is an LPHMIDIOUT and specifies a far pointer to a memory location the function fills with a handle to the open MIDI output device. Use this handle to identify the MIDI device when calling other MIDI output functions.

The *wDeviceID* parameter is a WORD that identifies the MIDI output device to be opened. See "Getting the Number of Devices," earlier in this chapter, for details on device IDs.

The *dwCallback* parameter is a DWORD that specifies either a window handle or the address of a low-level callback function. The callback can be used to monitor the progress of the playback of MIDI system-exclusive data so the application can determine when to send additional data blocks, or when to free data blocks that have been sent. You must specify the appropriate flag in the *dwFlags* parameter to indicate which type of callback you want. If no callback is needed, this parameter is NULL.

The *dwInstance* parameter is a DWORD that specifies 32 bits of instance data sent to the callback function each time it is called.

The *dwFlags* parameter is a DWORD and specifies one or more flags for opening the MIDI device. If you are specifying a window or low-level callback in the *dwCallback* parameter, you must specify either the CALLBACK_WINDOW or the CALLBACK_FUNCTION flag to indicate the type of callback used.

Sending MIDI Messages

Once you open a MIDI output device, you can begin sending it MIDI messages using the following function:

midiOutShortMsg
Sends a MIDI message to a specified MIDI output device.

Use **midiOutShortMsg** to send any MIDI message (except for system-exclusive messages). This function takes an HMIDIOUT parameter specifying the MIDI output device to send the message to, and a DWORD for the MIDI message. The message is packed into the DWORD, as shown in the following illustration:

HIWORD		LOWORD	
HIBYTE (not used)	**LOBYTE** MIDI Data 2 (optional)	**HIBYTE** MIDI Data 1 (optional)	**LOBYTE** MIDI Status

DWORD packing for the midiOutShortMsg function.

The two MIDI data bytes are optional, depending on the MIDI status byte. The following code fragment uses **midiOutShortMsg** to send a given MIDI event to a given MIDI output device:

```
/* Sends a given MIDI event to the given output device
 */
WORD sendMIDIEvent(hMidiOut, bStatus, bData1, bData2)
HMIDIOUT hMidiOut;  // handle to the output device
BYTE bStatus;       // MIDI status byte
BYTE bData1;        // first MIDI data byte
BYTE bData2;        // second MIDI data byte
{
    union {
        DWORD dwData;
        BYTE bData[4];
    } u;

    /* Construct the MIDI message */
    u.bData[0] = bStatus;
    u.bData[1] = bData1;
    u.bData[2] = bData2;
    u.bData[3] = 0;

    /* Send the message */
    return midiOutShortMsg(hMidiOut, u.dwData);
}
```

Note MIDI output drivers are not required to verify data before sending it to an output port. It is up to applications to ensure only valid data is sent using **midiOutShortMsg**.

Sending System-Exclusive Messages

MIDI system-exclusive messages are the only MIDI messages that will not fit into a single DWORD. System exclusive messages can be any length. The Multimedia extensions provide the following function for sending system-exclusive messages to MIDI output devices:

---

midiOutLongMsg
Sends a MIDI system-exclusive message to a specified MIDI output device.

Use the MIDIHDR data structure to specify MIDI system-exclusive data blocks. This structure contains a pointer to a locked data block, the data-block length, and some assorted flags. The MMSYSTEM.H file defines the MIDIHDR data structure as follows:

```
typedef struct midihdr_tag {
    LPSTR           lpData;             /* pointer to data block */
    DWORD           dwBufferLength;     /* length of data block */
    DWORD           dwBytesRecorded;    /* number of bytes recorded */
    DWORD           dwUser;             /* user instance data */
    DWORD           dwFlags;            /* assorted flags */
    struct wavehdr_tag far *lpNext;     /* private to the driver */
    DWORD           reserved;           /* private to the driver */
} MIDIHDR;
```

Memory for the MIDIHDR data structure and the data block pointed to by **lpData** must be allocated and prepared, as shown in "Allocating and Preparing Audio Data Blocks," earlier in this chapter.

After you send a system-exclusive data block using **midiOutLongMsg**, you must wait until the device driver is finished with the data block before freeing it. If you are sending multiple data blocks, you must monitor the completion of each data block so you know when to send additional blocks. For information on different techniques for monitoring data-block completion, see "Managing Audio Data Blocks," earlier in this chapter.

Note   Any MIDI status byte other than a system-real-time message will terminate a system exclusive message. If you are using multiple data blocks to send a single system-exclusive message, do not send any MIDI messages other than system-real-time messages between data blocks.

Using Window Messages to Manage System-Exclusive Playback

The following messages can be sent to a window-procedure function for managing MIDI system-exclusive playback:

Message	Description
MM_MOM_CLOSE	Sent when the device is closed using **midiOutClose**.
MM_MOM_DONE	Sent when the device driver is finished with a data block sent using **midiOutLongMsg**.
MM_MOM_OPEN	Sent when the device is opened using **midiOutOpen**.

A *wParam* and *lParam* parameter is associated with each of these messages. The *wParam* parameter always specifies a handle to the open MIDI device. For the MM_MOM_DONE message, *lParam* specifies a far pointer to a MIDIHDR structure identifying the completed data block. The *lParam* parameter is unused for the MM_MOM_CLOSE and MM_MOM_OPEN messages.

The most useful message is the MM_MOM_DONE message. Unless you need to allocate memory or initialize variables, you probably don't need to process the MM_MOM_OPEN and MM_MOM_CLOSE messages. When playback of a data block is completed, you can clean up and free the data block as described in "Allocating and Preparing Audio Data Blocks," earlier in this chaper.

Using a Callback to Manage System-Exclusive Playback

This syntax of the low-level callback function for MIDI output devices is as follows:

void FAR PASCAL midiOutCallback(*hMidiOut, wMsg, dwInstance, dwParam1, dwParam2*)

The following messages can be sent to the *wMsg* parameter of MIDI output callback functions:

Message	Description
MOM_CLOSE	Sent when the device is closed using **midiOutClose**.
MOM_OPEN	Sent when the device is opened using **midiOutOpen**.
MOM_DONE	Sent when the device driver is finished with a data block sent using **midiOutLongMsg**.

These messages are similar to those sent to window-procedure functions, but the parameters are different. A handle to the open MIDI device is passed as a parameter to the callback, along with the DWORD of instance data passed using **midiOutOpen**.

Message-Dependent Parameters

The callback has two message-dependent parameters: *dwParam1* and *dwParam2*. For the MOM_OPEN and MOM_CLOSE messages, these parameters are not used. For the MOM_DONE message, *dwParam1* specifies a far pointer to a MIDIHDR structure identifying the completed data block and *dwParam2* is not used.

After the driver is finished with a data block, you can clean up and free the data block. Because of the restrictions of low-level audio callbacks, you can't do this within the callback. See "Using a Callback Function to Process Driver Messages," earlier in this chapter, for details on the restrictions when using callback functions.

Using midiOutLongMsg to Send Regular MIDI Messages

In addition to system-exclusive data blocks, you can also use **midiOutLongMsg** to send regular MIDI messages. You can even mix complete system-exclusive messages with regular MIDI messages in a single data block. Regular MIDI messages should be packed into the data block with the most significant byte (the status byte) coming first—no DWORD padding is used.

Note MIDI output drivers are not required to verify any data in a MIDI data block before sending the data to an output port. It is up to applications to ensure only valid data is sent using **midiOutLongMsg**.

Sending MIDI Messages Using Running-Status

The MIDI 1.0 Specification allows the use of *running-status* when a message has the same status byte as the previous message. When running status is used, the status byte of subsequent messages can be omitted. You can send MIDI messages using running status with both **midiOutShortMsg** and **midiOutLongMsg**. To send a message using running status with **midiOutShortMsg**, pack the message into a DWORD, as shown in the following illustration:

HIWORD		LOWORD	
HIBYTE (not used)	**LOBYTE** (not used)	**HIBYTE** MIDI Data 2 (optional)	**LOBYTE** MIDI Data 1

DWORD packing for midiOutShortMsg when using running status.

To send a message using running status with **midiOutLongMsg**, pack the bytes into the data block with the most significant byte coming first—no DWORD padding is used.

Changing Internal MIDI Synthesizer Volume

The Multimedia extensions provide the following functions to query and set the volume level of internal MIDI synthesizer devices:

midiOutGetVolume
   Gets the volume level of the specified internal MIDI synthesizer device.

midiOutSetVolume
   Sets the volume level of the specified internal MIDI synthesizer device.

Not all MIDI output devices support volume changes. Some devices can support individual volume changes on both the left and the right channels. See "Determining Capabilities of Internal Synthesizers," earlier in this chapter, for information on how to determine if a particular device supports volume changes.

Note   Unless your application is designed to be a master volume-control application providing the user with volume control for all audio devices in a system, you should open an audio device before changing its volume. You should also query the volume level before changing it and restore the volume level to its previous level as soon as possible.

Volume is specified in a DWORD; the upper 16 bits specify the relative volume of the right channel, and the lower 16 bits specify the relative volume of the left channel, as shown in the following illustration.

HIWORD	**LOWORD**
Right-Channel Volume	Left- or Mono-Channel Volume

DWORD packing for internal MIDI synthesizer volume levels.

For devices that don't support individual volume changes on both the left and right channels, the lower 16 bits specify the volume level, and the upper 16 bits are ignored. Values for the volume level range from 0x0 (silence) to 0xFFFF (maximum volume) and are interpreted logarithmically. The perceived volume increase is the same when increasing the volume level from 0x5000 to 0x6000 as it is from 0x4000 to 0x5000.

When querying using **midiOutGetVolume**, the volume is returned in a DWORD location specified by a far pointer parameter.

Preloading Patches with Internal MIDI Synthesizers

Some internal MIDI synthesizer devices can't keep all of their patches loaded simultaneously. These devices must preload their patch data.

The Multimedia extensions provide the following functions to request that a synthesizer preload and cache specified patches:

midiOutCachePatches
Requests that an internal MIDI synthesizer device preload and cache specified melodic patches.

midiOutCacheDrumPatches
Requests that an internal MIDI synthesizer device preload and cache specified key-based percussion patches.

The PATCHARRAY Data Type

The **midiOutCachePatches** function takes a pointer to a PATCHARRAY to indicate the patches to be cached. The MMSYSTEM.H file defines the PATCHARRAY data type as follows:

```
typedef WORD PATCHARRAY[128];
```

Each element in the array corresponds to a patch with each of the 16 bits representing one of the 16 MIDI channels. Bits are set for each of the channels that use that particular patch. For example, if patch number 0 is used by physical MIDI channels 0 and 8, set element 0 of the array to 0x0101:

15	14	13	12	11	10	9	8	7	6	5	4	3	2	1	0
0	0	0	0	0	0	0	1	0	0	0	0	0	0	0	1

The KEYARRAY Data Type

The **midiOutCacheDrumPatches** function takes a pointer to a KEYARRAY to indicate the key-based percussion patches to be cached. The MMSYSTEM.H file defines the KEYARRAY data type as follows:

```
typedef WORD KEYARRAY[128];
```

Each element in the array corresponds to a key-based percussion patch with each of the 16 bits representing one of the 16 MIDI channels. Bits are set for each of the channels that use that particular patch. For example, if the percussion patch for key number 60 is used by physical MIDI channels 9 and 15, set element 60 of the array to 0x8200:

15	14	13	12	11	10	9	8	7	6	5	4	3	2	1	0
1	0	0	0	0	0	1	0	0	0	0	0	0	0	0	0

Using the MIDI Mapper with Low-Level MIDI Functions

The MIDI Mapper provides standard patch services for device-independent playback of MIDI files. Applications that use MIDI files for audio should use the MIDI Mapper. For information on the MIDI Mapper, see "The MIDI Mapper" in Chapter 4, "High-Level Audio Services." For information on authoring device-independent MIDI files, see "Authoring MIDI Files," also in Chapter 4.

To use the MIDI mapper, open it using the **midiOutOpen** function with the *wDeviceID* parameter set to the constant MIDIMAPPER. Then you can send it MIDI messages using **midiOutShortMsg** or **midiOutLongMsg**.

Recording MIDI Audio

To record MIDI audio data, you must use low-level MIDI input functions. MCI does not currently provide a device handler for recording MIDI audio.

MIDI Input Data Types

The MMSYSTEM.H file defines data types and function prototypes for all of the low-level audio functions. MMSYSTEM.H defines the following data types for low-level MIDI input functions:

HMIDIIN
  A handle to a MIDI input device.

MIDIHDR
  A data structure that is a header for a block of MIDI system-exclusive data. This data structure is used for input as well as output.

MIDIINCAPS
  A data structure used to inquire about the capabilities of a MIDI input device.

Querying MIDI Input Devices

Before recording MIDI audio, you should call the **midiInGetDevCaps** function to determine the capabilities of the MIDI input hardware present in the system. This function takes a pointer to a MIDIINCAPS structure, which it fills with information about the capabilities of a given device. This information includes the manufacturer and product IDs, a product name for the device, and the version number of the device driver. MMSYSTEM.H defines the MIDIINCAPS structure as follows:

```
typedef struct midiincaps_tag {
  WORD  wMid;                    /* manufacturer ID */
  WORD  wPid;                    /* product ID */
  VERSION vDriverVersion;        /* driver version */
  char  szPname[MAXPNAMELEN];    /* product name */
} MIDIINCAPS;
```

Opening MIDI Input Devices

Use the **midiInOpen** function to open a MIDI input device for recording. This function opens the device associated with the specified device ID and returns a handle to the open device by writing the handle to a specified memory location. The syntax of **midiInOpen** is as follows:

WORD midiInOpen*(lphMidiIn, wDeviceID, dwCallback, dwInstance, dwFlags)*

The *lphMidiIn* parameter is an LPHMIDIIN and specifies a far pointer to a memory location the function fills with a handle to the open MIDI input device. Use this handle to identify the MIDI device when calling other MIDI input functions.

The *wDeviceID* parameter is a WORD that identifies the MIDI input device to be opened. See "Getting the Number of Devices," earlier in this chapter, for details on device IDs.

The *dwCallback* parameter is a DWORD and specifies either a window handle or the address of a low-level callback function. You must specify the appropriate flag in the *dwFlags* parameter to indicate which type of callback you want.

The *dwInstance* parameter is a DWORD that specifies 32 bits of instance data sent to the callback function each time it is called.

The *dwFlags* parameter is a DWORD and specifies one or more flags for opening the MIDI device. You must specify either the CALLBACK_WINDOW or the CALLBACK_FUNCTION flag to indicate the type of callback you are using.

Managing MIDI Recording

Once you open a waveform input device, you can begin recording MIDI data. The Multimedia extensions provide the following functions for managing MIDI recording:

midiInAddBuffer
  Sends a buffer to the device driver so it can be filled with recorded MIDI data.

midiInReset
  Stops MIDI recording and marks all pending buffers as done.

midiInStart
  Starts MIDI recording and resets the time stamp to zero.

midiInStop
  Stops MIDI recording.

Use the **midiInAddBuffer** function to send data buffers to the device driver for recording system-exclusive messages. As the buffers are filled with recorded data, the application is notified by one of the techniques discussed in "Managing Audio Data Blocks," earlier in this chapter.

Use the **midiInStart** function to begin recording. To record system-exclusive messages, send at least one buffer to the driver before starting recording. To stop recording, use **midiInStop**. Before closing the device using **midiInClose**, call **midiInReset** to mark any pending data blocks as being done.

You must use either a window-procedure function or a low-level callback function to receive MIDI data. If you want time-stamped data, you must use a low-level callback function.

To record system-exclusive messages, you must supply the device driver with data buffers. These buffers are specified by a MIDIHDR data structure. This is the same data structure used for MIDI system-exclusive playback described in "Sending System-Exclusive Messages," earlier in this chapter. Memory for the MIDIHDR structure and its accompanying data buffer must be allocated and prepared as shown in "Allocating and Preparing Audio Data Blocks," earlier in this chapter.

Using Window Messages to Manage MIDI Recording

The following messages can be sent to a window-procedure function for managing MIDI recording:

Message	Description
MM_MIM_CLOSE	Sent when the device is closed using **midiInClose**.
MM_MIM_DATA	Sent when a complete MIDI message is received (this message is used for all MIDI messages except system-exclusive messages).
MM_MIM_ERROR	Sent when an invalid MIDI message is received (this message is used for all MIDI messages except system-exclusive messages).

Message	Description
MM_MIM_LONGDATA	Sent when either a complete MIDI system-exclusive message is received, or when a data buffer sent using **midiInAddBuffer** is filled with system-exclusive data.
MM_MIM_LONGERROR	Sent when an invalid MIDI system-exclusive message is received.
MM_MIM_OPEN	Sent when the device is opened using **midiInOpen**.

A *wParam* and *lParam* parameter is associated with each of these messages. The *wParam* parameter always specifies a handle to the open MIDI device. The *lParam* parameter is unused for the MM_MIM_CLOSE and MM_MIM_OPEN messages.

Receiving Regular MIDI Data
For the MM_MIM_DATA message, *lParam* specifies the received MIDI data. This data is packed into a DWORD, as shown in the following illustration:

HIWORD		LOWORD	
HIBYTE (Unused)	**LOBYTE** MIDI Data 2 (optional)	**HIBYTE** MIDI Data 1 (optional)	**LOBYTE** MIDI Status

DWORD packing for recorded MIDI data.

Receiving System-Exclusive MIDI Data
For the MM_MIM_LONGDATA message, *lParam* specifies a far pointer to a MIDIHDR structure that identifies the data buffer for system-exclusive messages. The data buffer might not be completely filled—you usually don't know the size of the system-exclusive messages before recording them and must allocate a buffer large enough for the largest expected message. Use the **dwBytesRecorded** field of the MIDIHDR structure to determine the amount of valid data present in the buffer.

Using a Low-Level Callback to Manage MIDI Recording

This syntax of the low-level callback function for MIDI input devices is as follows:

void FAR PASCAL midiInCallback(*hMidiIn, wMsg, dwInstance, dwParam1, dwParam2*)

The following messages can be sent to the *wMsg* parameter of MIDI input callback functions:

Message	Description
MIM_CLOSE	Sent when the device is closed using **midiInClose**.
MIM_DATA	Sent when a complete MIDI message is received (this message is used for all MIDI messages except system-exclusive messages).
MIM_ERROR	Sent when an invalid MIDI message is received (this message is used for all MIDI messages except system-exclusive messages).
MIM_LONGERROR	Sent when an invalid MIDI system-exclusive message is received.
MIM_LONGDATA	Sent when either a complete MIDI system-exclusive message is received, or when a data buffer is filled with system-exclusive data.
MIM_OPEN	Sent when the device is opened using midiInOpen.

These messages are similar to those sent to window-procedure functions, but the parameters are different. A handle to the open MIDI device is passed as a parameter to the callback, along with the DWORD of instance data that was passed using **midiInOpen**.

The callback has two message-dependent parameters: *dwParam1* and *dwParam2*. For the MIM_OPEN and MIM_CLOSE messages, these parameters are unused.

For the MIM_DATA message, *dwParam1* specifies the received MIDI data and *dwParam2* specifies a time stamp for the data. The data is packed into a DWORD, as shown in the previous section on using window messages.

For the MIM_LONGDATA message, *dwParam1* specifies a far pointer to a MIDIHDR structure that identifies the data buffer for system-exclusive messages. As with the MIM_DATA message, *dwParam2* specifies a time stamp for the data. The data buffer might not be completely filled. Use the **dwBytesRecorded** field of the MIDIHDR structure to determine the amount of valid data present in the buffer.

After the device driver is finished with a data block, you can clean up and free the data block. Because of the restrictions of low-level audio callbacks, you can't do this within the callback. You must set some semaphores and do this outside of the callback.

Receiving Time-Stamped MIDI Messages

Because of the delay between when the device driver receives a MIDI message and the time the application receives the message, MIDI input device drivers time stamp the MIDI message with the time the message was received. MIDI time stamps are defined as the time the first byte of the message was received and are specified in milliseconds. The **midiInStart** function resets the time stamps for a device to zero.

As stated earlier, to receive time stamps with MIDI input, you must use a low-level callback function. The *dwParam2* parameter of the callback function specifies the time stamp for data associated with the MIM_DATA and MIM_LONGDATA messages.

Receiving Running-Status Messages

The MIDI 1.0 Specification allows the use of *running-status* when a message has the same status byte as the previous message. When running status is used, the status byte of subsequent messages can be omitted. All MIDI input device drivers are required to expand messages using running status to complete messages—you always receive complete MIDI messages from a MIDI input device driver.

Auxiliary Audio Devices

Auxiliary audio devices are audio devices whose output is mixed with the MIDI and waveform output devices in a multimedia computer. An example of an auxiliary audio device is the compact disc audio output from a CD-ROM drive.

Control for auxiliary audio devices is provided by a software-controlled audio mixer. The mixer can reside on the motherboard of a multimedia computer, or it can be on an add-in sound card. The following illustration shows the conceptual audio-signal routing in a multimedia computer:

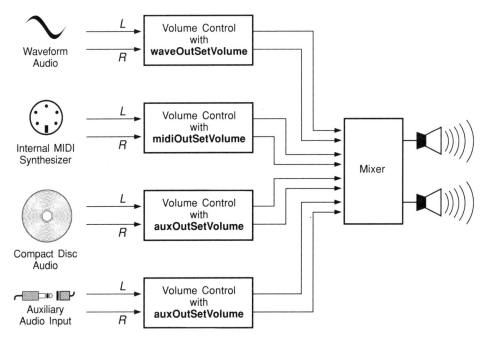

Audio signal routing for a multimedia computer.

In this multimedia computer, there are two auxiliary audio devices: the CD-ROM and the external audio input. The external audio input is an input jack that allows the user to connect other audio devices.

Querying Auxiliary Audio Devices

Not all multimedia systems have auxiliary audio support. You can use the **auxGetNumDevs** function to determine the number of controllable auxiliary devices present in a system.

To get information on a particular auxiliary audio device, use the **auxGetDevCaps** function. This function takes a pointer to an AUXCAPS structure, which it fills with information on the capabilities of a given device. This information includes the manufacturer and product IDs, a product name for the device, and the device-driver version number. For information on these fields, see "Getting the Capabilities of a Device," earlier in this chapter. The AUXCAPS structure also contains information on the device type and the functionality the device supports. The MMSYSTEM.H file defines the AUXCAPS structure as follows:

```
typedef struct auxcaps_tag {
    WORD    wMid;                       /* manufacturer ID */
    WORD    wPid;                       /* product ID */
    VERSION vDriverVersion;             /* driver version */
    char    szPname[MAXPNAMELEN];       /* product name */
    WORD    wTechnology;                /* device type */
    DWORD   dwSupport;                  /* functionality supported */
} AUXCAPS;
```

Determining Auxiliary Audio Device Types

The MMSYSTEM.H file defines the following flags for the **wTechnology** field of the AUXCAPS structure to determine the device type of an auxiliary audio device:

Flag	Description
AUXCAPS_CDAUDIO	The device is an internal CD-ROM drive.
AUXCAPS_AUXIN	The device is an auxiliary audio input jack.

Determining Capabilities of Auxiliary Audio Devices

The **dwSupport** field of the AUXCAPS structure indicates whether the device driver supports volume changes. The MMSYSTEM.H file defines the following flags for the **dwSupport** field:

Flag	Description
AUXCAPS_VOLUME	Volume-control support.
AUXCAPS_LRVOLUME	Individual volume-control support for both the left and right channels.

Changing Auxiliary Audio-Device Volume

The Multimedia extensions provide the following functions to query and set the volume for auxiliary audio devices:

---

auxGetVolume
   Gets the volume level of the specified auxiliary audio device.

auxSetVolume
   Sets the volume level of the specified auxiliary audio device.

Not all auxiliary audio devices support volume changes. Some devices can support individual volume changes on both the left and the right channels. See "Determining Capabilities of Auxiliary Audio Devices," earlier in this chapter, for information on how to determine if a particular device supports volume changes.

Note Unless your application is designed to be a master volume-control application providing the user with volume control for all audio devices in a system, you should open an audio device before changing its volume. You should also query the volume level before changing it and restore the volume level to its previous level as soon as possible.

The volume level is specified as in the waveform and MIDI volume-control functions: in a DWORD with the upper 16 bits specifying the relative volume of the right channel and the lower 16 bits specifying the relative volume of the left channel. For devices that don't support individual volume control on both the left and right channels, the lower 16 bits specify the volume level, and the upper 16 bits are ignored.

Values for the volume level range from 0x0 (silence) to 0xFFFF (maximum volume) and are interpreted logarithmically. This means the perceived volume increase is the same when increasing the volume level from 0x5000 to 0x6000 as it is from 0x4000 to 0x5000.

When querying with **auxGetVolume**, the volume is returned in a DWORD location specified by a far pointer parameter.

Chapter 6

The Multimedia Movie Player

The Movie Player provides the ability to play animation files in Windows with Multimedia. These animation files, called Multimedia Movie Files, can be created on the Macintosh using MacroMind Director, a multimedia authoring tool. Movie files can contain animation data, audio data, Media Control Interface (MCI) script commands, and user-defined script commands.

This chapter covers the following topics:

- The Movie Player and its capabilities and architecture

- The different ways to play movies

- Using the MCI Multimedia Movie Driver

About the Movie Player

The Movie Player API is supported by a single dynamic-link library (DLL) called MMP.DLL. The Movie Player can load and play movie files that include animated graphics, sound, and commands for controlling MCI devices. The Movie Player performs the animation sequences, using other parts of the Multimedia extensions to play embedded audio and handle MCI commands.

The Movie Player loads the animation data in the movie file at the time the file is opened; it does not perform any streaming techniques to incrementally load the bitmaps and other animation objects during playback. If a movie contains a large number of bitmaps and other objects, the load time might be perceptible to the user. To avoid long pauses during presentations that display movies, you might consider loading the movie files while the presentation is paused, or perhaps load the movie files at the beginning of the presentation. The Movie Player gives you full control over the playback window; you don't need to display the movie frame until you're ready.

Like all Windows applications, the Movie Player uses the Windows palette manager to map the colors it needs into the limited range of colors supported by the display driver. If your movie uses a 256-color palette, the palette manager might have difficulty mapping the colors when the playback window is inactive. The Movie Player includes an option you can use to borrow all but two of the Windows static colors, providing 18 additional colors when the playback window is active. Using this option reduces all inactive windows to black and white, so you probably won't want to use it unless you're displaying the movie on a full-screen window.

For a complete discussion of authoring considerations for movies created for use with the Multimedia extensions, see the *Multimedia Authoring Guide*.

Multimedia Movie Files

Movie files, which typically have a .MMM filename extension, contain all the information necessary to present movie animation and sound sequences. These files use a RIFF-based format called the Multimedia Movie File (RMMP) format. Movies created on the Macintosh using MacroMind Director can be converted to RMMP format using the Microsoft Movie Convertor utility. The *Multimedia Authoring Guide* describes how to use this utility. For more information on the RMMP format, see the *Programmer's Reference*.

The Movie Player uses *cast-based animation*, also known as *object animation*. In cast-based animation, each object involved in the presentation is an individual element with its own movement pattern, color, size, shape, and speed. These presentation objects are called *cast members* and can be graphics, sounds, text, and palettes. Collectively, the group of cast members for a movie is called the *cast*.

The term *frame* refers to a segment of time in a movie. A movie is divided into a series of frames; the first frame in the movie is frame number 1. Each frame has a list of specifications defining the behavior of any cast members used at that point in the presentation. Movie files store frames not as complete pictures, but as a series of instructions defining the behavior of cast members, the display duration of the frame, and *transitions*, or special ways to move from frame to frame. Some frames contain *subframes*; subframes are mostly used with special transition effects in which cast members are drawn incrementally to the stage window.

The cast is controlled by a movie *score*. You might think of the score as a grid in which columns represent frames and rows represent instructions that define the appearance and behavior of a movie at the given frame. Not all cast members included in a movie file are necessarily involved in the presentation; cast members must be referenced in the score to play a part in the animation. The rows in the score are called *channels* and include the following:

- Instructions for graphic objects, bitmaps, and text

- A tempo channel defining the amount of time each frame is displayed

- A palette channel defining the color table for the frame

- A transition channel defining how the previous frame is replaced by the current frame

- A sound channel referencing audio cast members for each frame

- A script channel referencing textual script commands to be executed after each frame is displayed

For more information on cast-based animation, see the MacroMind Director documentation.

Using Script-Channel Commands

Movie files can include textual script commands. Script statements are entered in a movie file and referenced in the script channel. The Movie Player recognizes two script-channel commands that allow a movie to send command strings to MCI. For example, a movie can use MCI to play a MIDI file during a specific range of frames.

MacroMind Director includes a script language, Lingo, that allows authors to create interactive movies. The Movie Player does not support Lingo and ignores any Lingo statements in the script channel. Contact MacroMind for information on licensing a version of the Movie Player that supports Lingo.

The Movie Player can pass script commands to a movie player application for processing. This allows you to define and process your own set of script commands.

Script Commands for Controlling MCI Devices

The following commands allow you to control MCI devices from a movie (these commands are not case sensitive):

Command	Description
mci <*MCI command string*>	Sends the specified command string to MCI for processing. The <*MCI command string*> consists of an MCI command string, optionally enclosed in single or double quotation marks.
mciWait <*DeviceName*>	Pauses frame advancement until the previous MCI command sent to the device is complete. If no command is outstanding, the movie continues to play. The <*Device Name*> is a valid MCI device name opened in a previous frame.

You most open the MCI device before sending commands to it. See Chapter 2, "The Media Control Interface (MCI)," for information on using MCI command strings.

Multiple MCI commands can be called from one script-channel command; just separate each MCI command with a semicolon (;). However, a series of MCI commands called from one script-channel command will not necessarily execute sequentially. If the commands need to be processed in a specific order, place them in separate frames.

Note Before the playback application ends, the Movie Player automatically closes any open MCI devices.

For example, a movie can open a waveform audio file at frame number 25 and start playback at frame 26. At frame 30, it could pause the frame advance until MCI finishes playing the audio file. The following script-channel commands would accomplish this:

Frame	Script-Channel Text
25	`mci open firetruk.wav type waveaudio alias truck`
26	`mci play truck`
30	`mciWait truck`
31	`mci close truck`

For more detailed examples on using the MCI script-channel commands, see the *Multimedia Authoring Guide*.

Application-Specific Script Commands

The Movie Player can pass the contents of the script channel to an application. The application assigns a callback function that the Movie Player executes at the following times:

- After the Movie Player completes frame and subframe updates

- Before the Movie Player processes the script-channel text for the frame

Chapter 7, "Using the Movie Player Functions," describes how you might create a simple script-channel command processor using this capability.

Movie Player Instances

Up to eight instances of the Movie Player can be resident simultaneously, allowing a single application to simultaneously load and play multiple movie files. Also, multiple applications can simultaneously load and play movie files, as long as the total number of movies does not exceed eight. Each Movie Player instance is associated with the following:

- An instance identifier called a *movie ID*

- A playback window called a *stage window* (the stage window is required only during playback)

- A *movie file* (containing all animation and sound information)

The following illustration uses the analogy of a movie projector to show how the movie ID, stage window, and movie file all work together:

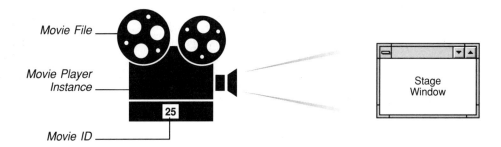

Relationship of Movie Player components.

The Movie Player instance also uses the following items when playing a movie:

- An *off-screen buffer* that allows frames to be drawn in memory before being displayed. If you're using the Movie Player functions, you can direct the Movie Player to omit the off-screen buffer, thus reducing memory requirements.

- A *frame index* that keeps track of the current movie-frame number. The frame index references the frame displayed in the stage window.

Identifying Movie Player Instances   The following illustration shows three Movie Player instances, each with associated data objects. An **mmpAnimate** function call, which advances the movie one frame, is directed to the Movie Player instance with movie ID *idMovie1*.

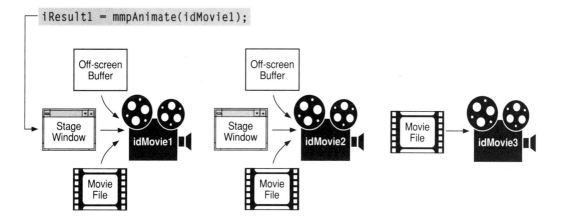

Movie Player instances.

Movie Playback Methods

You can play MacroMind Director movies by doing the following:

■ Using the MCI animation commands

■ Using the Movie Player functions

The following illustration shows the different ways your application can access the Movie Player:

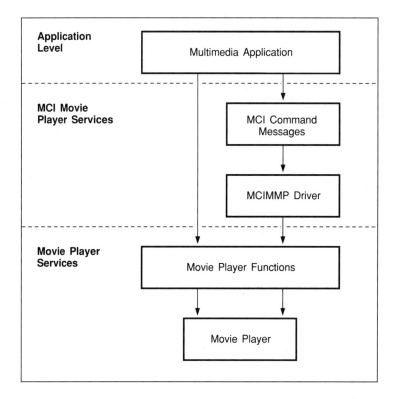

Methods of playing a movie file from Windows with Multimedia.

The method you use depends on the amount of control you want over playback. MCI provides the easiest way to play movies.

Playback Using MCI Command Messages

Using MCI commands, your application can supply a movie filename with the MCI_OPEN command message and then send an MCI_PLAY command message to start playback. Using the MCI Multimedia Movie Driver (hereafter called the MCI Movie Driver), you can do the following:

- Start the Movie Player and load a movie file

- Play a movie file from start to finish or through a range of frames; play forward or reverse; play fast or slow; step frame by frame; stop and restart playback; and receive notification when playback is complete

- Use a default playback window or a playback window created by the application; specify the size and location of the playback area within the window; minimize, maximize, move, hide, or show the window; and change the window caption

- Control the usage of the system colors and turn sound playback off or on

- Get status information, including playback state, current frame number, window handle, and palette handle

Playback Using Movie Player Functions

Using the Movie Player functions is more work because your application is responsible for starting the Movie Player, loading the movie, creating the stage window, starting the movie, and advancing the frames. It must keep track of the movie ID of each Movie Player instance and tell the Movie Player to update the stage window when the window is invalidated. The Movie Player API provides the following capabilities beyond the basic MCI playback functions:

- The ability to load an RMMP chunk from an open data file

- Control over the loading of cast members and the use of the image buffer

- Control over frame advancement

- The ability to specify a device context for the display of movie frames

- The ability to specify tempo settings for the movie

- The ability to set the movie to automatically repeat

- The ability to specify a callback function that is executed after frame updates and before script-channel processing

- The ability to retrieve detailed information on movie files on disk and in memory, and get detailed error information

Chapter 7, "Using the Movie Player Functions," describes how to use the Movie Player functions. The rest of this chapter discusses the MCI Movie Driver.

About the MCI Movie Driver

The MCI Movie Driver is an MCI device driver called MCIMMP.DRV. Using MCI can simplify your code development because your application is responsible only for opening the movie file, telling MCI to begin playback, and closing the movie file. Also, once you have added MCI support to your application, you can easily add support for other media devices and animation players; the MCI interface is standard across different types of devices.

In contrast, the Movie Player functions work only with the Movie Player. They can require more coding than the MCI commands; applications using Movie Player functions must open the Movie Player, load the movie, register and create the stage window, start playback, advance the frames, update the stage window, and then close the Movie Player instance.

MCI controls many device types and supports both the command-string and command-message interfaces. This section covers the basic command-message interface for animation. See the following documentation for more information on MCI:

- Chapter 2, "The Media Control Interface (MCI)," for general information on MCI

- The *Programmer's Reference* for a complete description of each MCI command message and its flags and data structures (the *Programmer's Reference* also describes the command strings supported by each MCI device)

The MMSYSTEM.H file defines messages, flags, data types, and function prototypes for MCI. You must include this header file in any source module that uses MCI.

MCI Movie Playback Commands

The following MCI command messages can be used to perform common movie-playback tasks:

Task	Command Message
Open and close movie files	
Open a movie file, specify stage-window style, specify color-palette usage	MCI_OPEN
Close a movie file	MCI_CLOSE
Play movie frames	
Play any range of frames, forward or reverse, fast or slow	MCI_PLAY
Play from the current position, one or more frames, forward or reverse	MCI_STEP
Stop playback	MCI_PAUSE, MCI_STOP
Seek to a specific frame number or to the beginning or end of the movie file	MCI_SEEK
Update an invalid rectangle on a stage window	MCI_UPDATE
Change playback options	
Supply the application-created playback window, change the display state of the window, change the window caption	MCI_WINDOW
Specify the location and size of the playback area within the stage window	MCI_PUT
Mute sound playback	MCI_SET
Get playback information	
Get the current frame number, handle to the palette, or handle to the stage window	MCI_STATUS
Get the origin and size of the movie frame	MCI_WHERE
Get product name, movie filename, or stage window caption	MCI_INFO

For a comprehensive list of MCI commands, and their flags and associated data structures, see the *Programmer's Reference*.

MCI Movie Playback Data Types

The following are the MCI data types specific to movie playback. These data types all specify parameter blocks for MCI command messages. For a complete list of MCI data types, see the *Programmer's Reference*.

MCI_ANIM_OPEN_PARMS
A data structure specifying a parameter block for the MCI_OPEN command message.

MCI_ANIM_PLAY_PARMS
A data structure specifying a parameter block for the MCI_PLAY command message.

MCI_ANIM_RECT_PARMS
A data structure specifying a parameter block for the MCI_PUT and MCI_WHERE command messages.

MCI_ANIM_SET_PARMS
A data structure specifying a parameter block for the MCI_SET command message.

MCI_ANIM_STEP_PARMS
A data structure specifying a parameter block for the MCI_STEP command message.

MCI_ANIM_UPDATE_PARMS
A data structure specifying a parameter block for the MCI_UPDATE command message.

MCI_ANIM_WINDOW_PARMS
A data structure specifying a parameter block for the MCI_WINDOW command message.

Loading a Movie File

To load a movie file, send the MCI_OPEN command message to the MCI Movie Driver using the **mciSendCommand** function. Because the MCI Movie Driver is a compound device (one that can handle multiple instances), you must set the MCI_OPEN_ELEMENT flag in the *dwParam1* parameter of **mciSendCommand**.

The MCI_OPEN command starts a Movie Player instance and loads the movie file. The playback window is hidden until you send an MCI_PLAY or MCI_WINDOW command message to the driver. When the movie is open, the current position is the first frame. There can be up to eight movie files open simultaneously.

The device name on compound devices like the MCI Movie Driver is the same as the filename. The MCI Movie Driver is a non-shareable device, so subsequent attempts to open an already open movie file will fail.

In the MCI_ANIM_OPEN_PARMS parameter block that you pass with the MCI_OPEN command, specify the name of the movie file you want to load. You can also specify the following playback options using flags and the fields of the MCI_ANIM_OPEN_PARMS structure:

Option	Flag	Field
Specify filename	MCI_OPEN_ELEMENT	**lpstrElementName**
Specify MCI device type	MCI_OPEN_TYPE	**lpstrDeviceType**
Use static colors for playback	MCI_ANIM_OPEN_NOSTATIC	None
Specify playback-window style	MCI_ANIM_OPEN_WS	**dwStyle**
Specify parent-window handle	MCI_ANIM_OPEN_PARENT	**hWndParent**

The MCI_ANIM_OPEN_PARMS parameter block is defined as follows:

```
typedef struct {
    DWORD   dwCallback;              // Callback function to notify
    WORD    wDeviceID;              // Device ID returned to user
    WORD    wReserved0;
    LPSTR   lpstrDeviceType;        // Device name from SYSTEM.INI
    LPSTR   lpstrElementName;       // Filename of movie file
    LPSTR   lpstrAlias;             // Optional device alias
    DWORD   dwStyle;                // Window styles (WS_CHILD, etc.)
    WORD    hWndParent;             // Handle of parent window
    WORD    wReserved1;
} MCI_ANIM_OPEN_PARMS;
```

The MCI device ID is returned in the **wDeviceID** field. Subsequent commands to the MCI Movie Driver require the MCI device ID. You should always check the return value of the MCI_OPEN command before using this device ID. A nonzero return value indicates an error occurred in opening the device.

Set the **lpstrElementName** field to point to a string containing the filename of the movie file. The **lpstrDeviceType** field is optional if the [mci extensions] section in the WIN.INI file has an entry for .MMM, the standard movie filename extension. By default, this entry is automatically created when Windows with Multimedia is installed.

If you specify a device type, you can use "mmmovie," the device name of the MCI Movie Driver. To specify the device type, you must also set the MCI_OPEN_TYPE flag in the *dwParam1* parameter of **mciSendCommand**.

To specify window styles for the playback window, set the **dwStyle** field to any valid combination of window-style flags. By default, the MCI Movie Driver creates a pop-up window with a caption, a thick frame, a system menu, and minimize and maximize boxes. If you fill in the **dwStyle** field, pass the MCI_ANIM_OPEN_WS flag to the *dwParam1* parameter of the **mciSendCommand** function.

Some window styles require a parent window; if you specify such a style, set the **hWndParent** field of the MCI_ANIM_OPEN_PARMS structure to a valid window handle, and set the MCI_ANIM_OPEN_PARENT flag in the *dwParam1* parameter. If you don't specify a parent window handle, the MCI Movie Driver won't be able to create a playback window, and the MCI_OPEN command will fail.

Closing a Movie File

After you finish showing the movie, use the MCI_CLOSE command message to close the movie file. This also closes the Movie Player instance.

Before exiting, your application must close any MCI devices it opened. Each movie file an application opens is a separate MCI device. If an application fails to close a device, the device remains open after the application ends. This can prevent your application or other applications from reopening MCI devices or accessing movie files and might also cause unrecoverable application errors.

You can use the MCI_ALL_DEVICE_ID constant with the MCI_CLOSE command; using this constant closes all devices that your application opened. For example, the code in the following example closes all devices opened by the application:

```
dwError = mciSendCommand(MCI_ALL_DEVICE_ID, MCI_CLOSE, 0, NULL);

if(dwError)                               // Check return value
    showError(dwError);
```

This code fragment (as well as the others in this chapter) tests the values returned from the **mciSendCommand** function. It calls a showError function if an error occurs; the showError function uses the **mciGetErrorString**, **MessageBeep**, and **MessageBox** functions to display the MCI error message. The showError function is described in Chapter 4, "High-Level Audio Services."

Your application should test the **mciSendCommand** return values; when learning to use MCI, it's easy to omit a required flag or constant.

Opening a Movie File

The following code fragment opens a movie file. It specifies an overlapped window with a thick frame for the stage window. It records the MCI device ID in a global variable called wDeviceID. After opening the movie file, it uses the MCI_STATUS message to retrieve the handle to the stage window.

```
BOOL OpenMovie(HWND hWnd)
{
    char szName[145];                      // Buffer for filename
    MCI_ANIM_OPEN_PARMS mciOpen;
    MCI_STATUS_PARMS    mciStatus;
    HCURSOR hSaveCursor;
    DWORD dwError;
```

```
    .
    .                                               // Get a filename
    .
// If a movie is loaded, unload it.
if(wDeviceID)
{
    dwError = mciSendCommand(wDeviceID, MCI_CLOSE, MCI_WAIT, NULL);

    if(dwError)                          // Check return value
        showError(dwError);
}

// Load the new movie file.

mciOpen.lpstrDeviceType = "mmmovie";
mciOpen.lpstrElementName = (LPSTR)szName;
mciOpen.dwStyle = WS_OVERLAPPED | WS_THICKFRAME;

hSaveCursor = SetCursor(LoadCursor(NULL, IDC_WAIT));
dwError = mciSendCommand(NULL, MCI_OPEN,
                    MCI_OPEN_ELEMENT | MCI_OPEN_TYPE | MCI_ANIM_OPEN_WS,
                    (DWORD)(LPVOID)&mciOpen);
SetCursor(hSaveCursor);

// If open failed, set the device ID to NULL and display a message

if(dwError)
{
    wDeviceID = NULL;
    showError(dwError);
    return FALSE;
}

wDeviceID = mciOpen.wDeviceID;              // Save the device ID

mciStatus.dwItem = MCI_ANIM_STATUS_HWND;
dwError = mciSendCommand(wDeviceID, MCI_STATUS, MCI_STATUS_ITEM,
                              (DWORD)(LPVOID)&mciStatus);
if(dwError)
{
    hWndStage = NULL;
    showError(dwError);
}
else
    hWndStage = (HWND)LOWORD(mciStatus.dwReturn);

return TRUE;
}
```

Playing a Movie File

Once you open a movie file, you can use the MCI_PLAY command message to begin playing a movie. If the stage window is hidden or overlapped, the MCI Movie Driver displays the stage window before starting the playback.

The MCI Movie Driver handles all tasks associated with the playback, including starting the animation, updating the window, and advancing the frames. Using the flags for the MCI_PLAY command, you can play the movie reverse or forward and specify a starting and/or ending frame for the playback.

If an application sends an MCI_PLAY command message while the movie is already playing, one or both of the following might occur:

- If the new playback request specifies a starting or stopping frame number, or if it specifies a different playback direction, the MCI Movie Driver stops playback and then restarts playback using the parameters specified by the new request.

- If the new playback request specifies the MCI_NOTIFY flag, and notification is pending on the previous playback request, the new notification request supersedes the previous one. The MCI Movie Driver posts an MCI_NOTIFY_SUPERSEDED or an MCI_NOTIFY_ABORTED message to the notification function specified by the previous playback request.

Reverse Playback   To play a movie in reverse, you can use one of the following techniques:

- Specify an ending frame number less than the starting frame number. The MCI Movie Driver plays the movie in reverse, from the starting frame number to the ending frame number.

- Specify the MCI_REVERSE flag with the MCI_PLAY command. The MCI Movie Driver plays the movie in reverse from the current position (or the specified starting position) through the first frame in the movie. You can't specify an ending frame with the MCI_REVERSE flag.

MCI_PLAY Parameter Block

For animation devices, the MCI_PLAY command requires either the MCI_PLAY_PARMS or MCI_ANIM_PLAY_PARMS parameter blocks. The MCI_ANIM_PLAY_PARMS block is defined as follows:

```
typedef struct {
    DWORD    dwCallback;        // Callback for MCI_NOTIFY flag
    DWORD    dwFrom;            // Optional starting position
    DWORD    dwTo;              // Optional ending position
    DWORD    dwFPS;             // Not used with the MCI Movie Driver
} MCI_ANIM_PLAY_PARMS;
```

Since the MCI Movie Driver cannot use the frames-per-second setting, you can use the MCI_PLAY_PARMS parameter block when playing movie files. Playback begins at the current frame or the frame specified in the **dwFrom** field. Playback continues through the last frame or through the frame specified in the **dwTo** field (or, in the case of the MCI_REVERSE flag, through the first frame in the movie). You must specify the MCI_FROM and/or MCI_TO flags to notify the MCI Movie Driver that there are values in the **dwFrom** and **dwTo** fields.

Playing a Movie File

This section discusses one possible use of the MCI_PLAY and MCI_STOP commands. For example, if an application responds to a WM_COMMAND message by sending the MCI_PLAY or MCI_STOP commands to the MCI Movie Driver. The application uses the MCI_NOTIFY flag with the MCI_PLAY command, so the MCI Movie Driver notifies the window function when playback is finished. The application uses a global variable to identify the last operation that requested notification.

The following code fragment shows the IDM_STARTSTOP block of the main message handler for such an application:

```
long FAR PASCAL MainWndProc(HWND hWnd, unsigned iMessage, WORD wParam,
    LONG lParam)
{
    MCI_ANIM_PLAY_PARMS    mciPlay;
    .
    .                                          // Other message cases
    .
```

```
case WM_COMMAND :
    switch(wParam)
    {
        case IDM_STARTSTOP :
            if(bRunning = !bRunning)
            {
                // Create window if in full-screen mode
                if(bFull)
                    CreateStage(hWnd);

                // Record source of last notify request
                wNotify = IDM_STARTSTOP;

                mciPlay.dwCallback = hWnd;
                dwError = mciSendCommand(wDeviceID, MCI_PLAY,
                            MCI_NOTIFY, (DWORD)(LPVOID)&mciPlay);
                if(dwError)
                    showError(dwError);
            }
            else
            {
                dwError = mciSendCommand(wDeviceID, MCI_STOP, 0,
                                            NULL);
                if(dwError)
                    showError(dwError);
            }
            ChangeMenuItem(hWnd, bRunning, IDM_STARTSTOP,
                        "&Stop animating", "&Start animating");
            break;
```

Using the Notification Message

The MCI Movie Driver sends the MM_MCINOTIFY message to the window function when it finishes an operation that was started with the MCI_NOTIFY flag. In the following code fragment, an application responds to the notification message by setting some global variables and, if the movie is being played on a full-screen window, destroying the stage window:

```
case MM_MCINOTIFY:
    switch(wNotify)             // Global variable identifies the source
    {                           // of the notification request.
        case IDM_STARTSTOP:
            bRunning = FALSE;
            if(bFull)           // If playing on a full-screen window.
            {
                MessageBeep(MB_ICONINFORMATION);
                MessageBox(hWnd, "The movie's over!", szAppName,
                            MB_OK | MB_ICONINFORMATION);

                // Note: In the WM_DESTROY case of the full-screen window
                // function, the application switches playback to the
                // default window.

                DestroyWindow(hWndFull);
            }
            ChangeMenuItem(hWnd, bRunning, IDM_STARTSTOP,
                            "&Stop animating", "&Start animating");
            break;

        default:
            break;
    }
    wNotify = NULL;
    return 0L;
```

Routing Messages

The MCI Movie Driver handles all updates to its default stage window. However, your application must route Windows messages to the stage window. Your application owns all windows created by the driver.

It is recommended that you specify a NULL window handle in the message-loop **GetMessage** or **PeekMessage** function; this collects messages for all windows owned by the application. For example, the following message loop ensures that Windows messages are properly routed to the driver's default playback window.

```
while(GetMessage(&msg, NULL, 0, 0))   // Gets messages for all owned windows
{
    TranslateMessage(&msg);
    DispatchMessage(&msg);
}
```

If you are using the default stage window, and you want to specify a window handle in the **GetMessage** function, you can get the handle to the stage window using the MCI_STATUS command message.

Controlling the Stage Window

When you open a movie file, the MCI Movie Driver loads the movie file but does not display the stage window. The MCI Movie Driver creates a default stage window when it opens the movie; the window remains hidden until you issue an MCI_PLAY or MCI_WINDOW command message. By default, the driver creates a pop-up window with a caption, a thick frame, a system menu, and minimize and maximize boxes. You can change the default options when you open the movie.

An application can create its own window and then supply the window handle to the MCI Movie Driver. To do this, use the MCI_WINDOW command message with the MCI_ANIM_WINDOW_HWND flag. The MCI_WINDOW command message can also display the current stage window in various states (for example, restored, minimized, maximized, or hidden) and set the window-caption text.

You can get a handle to the default stage window using the MCI_STATUS command. See "Opening a Movie File," earlier in this chapter, for a code fragment that obtains the stage-window handle. With this handle, you can use any window-manager functions to manipulate the stage window.

Showing the Stage Window

Use the MCI_WINDOW command message to change the display state of the stage window. The parameter block for the MCI_WINDOW message is as follows:

```
typedef struct {
    DWORD   dwCallback;                 // Callback function to notify
    WORD    hWnd;                       // Supplied window handle
    WORD    wReserved1;
    WORD    nCmdShow;                   // Display styles
    WORD    wReserved2;
    LPSTR   lpstrText;                  // Pointer to window-caption text
} MCI_ANIM_WINDOW_PARMS;
```

The MCI_WINDOW message also allows you to set the stage-window caption and to provide a handle to a window that your application creates.

To change the display state of the stage window, set the **nCmdShow** field of the structure to any of the window-state flags used with the **ShowWindow** function. Pass the MCI_ANIM_WINDOW_STATE flag with the MCI_WINDOW command message. For example, the following code fragment hides the playback window:

```
MCI_ANIM_WINDOW_PARMS mciWindow;
DWORD dwError;

mciWindow.nCmdShow = SW_HIDE;

dwError = mciSendCommand(wDeviceID, MCI_WINDOW, MCI_ANIM_WINDOW_STATE,
                (DWORD)(LPVOID)&mciWindow);
if(dwError)
    showError(dwError);                     // Display MCI error string
```

Using window-manager functions, the application could do the following:

```
MCI_STATUS_PARMS mciStatus;

// Retrieve the handle to the stage window

mciStatus.dwItem = MCI_ANIM_STATUS_HWND;
dwError = mciSendCommand(wDeviceID, MCI_STATUS, MCI_STATUS_ITEM,
                        (DWORD)(LPVOID)&mciStatus);

if(dwError)
    showError(dwError)                       // If error, display error string
else
{
    if(!IsHidden((HWND)mciStatus.dwReturn))
        ShowWindow((HWND)mciStatus.dwReturn, SW_HIDE);
}
```

Specifying the Playback-Area Origin and Extents

You can specify the origin and extents of the playback area within the stage window. Use the following command messages and flags to specify the origin and extents of the playback area, and to obtain the authored frame size.

Message	Flag	Description
MCI_WHERE	MCI_ANIM_WHERE_SOURCE	Obtains original frame size.
	MCI_ANIM_WHERE_DESTINATION	Obtains origin and size of the frame as displayed in the playback window.
MCI_PUT	MCI_ANIM_PUT_SOURCE	Not supported.
	MCI_ANIM_PUT_DESTINA TION	Sets the origin and size of the movie frame within the playback window.

In the following code fragment, an application centers the playback area within the stage-window client area:

```
MCI_ANIM_RECT_PARMS mciRect;
RECT rc;

// Get height and width of movie frames

dwError = mciSendCommand(wDeviceID, MCI_WHERE,
                        MCI_ANIM_WHERE_SOURCE | MCI_ANIM_RECT,
                        (DWORD)(LPVOID)&mciRect);

if(dwError)
    showError(dwError);
else
{
    // Get height and width of window client area
    GetClientRect(hWndFull, (LPRECT)&rc);

    // Top =  client height - frame height / 2
    // Left = client width  - frame width  / 2
    mciRect.rc.top  = max(0, ((rc.bottom - mciRect.rc.bottom) / 2));
    mciRect.rc.left = max(0, ((rc.right  - mciRect.rc.right)  / 2));

    dwError = mciSendCommand(wDeviceID, MCI_PUT,
                MCI_ANIM_PUT_DESTINATION | MCI_ANIM_RECT,
                (DWORD)(LPVOID)&mciRect);
    if(dwError)
        showError(dwError);
}
```

Using Your Own Stage Window

You can switch playback to a window created by your application. If you supply your own window for movie playback, your window function must update the window when it is invalidated (see "Updating the Invalid Rectangle," later in this chapter, for more information).

Supplying the Stage-Window Handle

Use the MCI_WINDOW command to switch playback to a window created by your application. Set the **hWnd** field of the MCI_ANIM_WINDOW_PARMS structure to the window handle. Then, send the MCI_WINDOW command with the MCI_ANIM_WINDOW_HWND flag.

The MCI Movie Driver hides the default stage window and uses the application-created window as the stage window. Your application owns the window function for the playback window, so it can monitor any user actions directed toward the stage window.

Use the MCI_ANIM_WINDOW_DEFAULT constant instead of a window handle to switch to the default window. The following code fragment shows how to do this:

```
MCI_ANIM_WINDOW_PARMS mciWindow;

mciWindow.hWnd = MCI_ANIM_WINDOW_DEFAULT;
dwError = mciSendCommand(wDeviceID, MCI_WINDOW, MCI_ANIM_WINDOW_HWND,
                         (DWORD)(LPVOID)&mciWindow);

if(dwError)                          // Check return value
    showError(dwError);
```

If the default window does not exist when an application sends a window-related command to the MCI Movie Driver, the driver creates a new default window; the application never loses the default playback window.

Updating the Invalid Rectangle

The window function for the stage window must handle WM_PAINT messages generated when the stage window is invalidated. In response to the WM_PAINT message, the stage-window function sends the MCI_UPDATE command message to the MCI Movie Driver. The MCI Movie Driver then handles the screen updates. The MCI_ANIM_UPDATE_PARMS parameter block specifies the handle to the device context and the invalid rectangle.

The following code fragment shows how to use the MCI_UPDATE message:

```
MCI_ANIM_UPDATE_PARMS mciUpdate;
PAINTSTRUCT ps;
    .
    .
    .
case WM_PAINT:
    hDC = BeginPaint(hWnd, &ps);
    mciUpdate.rc  = ps.rcPaint;
    mciUpdate.hDC = ps.hdc;
    dwError = mciSendCommand(wDeviceID, MCI_UPDATE,
                 MCI_ANIM_RECT | MCI_ANIM_UPDATE_HDC,
                 (DWORD)(LPVOID)&mciUpdate);
    EndPaint(hWnd, &ps);
    if(dwError)                            // Check return value
        showError(dwError);
    break;
```

Creating a Full-Screen Playback Window

The following code fragment creates a full-screen stage window, sends the window handle to the MCI Movie Driver, and centers the playback area within the window: example

```
BOOL CreateStage(HWND hWnd)
{
    MCI_ANIM_WINDOW_PARMS mciWindow;
    MCI_ANIM_RECT_PARMS   mciRect;
    DWORD dwError;
    RECT rc;

    hWndFull = CreateWindow( szFullScreenName, NULL, WS_POPUP,
        0, 0, GetSystemMetrics(SM_CXSCREEN), GetSystemMetrics(SM_CYSCREEN),
        hWnd, NULL, hInst, NULL);

    if(hWndFull == NULL)
        return FALSE;

    // Pass handle to MCI Movie Driver, and center playback area

    mciWindow.hWnd = hWndFull;
    dwError = mciSendCommand(wDeviceID, MCI_WINDOW,
                        MCI_ANIM_WINDOW_HWND | MCI_WAIT,
                        (DWORD)(LPVOID)&mciWindow);
```

```
        if(dwError)                            // If MCI_WINDOW failed, exit
        {
            showError(dwError);
            return FALSE;
        }
        dwError = mciSendCommand(wDeviceID, MCI_WHERE,
                                 MCI_ANIM_WHERE_SOURCE | MCI_ANIM_RECT,
                                 (DWORD)(LPVOID)&mciRect);

        if(dwError)
            showError(dwError);
        else
        {

            GetClientRect(hWndFull, (LPRECT)&rc);

            mciRect.rc.top =  max(0, ((rc.bottom - mciRect.rc.bottom) / 2));
            mciRect.rc.left = max(0, ((rc.right  - mciRect.rc.right)  / 2));

            dwError = mciSendCommand(wDeviceID, MCI_PUT,
                                     MCI_ANIM_PUT_DESTINATION | MCI_ANIM_RECT,
                                     (DWORD)(LPVOID)&mciRect);
            if(dwError)
                showError(dwError);
        }

        // Rewind

        dwError = mciSendCommand(wDeviceID, MCI_SEEK, MCI_SEEK_TO_START,
                                      (DWORD)(LPVOID)&mciSeek);
        if(dwError)
            showError(dwError);
        ShowWindow(hWndFull, SW_SHOW);
        return TRUE;
}
```

An application can specify the MCI_NOTIFY flag with the MCI_PLAY command that started the full-screen playback. The MCI Movie Driver then sends an MM_MCINOTIFY message to the specified window function when playback is finished. This capability is useful when playing on a full-screen window, because you need to give the user some way to get to the menu after playback is complete. See "Using the Notification Message," earlier in this chapter, for a description of how an application might handle the notification message when playing in a full-screen window.

Writing the Window Function The window function for the full-screen stage window handles WM_PAINT messages; it also captures WM_KEYDOWN messages, returning playback to the default stage window when the user presses the ESC key. The following code fragment shows the window function (note the use of the MCI_UPDATE command message):

```
LONG FAR PASCAL StageWndProc(HWND hWnd, WORD wMsg, WORD wParam, LONG lParam)
{
    PAINTSTRUCT ps;
    HDC hDC;
    MCI_ANIM_WINDOW_PARMS mciWindow;
    MCI_ANIM_UPDATE_PARMS mciUpdate;
    MCI_ANIM_RECT_PARMS   mciRect;

    switch(wMsg)
    {
        case WM_DESTROY:
            ShowWindow(hWnd, SW_HIDE);

            // Transfer playback to default stage window
            mciWindow.hWnd = MCI_ANIM_WINDOW_DEFAULT;
            mciWindow.nCmdShow = SW_SHOW;
            dwError = mciSendCommand(wDeviceID, MCI_WINDOW,
                MCI_ANIM_WINDOW_HWND | MCI_ANIM_WINDOW_STATE,
                (DWORD)(LPVOID)&mciWindow);
            if(dwError)
                showError(dwError);
            break;

        case WM_KEYDOWN:
            if(wParam == VK_ESCAPE)
                DestroyWindow(hWnd);
            break;

        case WM_PAINT:
            hDC = BeginPaint(hWnd, &ps);
            mciUpdate.rc  = ps.rcPaint;
            mciUpdate.hDC = ps.hdc;
            dwError = mciSendCommand(wDeviceID, MCI_UPDATE,
                MCI_ANIM_UPDATE_HDC | MCI_ANIM_RECT,
                (DWORD)(LPVOID)&mciUpdate);
            EndPaint(hWnd, &ps);
            if(dwError)
                showError(dwError);
            break;

        default:
            return DefWindowProc(hWnd, wMsg, wParam, lParam);
    }
    return 0L;
}
```

Copying a Frame to the Clipboard

The following code fragment copies a frame to the Clipboard. It uses the MCI_STATUS and MCI_WHERE commands to get the movie palette and playback-area extents. With this information, it can make a copy of the movie palette and create a bitmap sized to match the stage window. It then uses the MCI_UPDATE command to draw the current movie frame into the bitmap.

This example is similar to one presented in Chapter 7, "Using the Movie Player Functions." The CopyPalette function, which makes a copy of the logical palette for the movie, is defined in the MMPLAY sample application included on your MDK disc.

```
void CopyFrame(HWND hWnd)              // hWnd is a handle to the stage window
{
    HPALETTE hPalette, hClipPalette;
    HDC hDC, hMemoryDC;
    HBITMAP hBitmap;

    MCI_STATUS_PARMS      mciStatus;
    MCI_ANIM_RECT_PARMS   mciRect;
    MCI_ANIM_UPDATE_PARMS mciUpdate;

    /* Get handle to movie palette, and make a copy of the palette.
     */
    mciStatus.dwItem = MCI_ANIM_STATUS_HPAL;
    dwError = mciSendCommand(wDeviceID, MCI_STATUS, MCI_STATUS_ITEM,
                        (DWORD)(LPVOID)&mciStatus);

    if(dwError)
    {
        showError(dwError);
        return;
    }
    hPalette = mciStatus.dwReturn;

    if((hClipPalette = CopyPalette(hPalette)) == NULL)
    {
        MessageBox(hWndMain, "Could not copy palette.", szAppName, MB_OK);
        return;
    }

    /* Get playback area extents.
     */
    dwError = mciSendCommand(wDeviceID, MCI_WHERE,
                    MCI_ANIM_WHERE_DESTINATION | MCI_ANIM_RECT,
                    (DWORD)(LPVOID)&mciRect);
```

```
    if(dwError)
    {
        showError(dwError);
        return;
    }

    /* Create bitmap, sized to match the playback area.
     */
    hDC = GetDC(hWnd);
    hMemoryDC = CreateCompatibleDC(hDC);
    hBitmap = CreateCompatibleBitmap(hDC, mciRect.rc.right,
                                          mciRect.rc.bottom);

    /* Select the bitmap into the memory DC and draw the
     * movie frame into the bitmap.
     */
    SelectObject(hMemoryDC, hBitmap);

    mciUpdate.hDC = hMemoryDC;
    dwError = mciSendCommand(wDeviceID, MCI_UPDATE, MCI_ANIM_UPDATE_HDC,
                             (DWORD)(LPVOID)&mciUpdate);

    if(dwError)
        showError(dwError)
    else
    {
        /* Place the bitmap and logical palette on the Clipboard.
         */
        if(OpenClipboard(hWnd))
        {
            EmptyClipboard();
            SetClipboardData(CF_BITMAP, hBitmap);
            SetClipboardData(CF_PALETTE, hClipPalette);
            CloseClipboard();
        }
        else
            MessageBox(hWndMain, "Could not open Clipboard.",
                       szAppName, MB_OK | MB_ICONEXCLAMATION);
    }
    DeleteDC(hMemoryDC);
    ReleaseDC(hWnd, hDC);
}
```

C h a p t e r   7
Using the Movie Player Functions

Movie Player functions provide more flexibility than the MCI animation commands, but they require more work. This chapter covers the following topics:

- An overview of the Movie Player functions

- Opening and closing a Movie Player instance, and getting error information

- Loading, unloading, and getting information on movie files

- Managing the playback window

- Starting playback, advancing frames, and stopping playback

- Changing playback options and jumping to specific frames in a movie

- Using frame callback functions

For an overview of the Movie Player, including a description of the MCI animation commands, see Chapter 6, "The Multimedia Movie Player." Also, the MMPLAY sample application on your MDK disc is a Movie Player application that uses many of the Movie Player features.

About the Movie Player Functions

Movie Player functions all have an **mmp** prefix. The MMP.H file defines new data types and function prototypes for Movie Player functions. You must include this header file in any source module that uses Movie Player functions and data types.

The MMP.H file defines the following new data types:

MMPID
  A Movie Player instance identifier.

MMPMOVIEINFO
  A data structure used for obtaining information on movies.

To use Movie Player functions in your application, you must use the following header files and libraries in addition to the standard Windows and C files:

File	Description
MMP.H	C header file containing Movie Player function and data declarations.
MMP.LIB	Import library used to resolve function-call references.
MMP.DLL	Windows dynamic-link library containing code used by Movie Player functions.

The Animation Process

Several Movie Player functions work together to load and play movie files. The following functions are commonly used by movie player applications:

Function	Description
mmpOpen	Opens a Movie Player instance.
mmpLoadFile	Loads a movie file and specifies playback options.
mmpStartAnimating	Starts frame advance.
mmpAnimate	Advances the frames.
mmpUpdate	Updates an invalid rectangle in the stage window.
mmpClose	Closes the Movie Player instance.
mmpGetError	Get detailed error information.

Deciding on Movie-Playback Options

The Movie Player provides several playback options that allow flexibility in dealing with low-memory situations and performance problems. When working with the Movie Player API, keep in mind the following options:

Option and Description	Tradeoffs
Load referenced cast members The movie file can contain unused cast members; without this option, the Movie Player loads all cast members regardless of whether they are referenced in the score. Specify the MMP_LOAD_REFERENCED flag with the **mmpLoadFile** function. See "Handling Movie Files," later in this chapter, for more information.	Reduces memory consumption for some movie files. Increases the loading time, since the Movie Player must scan the score to determine which cast members are used.
Omit image buffer By default, the Movie Player builds the frame in an off-screen buffer before displaying it on the stage window. Use this option only if there is insufficient memory to load the movie file. Specify the MMP_LOAD_NOBUFFER flag with the **mmpLoadFile** function. See "Handling Movie Files," later in this chapter, for more information.	Reduces memory consumption but degrades animation performance. Can cause flashing in movies that draw multiple bitmaps to the frames.
Steal system colors This option lets the Movie Player take over all but two of the twenty system colors, reducing the system colors to black and white while the stage window is active. Specify the MMP_LOAD_NOSTATIC flag with the **mmpLoadFile** function. See "Handling Movie Files," later in this chapter, for more information.	Provides 18 more colors for the movie but reduces the rest of the system to black and white while the stage window is active.
Use private device context By default, the Movie Player calls **GetDC** and **ReleaseDC** with most operations. Providing the alternate device context lets the Movie Player bypass this step, thus improving performance. Use the **mmpSetDC** function. See "Managing the Stage Window," later in this chapter, for more information.	Improves performance for some movies but uses more memory.

Starting and Stopping the Movie Player

Before calling any Movie Player functions, you must start an instance of the Movie Player. When you start a Movie Player instance, you receive a movie ID that you use when calling any further Movie Player functions.

You can open multiple instances of the Movie Player and assign a movie to each instance. You can also consecutively load and play multiple movies from a single Movie Player instance. Before your application ends, it should close any Movie Player instances it has opened.

The following functions start and stop a Movie Player instance and obtain error information:

mmpOpen
  Initializes an instance of the Movie Player.

mmpClose
  Closes an instance of the Movie Player.

mmpError
  Returns an error code and optional error message.

Getting Error Information

Most Movie Player functions return a FALSE or NULL value to indicate errors. Use the **mmpError** function to obtain a specific error code and error message. The syntax of this function is as follows:

int mmpError(*idMovie, lpszError, wLen*)

Pass the movie ID to the *idMovie* parameter. To return the last Movie Player error occurring with any instance, pass a NULL value to the *idMovie* parameter.

To get an error message string, pass a far pointer to a character buffer to the *lpszError* parameter. The *wLen* parameter indicates the maximum number of characters to copy to the *lpszError* buffer. The MMP_MAXERRORLENGTH constant specifies the maximum length of Movie Player error strings. You can pass a NULL pointer to the *lpszError* parameter to obtain only the numeric error code returned by the function.

Error-code values returned by **mmpError** are defined in the MMP.H header file. For more information on error return codes, see the description of **mmpError** in the *Programmer's Reference*.

The following function is used in many of the code samples in this chapter. It calls **mmpGetError** to get a detailed error message and displays the error message in a message box.

```
void PrintError(MMPID idMovie, LPSTR lpszIntro)
{
    char szErrorBuf[MMP_MAXERRORLENGTH];

    mmpError(idMovie, szErrorBuf, MMP_MAXERRORLENGTH);

    MessageBeep(MB_ICONEXCLAMATION);
    MessageBox(hFullWnd ? hFullWnd : hMainWnd, szErrorBuf, lpszIntro,
               MB_OK | MB_ICONEXCLAMATION);
}
```

Opening the Movie Player Instance

Each Movie Player instance can load and play one movie file. To load multiple movies and display them simultaneously on screen, you must open a Movie Player instance for each movie file.

Although the Movie Player can support a total of eight instances system-wide, displaying multiple movies can result in poor color mapping for movies running in inactive windows. For best results, display only one movie at a time, or limit the number of colors in the movie palettes.

Call the **mmpOpen** function to open a single Movie Player instance. The **mmpOpen** function can also assign a playback window, or *stage window*, to the Movie Player. The stage window can be any overlapped or pop-up window. The **mmpOpen** function has the following syntax:

MMPID mmpOpen(*hWndStage, wOptions*)

When you open the Movie Player instance, you can specify a handle to a window in the *hWndStage* parameter of the **mmpOpen** function. This becomes the stage window for the Movie Player instance. The **mmpSetStage** function provides another way to supply a stage-window handle for a Movie Player instance. For more information on the **mmpSetStage** function, see "Managing the Stage Window," later in this chapter.

The *wOptions* parameter is not used. Set this parameter to NULL.

The **mmpOpen** function returns a movie ID of type MMPID. This movie ID identifies the Movie Player instance. Most Movie Player functions require this movie ID. The function returns NULL if it fails to start the Movie Player instance.

Note   To obtain error information after receiving a NULL movie ID from **mmpOpen**, immediately call the **mmpError** function with a NULL movie ID. If another Movie Player command is run before the application calls **mmpError**, the error result will be incorrect.

To play more than one movie at the same time, you must call **mmpOpen** for each movie you want to play, saving the movie IDs returned by each call.

Closing the Movie Player

When you finish using the Movie Player instance, close it using **mmpClose**. The syntax of this function is as follows:

BOOL mmpClose(*idMovie, wOptions*)

Pass the movie ID of the Movie Player instance to the *idMovie* parameter. The *wOptions* parameter is reserved for future use; set it to NULL.

When called, **mmpClose** clears the stage window, unloads any file currently loaded, and frees memory allocated during **mmpOpen**. This function returns TRUE if successful.

Note   If **mmpClose** returns FALSE, you can get error information by immediately calling **mmpError** with a NULL movie ID.

Opening the Movie Player

The following code fragment shows how an application might open a Movie Player instance and save the resulting movie ID. This code might be called in response to the WM_CREATE message sent to the main window.

```
// Open a Movie Player instance

if((idMovie = mmpOpen(hWnd, NULL)) == NULL)
{
    PrintError(idMovie, "Closing MMPLAY.");
    return FALSE;
}
```

If **mmpOpen** fails, the PrintError function calls **mmpError** to retrieve error information. Because the movie ID is NULL, **mmpError** retrieves the last Movie Player error.

Handling Movie Files

Once you start the Movie Player instance, you can load, unload, and get information on a movie file using the following functions:

mmpLoadFile
Loads a movie file into the Movie Player instance and specifies playback options.

mmpFileLoaded
Checks whether a movie file is loaded in the Movie Player instance.

mmpFreeFile
Clears the movie file from the Movie Player instance and frees memory used by the file.

mmpGetFileInfo
Returns information on a movie file on disk.

mmpGetMovieInfo
Returns information on a movie file in memory.

Loading and Unloading a Movie File

After getting a movie ID from **mmpOpen**, you can load a movie using **mmpLoadFile**. This function also establishes playback options for the movie file. The **mmpLoadFile** function has the following syntax:

BOOL mmpLoadFile(*idMovie, lpszFileName, wOptions*)

The *idMovie* parameter contains the movie ID returned from **mmpOpen**. If you start multiple instances of the Movie Player, you can load multiple movies simultaneously by calling **mmpLoadFile** to load a movie file into each Movie Player instance.

In the *lpszFileName* parameter, you can specify one of the following:

- An LPSTR pointer to the movie filename.

- A DWORD value in which the high-order word is set to zero and the low-order word is a file handle to an open file. The file pointer of the specified file must be positioned at the start of the RMMP chunk (at the first byte of the "RIFF" FOURCC code).

If the Movie Player fails to load the file, **mmpLoadFile** returns FALSE.

The following flags, passed in any combination to the *wOptions* parameter, specify load and playback options for the movie file:

Flag	Description
MMP_DRAW_FRAME	Draws the first frame to the stage window after loading the movie file. By default, the Movie Player does not display the first frame.
MMP_ERASE_FRAME	Clears the stage window before loading the new movie file.
MMP_LOAD_REFERENCED	Loads only those cast members referenced in the score. By default, the Movie Player loads all cast members.
MMP_LOAD_NOBUFFER	Omits off-screen image buffer.
MMP_LOAD_NOSTATIC	When the stage window is active, reduces the system colors to black and white, providing 18 more colors for use by the Movie Player.

To determine if the Movie Player currently has a movie file loaded, call **mmpFileLoaded**. This function has the following syntax:

BOOL mmpFileLoaded(*idMovie*)

This returns TRUE if the Movie Player instance identified by the given movie ID currently has a movie loaded.

Unloading the Movie File   To unload the movie file, you can call the **mmpFreeFile** function. This function has the following syntax:

BOOL mmpFreeFile(*idMovie, wOptions*)

This function frees memory associated with the movie file loaded in the Movie Player instance. The **mmpFreeFile** function returns TRUE if it successfully frees the memory. If the function returns FALSE, you should close the Movie Player instance.

To clear the stage window after clearing a file from memory, pass the MMP_ERASE_FRAME flag to the *wOptions* parameter. Without this flag, the last movie frame shown remains on screen.

The Movie Player automatically unloads the current movie file before attempting to load a new movie file. Also, you don't need to call **mmpFreeFile** when you close the Movie Player instance using **mmpClose**—the Movie Player automatically frees resources when the instance is closed.

Getting Information on a Movie File

The Movie Player provides two functions that return information about a movie file on disk and in memory. The **mmpGetFileInfo** function fills an MMPMOVIEINFO movie-information structure for a movie file on disk, and the **mmpGetMovieInfo** function fills the structure for the currently loaded movie. The MMPMOVIEINFO structure has the following fields:

Field	Description
dwFileVersion	Version of the authoring system used to create the movie.
dwTotalFrames	Number of movie frames.
dwInitialFramesPerSecond	Tempo value of the first frame (expressed as a frames-per-second value).
wPixelDepth	Number of bits per pixel.
dwMovieExtentX	Width of the playback area (in pixels).
dwMovieExtentY	Height of the playback area (in pixels).
chFullMacName[128]	Movie title contained in a null-terminated string.

The syntax of **mmpGetFileInfo** is as follows:

BOOL mmpGetFileInfo(*idMovie, lpszFileName, lpMovieInfo*)

Pass the movie ID of the Movie Player instance to *idMovie* and a far pointer to a MMPMOVIEINFO structure to *lpMovieInfo*. In the *lpszFileName* parameter, you can specify one of the following:

- An LPSTR pointer to the movie filename.

- A DWORD value in which the high-order word is set to zero and the low-order word is a file handle to an open file. The file pointer of the specified file must be positioned at the start of the RMMP chunk (at the first byte of the "RIFF" FOURCC code).

The **mmpGetFileInfo** function returns TRUE if successful.

The **mmpGetMovieInfo** function has similar syntax but omits the filename parameter. For this function to return useful information, a movie file must be loaded into the Movie Player instance. The **mmpGetMovieInfo** has the following syntax:

BOOL mmpGetMovieInfo(*idMovie, lpMovieInfo*)

This function retrieves the movie-information structure for the currently loaded movie file.

Loading a Movie File

The following code fragment shows a function that loads a movie file. Several Movie Player playback options can be specified at load time. Therefore, the following function can be used to load the same movie file with different playback options:

```
BOOL OpenMovie(BOOL bReload)          // bReload is TRUE if loading same file
{                                     // Global szFilename holds the filename
    BOOL bLoadResult;
    WORD wOptions = 0;
    HCURSOR hSaveCursor;

    if(bNoStatic)       wOptions |= MMP_LOAD_NOSTATIC;
    if(bLoadReferenced) wOptions |= MMP_LOAD_REFERENCED;
    if(bNoBuffer)       wOptions |= MMP_LOAD_NOBUFFER;
```

```
// If loading a new movie file, draw the first frame
// to the stage window.

if(!bReload)          wOptions |= MMP_DRAW_FRAME;

// If the Movie Player is in animation mode, stop playback first.

if(iState == MOVIE_RUNNING)
    mmpStopAnimating(idMovie, 0);

hSaveCursor = SetCursor(LoadCursor(NULL, IDC_WAIT));
bLoadResult = mmpLoadFile(idMovie, szFilename, wOptions);
SetCursor(hSaveCursor);

if(!bLoadResult)
    PrintError(idMovie, "Could not load movie file.");

return bLoadResult;
}
```

The following SetupStageWindow function changes the window caption and adjusts the window size based on information returned by the **mmpGetMovieInfo** function:

```
void SetupStageWindow(HWND hWndStage, MMPID idMovie)
{
    RECT rc;
    MMPMOVIEINFO mmpInfo;

    mmpInfo.chFullMacName[0] = 0;
    mmpGetMovieInfo(idMovie, &mmpInfo);

    if(mmpInfo.chFullName[0])
        SetWindowText(hWndStage, mmpInfo.chFullMacName);
    else
        SetWindowText(hWndStage, szFilename);        // szFilename is global

    if(mmpInfo.dwMovieExtentX && mmpInfo.dwMovieExtentY)
    {
        SetRect(&rc, 0, 0, (WORD)mmpInfo.dwMovieExtentX,
                           (WORD)mmpInfo.dwMovieExtentY);
        AdjustWindowRect(&rc, GetWindowLong(hWndStage, GWL_STYLE), TRUE);
        SetWindowPos(hWndStage, NULL,
                    0, 0, rc.right-rc.left, rc.bottom-rc.top,
                    SWP_NOMOVE | SWP_NOZORDER | SWP_NOACTIVATE);
    }
}
```

Playing a Movie File

Once you complete all the preparatory steps, you can play your movie. The following Movie Player functions start and stop a movie, check playback status, and advance the movie frames:

mmpStartAnimating
Prepares the stage window and starts playback.

mmpStopAnimating
Stops playback with an optional final update.

mmpAnimate
Prompts the Movie Player to perform the transition to the next segment in the animation.

mmpAnimStatus
Checks the animation status.

mmpAnimStopped
Checks whether a movie is currently running.

Calling **mmpStartAnimating** notifies the Movie Player that playback is to start. The **mmpAnimate** function, however, actually advances the movie frames. Before you start playback using **mmpStartAnimating**, **mmpAnimate** returns without advancing the animation.

Starting and Stopping Playback

The **mmpStartAnimating** function notifies the Movie Player that playback is to start. This function has the following syntax:

BOOL mmpStartAnimating(*idMovie, wOptions*)

Pass a valid movie ID to *idMovie*. You can pass the MMP_DRAW_FRAME flag to the *wOptions* parameter to display the next frame in the stage window. This function returns FALSE if the movie is already running; TRUE if it succeeds in starting animation.

The Movie Player automatically stops playback when it reaches the last frame in a movie. You can call **mmpStopAnimating** to stop playback before the end of the movie. This function has the following syntax:

BOOL mmpStopAnimating(*idMovie, wOptions*)

If you set the MMP_DRAW_FRAME flag in the *wOptions* parameter, the Movie Player displays the next frame before stopping the movie. This function returns FALSE if the movie isn't running. If it succeeds in stopping animation, it returns TRUE.

You can call **mmpStartAnimating** and **mmpStopAnimating** functions anytime after the Movie Player is open and a movie file is loaded. Use these functions as pause and resume controls for the Movie Player.

Advancing the Frames

Although the **mmpStartAnimating** function notifies the Movie Player to start playback, your application must advance the animation using **mmpAnimate**. Your application calls **mmpAnimate** at regular intervals, generally in the message loop, and prompts the Movie Player to advance the animation.

It's useful to think of the movie frame as an expanse of time rather than a collection of animation data elements. Your application can call **mmpAnimate** many times during a given movie frame; with each call, the Movie Player performs whatever task is appropriate given the current state of the animation. These tasks can include the following:

- Drawing a subframe or frame. On frames that use complex transitions, each **mmpAnimate** call completes one subframe, and the transition occurs over a series of **mmpAnimate** calls. For simpler transitions such as a straight copy, only one **mmpAnimate** call is required to complete the frame drawing.

- Processing script-channel commands.

- Waiting for a tempo period to expire.

- Waiting for an MCI device to finish processing a script-channel command.

- Noting the end of the frame.

Because **mmpAnimate** might be called while the animation is stopped, or while a device or tempo wait is in effect, the Movie Player might not perform any animation task in response to the **mmpAnimate** call.

The **mmpAnimate** function has the following syntax:

int mmpAnimate(*idMovie*)

The return value of **mmpAnimate** indicates the current state of the animation. The **mmpAnimate** return values are described in the *Programmer's Reference*. A positive return value indicates the animation is progressing, and a negative return value indicates the Movie Player is waiting for a Windows message to proceed to the next frame.

The following diagram shows a typical movie frame (including subframes, script-channel text, and a tempo wait period) and the values returned by **mmpAnimate** as the Movie Player advances through the frame.

Frame 10		
	Subframe	MMP_ANIM_DRAW
	Subframe	MMP_ANIM_DRAW
	Subframe	MMP_ANIM_DRAW
	Subframe	MMP_ANIM_DRAW
	Subframe	MMP_ANIM_DRAWN
	Tempo Wait	MMP_TEMPO_WAIT MMP_TEMPO_WAIT MMP_TEMPO_WAIT
	Script Text	MMP_ANIM_SCRIPT_PROCESSED
	Device Wait (from mciWait command)	MMP_DEVICE_WAIT (Application calls **WaitMessage**) MMP_FRAME_DONE
Frame 11	. . .	

The rest of this section describes how to structure your message loop to keep the movie frames advancing while allowing other applications to run.

**Calling
mmpAnimate in
the Message Loop**
You must call **mmpAnimate** for each Movie Player instance you loaded. The following code fragment shows the minimum message loop required to animate a single movie:

```
while(TRUE)
{
    if(PeekMessage(&msg, NULL, 0, 0, PM_REMOVE))
    {
        if(msg.message == WM_QUIT)
            break;
        TranslateMessage(&msg);
        DispatchMessage(&msg);
    }
    else
        if(mmpAnimate(idMovie) < 0)
            WaitMessage();
}
```

▶ **To process Windows messages, and yield control to other applications:**

1. Call **PeekMessage** to check the message queue for messages and yield control to other applications. **PeekMessage** does not wait for a message to enter the queue before returning, allowing your application to continue calling **mmpAnimate** at regular intervals.

2. Call **mmpAnimate** if no other program has a message to process.

3. Check the **mmpAnimate** return value.

4. If **mmpAnimate** returned a positive value, let the loop continue.

5. If **mmpAnimate** returned a negative value, call **WaitMessage**.

Note If **mmpAnimate** returns a negative value, don't loop around and call the function again (the frames won't advance until a message is received, and such a loop just uses CPU resources).

If your application loads multiple Movie Player instances, you might use a message loop like the following:

```
#define MAX_MOVIES 4
BOOL bRunning;
int i;
MMPID idMovies[MAX_MOVIES];
        .
        .
        .
while(TRUE)
{
    if(PeekMessage(&msg, NULL, 0, 0, PM_REMOVE))
    {
        if(msg.message == WM_QUIT)
            break;
        TranslateMessage(&msg);
        DispatchMessage(&msg);
    }
    else
    {
        bRunning = FALSE;
        for(i = 0; i < MAX_MOVIES; i++)
            if(idMovies[i] && mmpAnimate(idMovies[i]) > 0)
                bRunning = TRUE;
        if(!bRunning)
            WaitMessage();
    }
}
```

Checking Playback Status

The Movie Player provides two functions you can use to check the animation status without actually advancing the movie frames.

The **mmpAnimStatus** function reports the animation status but does not perform any animation tasks. The **mmpAnimStatus** function has the following syntax:

int mmpAnimStatus(*idMovie*)

The function returns an animation-status flag. The return values are a subset of those used by **mmpAnimate**. See the *Programmer's Reference* for a description of the **mmpAnimStatus** return values.

The **mmpAnimStopped** function indicates whether the movie is stopped. It has the following syntax:

BOOL mmpAnimStopped(*idMovie*)

It returns TRUE if the animation is stopped; FALSE if animation is running.

Managing the Stage Window

Each Movie Player instance is associated with a playback window called a *stage window*. The stage window can be any pop-up or overlapped window. You can use the following functions to manage the stage window:

mmpSetStage
Sets the stage window for a Movie Player instance and specifies the position of the playback area.

mmpGetStage
Gets the current stage information for a Movie Player instance.

mmpSetDC
Provides the Movie Player a handle to a device context.

mmpUpdate
Performs a screen update in the invalid rectangle.

mmpGetPaletteHandle
Returns a handle to the movie palette.

To correctly manage the movie palette, handle wait-for-mouse tempo commands, and process MCI script-channel commands, the Movie Player subclasses the stage window and handles the following messages:

Message	How Handled	Passed to Application?
MM_MCINOTIFY	Movie Player uses this message to properly handle the mciWait commands in the movie script channel.	Yes
WM_SETCURSOR WM_LBUTTONDOWN WM_RBUTTONDOWN WM_MBUTTONDOWN	Movie Player uses these messages to handle wait-for-mouse tempo commands.	Only if not waiting for a mouse click
WM_ACTIVATE WM_ACTIVATEAPP	Movie player sets system-palette usage as needed.	Yes
WM_QUERYNEWPALETTE	If movie has a palette, the Movie Player selects and realizes the palette.	Only if movie has no palette
WM_PALETTECHANGED	If another window caused the system palette change, the Movie Player invalidates the client area of the stage window.	No

Setting the Stage Window

The **mmpSetStage** function specifies the stage window for the Movie Player instance. It also specifies the size and placement of the playback area in the stage window. This function returns TRUE if it successfully sets the new stage window. Note that the Movie Player instance must have a movie file loaded at the time **mmpSetStage** is called; otherwise, the function fails and returns FALSE, reporting error code MMPERR_STAGE_ERROR.

The **mmpSetStage** function has the following syntax:

BOOL mmpSetStage(*idMovie, hWndStage, lprectStage, wOptions*)

The *idMovie* parameter identifies the Movie Player instance. The *hWndStage* parameter identifies the new stage window. When you call **mmpSetStage**, the new stage window is brought to the foreground.

The *lprectStage* parameter points to a **RECT** structure defining the placement of the image in the window. The **top** and **left** fields of the structure define the offset's playback area; the **bottom** and **right** fields define the playback-area extents. The rectangle figures are not used unless you pass the MMP_STAGE_OFFSET flag in *wOptions*. The *wOptions* parameter takes the following flags:

Flag	Description
MMP_DRAW_FRAME	Draws the next frame to the stage window.
MMP_STAGE_OFFSET	Places the playback-area origin at the offset specified by the **top** and **left** fields of the **RECT** structure pointed to by *lprectStage*.
MMP_STAGE_CENTER	Centers the playback area in the stage-window client area.
MMP_STAGE_BORDER	Draws a border around the playback area, if there is room for a border. To set the playback area away from the client-area border, use the MMP_STAGE_CENTER flag, or use the MMP_STAGE_OFFSET flag with an appropriate *lprectStage* value.
MMP_STAGE_FIXED	Fixes the size and position of the movie-playback area. When the window is resized, or when a new movie is loaded, the playback area remains fixed at either the size of the client area at the time **mmpSetStage** was called or, if the MMP_STAGE_OFFSET flag was specified, the location and size specified by the **RECT** values.

Getting Window Information

The **mmpGetStage** function returns stage-window information. This function has the following syntax:

BOOL mmpGetStage(*idMovie, lphWndStage, lprectStage, lpwOptions*)

Specify the Movie Player instance using *idMovie*. This function returns the handle of the current stage window in the address pointed to by *lphWndStage*. It returns the playback-area origin and extents in the **RECT** structure pointed to by *lprectStage*. It also returns the current stage options (for example, MMP_STAGE_OFFSET or MMP_STAGE_CENTER) in the **WORD** value pointed to by *lpwOptions*.

If the function retrieves the stage information successfully, it returns TRUE.

Processing WM_PAINT Messages

Your window function must notify the Movie Player when it receives WM_PAINT messages for the stage window. To prompt the Movie Player to update the frame, use the **mmpUpdate** function, which has the following syntax:

BOOL mmpUpdate(*idMovie, hDC, lpRect*)

The parameters are a movie ID, the device context from **BeginPaint**, and a pointer to the invalid rectangle. See "Creating a Full-Screen Stage Window," later in this chapter, for an example of how to handle a WM_PAINT message for a stage-window message handler.

Providing a Private Device Context

You can improve playback performance slightly by providing a private device context for the Movie Player. To do this, use the **mmpSetDC** function, which has the following syntax:

BOOL mmpSetDC(*idMovie, hDC*)

The *idMovie* parameter identifies the Movie Player instance. The *hDC* parameter should contain a handle to a private device context for the stage window. If you pass a NULL value to this parameter, the Movie Player stops using the private device context and resumes calling **GetDC** and **ReleaseDC** with each operation.

To obtain a private device context for the stage window, you must specify the CS_OWNDC flag in the **style** field of the **WNDCLASS** structure for the window. For example, an application uses the following sequence to register the window class for the main stage window:

```
WNDCLASS wndclass;
    .
    .
    .
wndclass.style = CS_HREDRAW | CS_VREDRAW | CS_OWNDC;
wndclass.lpfnWndProc = MainWndProc;
    .
    .
    .
wndclass.lpszClassName = szAppName;

if(!RegisterClass(&wndclass))
    return FALSE;
```

If you use this technique, be sure to use the CS_OWNDC flag when registering your stage window. Otherwise, you'll deprive other applications of one of five common device contexts. An application can use the following **mmpSetDC** function to provide the Movie Player with a handle to the private device context:

```
mmpSetDC(idMovie, GetDC(hWnd));
```

Creating A Full-Screen Stage Window

You can use your entire screen as the stage window by creating a full-screen pop-up window with no menu and assigning playback to it using **mmpSetStage**. This section describes how to create and then handle messages for a full-screen stage window.

Creating the Window

The following function creates a full-screen stage window using a previously registered window class:

```
BOOL CreateStage(void)
{
    hFullWnd = CreateWindow(szFullScreenName,
                            NULL, WS_POPUP | WS_VISIBLE,
                            0, 0,
                            GetSystemMetrics(SM_CXSCREEN),
                            GetSystemMetrics(SM_CYSCREEN),
                            hMainWnd, NULL, hInst, NULL);
    if(hFullWnd == NULL)
        return FALSE;

    /* Switch the stage to the full-screen window
     */
    if(mmpSetStage(idMovie, hFullWnd, NULL,
                   MMP_STAGE_BORDER | MMP_STAGE_CENTER))
    {
        return TRUE;
    }
    else
    {
        PrintError(idMovie, "Could not set stage.");
        return FALSE;
    }
}
```

Handling Messages

The message handler for a full-screen stage window must provide a way for a user to exit the stage window. For example, an application might stop the animation and close the stage window when the user presses the ESC key.

The following code fragment shows the message handler for a full-screen stage window:

```
LONG FAR PASCAL StageWndProc(HWND hWnd, WORD wMsg, WORD wParam, LONG lParam)
{
    PAINTSTRUCT ps;
    static BOOL bControl;

    switch(wMsg)
    {
        case WM_CREATE:
            bControl = FALSE;
            mmpSetDC(idMovie, GetDC(hWnd));
            break;

        case WM_DESTROY:
            if(iState == MOVIE_RUNNING)
            {
                iState = MOVIE_STOPPED;
                mmpStopAnimating(idMovie, 0);
            }

            /* Transfer the movie to the original stage window
             */
            if(mmpSetStage(idMovie, hMainWnd, NULL, NULL))
            {
                mmpSetDC(idMovie, GetDC(hMainWnd));
                SetMenuStates(hMainWnd);
            }
            else
                PrintError(idMovie, "Could not set stage.");

            break;

        case WM_PAINT:
            BeginPaint(hWnd, &ps);
            mmpUpdate(idMovie, ps.hdc, &ps.rcPaint);
            EndPaint(hWnd, &ps);
            break;
```

```
        case WM_KEYDOWN:
            switch(wParam)
            {
                case VK_ESCAPE:
                    DestroyWindow(hWnd);
                    break;


                case VK_SPACE:
                    iState = MOVIE_RUNNING ? MOVIE_STOPPED : MOVIE_RUNNING;
                    if(iState == MOVIE_RUNNING)
                        mmpStartAnimating(idMovie, 0);
                    else
                        mmpStopAnimating(idMovie, 0);
                    break;

                case VK_INSERT:
                    if(bControl)
                        CopyFrame(hWnd);
                    break;

                case VK_CONTROL:
                    bControl = TRUE;
                    break;

                case VK_LEFT:
                    SendMessage(hMainWnd, WM_COMMAND, IDM_STEPBACKWARD, 0L);
                    break;

                case VK_RIGHT:
                    SendMessage(hMainWnd, WM_COMMAND, IDM_STEPFORWARD, 0L);
                    break;
            }
            break;

        case WM_KEYUP:
            if(wParam == VK_CONTROL)
                bControl = FALSE;
            break;

        default:
            return DefWindowProc(hWnd, wMsg, wParam, lParam);
    }
    return 0L;
}
```

Getting a Handle to the Movie Palette

The Movie Player can provide your application a handle to the movie palette. This can be useful if, for example, you need to paint a movie frame into a bitmap and copy the bitmap to the Clipboard. Use the **mmpGetPaletteHandle** function to obtain a handle to the movie palette. This function has the following syntax:

HPALETTE mmpGetPaletteHandle(*idMovie***)**

Pass the movie ID of the Movie Player instance in *idMovie*. This function returns a handle to the palette of the currently loaded movie.

The following function creates a copy of the movie palette. It then creates a bitmap, draws the current movie frame into the bitmap device context, and copies the bitmap and palette to the Clipboard.

```
void CopyFrame(HWND hWnd)
{
    HPALETTE     hPalette, hClipPalette;
    HDC          hDC, hMemoryDC;
    HBITMAP      hBitmap;
    MMPMOVIEINFO    mmpInfo;
    int          nX, nY;

    hPalette = mmpGetPaletteHandle(idMovie);
    if((hClipPalette = CopyPalette(hPalette)) == NULL)
    {
        MessageBox(hWnd, "Could not copy palette.", szAppName, MB_OK);
        return;
    }

    hDC = GetDC(hWnd);
    hMemoryDC = CreateCompatibleDC(hDC);

    if(bFullScreen)
        mmpInfo.dwMovieExtentX = mmpInfo.dwMovieExtentY = 0;
     else
        mmpGetMovieInfo(idMovie, &mmpInfo);
```

```
/* Create bitmap, sized to match the movie frame area
 */
nX = (int)(mmpInfo.dwMovieExtentX ? mmpInfo.dwMovieExtentX :
                                    GetSystemMetrics (SM_CXSCREEN));
nY = (int)(mmpInfo.dwMovieExtentY ? mmpInfo.dwMovieExtentY :
                                    GetSystemMetrics (SM_CYSCREEN));
hBitmap = CreateCompatibleBitmap(hDC, nX, nY);

/* Select the bitmap in the memory DC and draw the
 * movie frame into the bitmap
 */
SelectObject(hMemoryDC, hBitmap);
mmpUpdate(idMovie, hMemoryDC, NULL);

/* Place the bitmap and logical palette on the Clipboard
 */
if(OpenClipboard(hWnd))
{
    EmptyClipboard();
    SetClipboardData(CF_BITMAP, hBitmap);
    SetClipboardData(CF_PALETTE, hClipPalette);
    CloseClipboard();
}
else
    MessageBox(hWnd, "Could not open Clipboard.", szAppName, MB_OK);

DeleteDC(hMemoryDC);
ReleaseDC(hWnd, hDC);
}
```

Controlling Playback

The Movie Player lets you control playback in several ways. It provides functions that allow you to do the following:

- Determine the current frame

- Jump to a specific frame

- Change the movie tempo

- Automatically repeat a movie

- Turn sound playback off or on

Setting and Tracking the Frame Index

The *frame index* keeps track of the current frame in a movie. The Movie Player provides the following functions to query and change the frame index:

---

mmpGetCurFrame
Gets the number of the currently displayed frame.

mmpGoToFrame
Jumps to a given frame in a movie.

Getting the Current Frame

You can call **mmpGetCurFrame** at any time—even if you haven't called **mmpStartAnimating**. This function has the following syntax:

short mmpGetCurFrame(*idMovie*)

Pass the movie ID of the Movie Player instance in *idMovie*. Frame numbering in a movie starts at 1. The **mmpGetCurFrame** function returns zero if it fails.

Jumping to a Frame

Use **mmpGoToFrame** to jump to any frame in a movie file. You can do this before starting playback. This function has the following syntax:

BOOL mmpGoToFrame(*idMovie, sFrame, wOptions*)

Pass the movie ID of the Movie Player instance to *idMovie*.

The *sFrame* parameter, passed as a short integer, can contain any valid frame number in the movie. The function returns FALSE if you pass an invalid frame number. The following constants can be passed in *sFrame*:

Value	Description
MMP_FRAME_FIRST	Jumps to the beginning of a movie.
MMP_FRAME_LAST	Jumps to the end of a movie.

You can pass the MMP_DRAW_FRAME flag to the *wOptions* parameter to jump to a specified movie frame and then display the image.

Frame-by-Frame Playback

Using the **mmpGoToFrame** and **mmpGetCurFrame** functions, you can play a movie one frame at a time. The following code fragment shows two cases of a message handler for a Movie Player application. This code sequence responds to user requests to step forward and backward frame-by-frame:

```
short nFrameNum;
    .
    .
    .
case IDM_STEPFORWARD:
    if((nFrameNum = mmpGetCurFrame(idMovie)) == MMP_FRAME_LAST)
    {
        MessageBox(hWnd, "Can't step beyond end.", szAppName, MB_OK);
        break;
    }

    if(! mmpGoToFrame(idMovie, ++nFrameNum, MMP_DRAW_FRAME))
        PrintError(idMovie, "Could not go to specified frame.");

    break;

case IDM_STEPBACKWARD:
    if((nFrameNum = mmpGetCurFrame(idMovie)) == MMP_FRAME_FIRST)
    {
        MessageBox(hWnd, "Can't step before beginning.",
                   szAppName, MB_OK);
        break;
    }

    if(! mmpGoToFrame(idMovie, --nFrameNum, MMP_DRAW_FRAME))
    {
        PrintError(idMovie, "Could not go to specified frame.");
        break;
    }
    break;
```

Changing the Movie Tempo

Movie files include a tempo channel that specifies the movie-playback rate. The tempo can change with each frame. The Movie Player can change the tempo setting for a movie loaded into memory. The tempo setting remains until the Movie Player encounters a change-tempo command in the tempo channel.

Use the following functions to set and get the tempo setting:

mmpSetTempo
Sets a new tempo value for the movie.

mmpGetTempo
Returns a frames-per-second tempo value for the movie.

The syntax of **mmpSetTempo** is as follows:

BOOL mmpSetTempo(*idMovie, nTempo*)

Pass the movie ID of the Movie Player instance to *idMovie* and one of the following integer values to *nTempo*:

Tempo Value	Description
1 through 60	Sets the tempo to *nTempo* frames per second.
-1 through -120	Specifies a delay for the current frame. The Movie Player waits -*nTempo* seconds before advancing the frame.
MMPTEMPO_MOUSEWAIT	Specifies a wait for the current frame. The Movie Player waits for the stage window to receive a mouse click or keystroke before advancing the frame.

For example, the following code fragment increases the play rate by 10 frames per second:

```
#define MAX_TEMPO 60
int nCurrent;

nCurrent = mmpGetTempo(idMovie);              // Get current tempo setting
nCurrent = min(nCurrent+10, MAX_TEMPO);

if(!mmpSetTempo(idMovie, nCurrent))
{
    // Error occurred.
}
```

Changing the Repeat and Mute Flags

The Movie Player can automatically repeat a movie once it reaches the end. It can also suppress playback of sound cast members and streamed audio (specified through movie script-channel commands).

The following functions set and check the Movie Player repeat and mute flags:

mmpSetRepeat
Tells the Movie Player to automatically repeat the movie.

mmpGetRepeat
Returns TRUE if the Movie Player repeat flag is set.

mmpSetMute
Tells the Movie Player to suppress playback of sound cast members.

mmpGetMute
Returns TRUE if the Movie Player mute flag is set.

The syntax of **mmpSetRepeat** is as follows:

BOOL mmpSetRepeat(*idMovie, bRepeat*)

Pass a TRUE value to *bRepeat*, along with the movie ID in *idMovie*, to make the Movie Player automatically repeat the movie. To turn off the automatic repeat, pass a FALSE to *bRepeat*.

Use the **mmpSetMute** function to cancel playback of sound cast members. The **mmpSetMute** function has the following syntax:

BOOL mmpSetMute(*idMovie, bMuteOn*)

Pass the movie ID of the Movie Player instance to *idMovie*. Pass a TRUE value to *bMuteOn* to turn off the sound playback; a FALSE value to restart the playback of sound cast members.

Note The **mmpSetMute** function does not stop the playback of streamed audio started using the **mci** script-channel command. To cancel processing of MCI commands in the script channel, you must use a frame callback function, as described in the following section.

Using Frame-Callback Functions

You can specify a callback function to be executed each time a frame is advanced. This is useful if you need to synchronize a special effect with the playback or execute a function at a particular frame. A frame-callback function also allows an application to monitor script-channel text. The MMPLAY sample application includes a script-parsing feature that recognizes break, goto, loop, and close commands.

The frame-callback function is called with each frame advance. Frame advances occur when **mmpAnimate** is called after sufficient time has elapsed for the display of the current frame (if sufficient time has not elapsed, **mmpAnimate** returns without advancing the frame and without calling the callback function). The callback function is not called with the **mmpGoToFrame**, **mmpSetStage**, and **mmpStartAnimating** functions. Although these functions can draw a frame to the stage window, they don't advance the frame.

With each frame advance, the Movie Player sends two messages to the callback function:

Message	Description
MMP_HOOK_FRAME	Sent after the frame counter is advanced but before the new frame is drawn.
	The Movie Player supplies the current frame and subframe number with the message.
MMP_HOOK_SCRIPT	Sent just before the next frame is advanced. Before sending this message, the Movie Player advances the frame counter, draws the frame, and waits for the frame tempo period to expire.
	The Movie Player supplies the frame number and the contents of the script channel with the message. The return value from the callback function determines whether the Movie Player processes the script-channel text; the function returns TRUE if it has processed the script-channel text, or FALSE if the Movie Player should process the text.

Use the following functions to hook a callback function into the playback:

mmpSetFrameHook
Specifies a function the Movie Player calls after advancing each frame.

mmpGetFrameHook
Gets a pointer to the function called after each frame is advanced.

The callback function is associated with a Movie Player instance, not a movie file. You can keep the callback function hooked into the Movie Player instance regardless of whether a movie file is loaded.

Specifying the Callback Function

Your callback function must have the following syntax:

```
BOOL FAR PASCAL FrameHook(
    MMPID idMovie,              // Instance identifier
    WORD  wMsg,                 // Message
    WORD  wParam,               // Frame index
    LONG  lParam)               // Message-dependent
```

FrameHook is a placeholder for an application-supplied function name. Like all callback functions, the function name must be listed in the EXPORTS section of the module definition (.DEF) file for your application.

Any Movie Player functions called from the callback function must be directed to the current Movie Player instance. For example, the movie ID used in the callback function should be the same one used in the call to **mmpSetFrameHook**. If the callback function calls a Movie Player function with a different movie ID, the Movie Player function will fail, returning an MMPERR_BAD_ID error code.

Don't close the current movie file while processing a frame hook message. If you need to implement a close command in your application, you can post a message to the main window and close the movie file (or Movie Player instance) from there.

Getting the Current Callback Function

Before inserting a callback function into the playback, you should determine whether another function is already attached. If a callback function does exist, you should call it from your callback function. Using this chaining technique, your application can hook multiple functions into the playback.

To get the procedure-instance address of the most recently attached callback function, call **mmpGetFrameHook**. This function returns a pointer to the current callback function and has the following syntax:

FARPROC mmpGetFrameHook(*idMovie*)

Pass the movie ID of the Movie Player instance to *idMovie*. If no callback function is attached, **mmpGetFrameHook** returns NULL.

Hooking the Callback Function into the Playback

Use the **mmpSetFrameHook** function to hook your callback function into the playback. This function returns TRUE if successful. It has the following syntax:

BOOL mmpSetFrameHook(*idMovie, lpFrameHook*)

Pass the movie ID of the Movie Player instance to *idMovie* and a FARPROC pointer containing the procedure-instance address of the callback function to *lpFrameHook*.

To remove the callback function from the playback, call **mmpSetFrameHook** to reset the callback function pointer to its original value (this might be NULL if no callback function was attached).

Note Don't free the procedure instance of the callback function before unhooking the callback function.

Example of a Callback Function

The remainder of this chapter presents code that implements a script-channel monitor. This script-channel monitor responds to the following commands:

Command	Description
!b *<text>*	Break command. This command tells the application to stop the movie and display the text string *<text>*.
!g *<frame>*	Goto command. This command tells the application to jump to frame number *<frame>*.
!l *<frame>*	Loop command. This command tells the application to enter a loop, returning to frame number *<frame>* until a Continue button (displayed in a small child window) is pressed.
!c *<text>*	Close command. This command tells the application to display the text string *<text>* and then exit.

Each command begins with an exclamation point (!); this makes it easy for the callback function to recognize commands. When the callback function encounters a script-channel command that it recognizes, it copies the command text and calls another function, Parse, to check the command syntax and break the script command into the window-message format. It then sends the resulting window message and parameters to the main message handler function.

The Callback Function

The callback function is shown in the following code fragment:

```
#define MAX_SCRIPT 1023
char szScriptText[MAX_SCRIPT+1];

BOOL FAR PASCAL
MyFrameHook(MMPID idMovie, WORD wMsg, WORD wParam, LONG lParam)
{
    WORD wMsgOut, wParamOut;
    LONG lParamOut;

    /* If another callback function is hooked, call it first.
     */
    if(lpfnCallback)
        (*lpfnCallback)(idMovie, wMsg, wParam, lParam);

    switch(wMsg)
    {
        case MMP_HOOK_FRAME :
            return FALSE;

        case MMP_HOOK_SCRIPT :

            // Check the script-channel text. If there's no text, or the
            // command is not recognized, let the Movie Player handle it.

            if(lParam == NULL || *((LPSTR)lParam) != '!')
                return FALSE;

            if(lstrlen((LPSTR)lParam) > MAX_SCRIPT)
                return FALSE;

            // Copy the script-channel text.
            lstrcpy(szScriptText, (LPSTR)lParam);

            // Convert the script-channel text to message format.
            // If the parsing succeeds, carry out the command.
            AnsiLower(szScriptText);
            if(Parse(szScriptText, &wMsgOut, &wParamOut, &lParamOut))
            {
                if(bFullScreen && hFullWnd)
                    DoCommand(hFullWnd, wMsgOut, wParamOut, lParamOut);
                else
                    DoCommand(hMainWnd, wMsgOut, wParamOut, lParamOut);
                return TRUE;                // Application handled it.
            }
```

```
        else
            return FALSE;                   // Let Movie Player handle it.
        break;

    default:
        return FALSE;
    }
}
```

The following DoCommand function, called in the previous frame-hook function, handles script-channel commands:

```
LONG DoCommand(HWND hWnd, int iMessage, WORD wParam, LONG lParam)
{
    switch(iMessage)
    {
    case WM_MMPLAY_GOTO:
        if(wParam)
            mmpGoToFrame(idMovie, wParam, MMP_DRAW_FRAME);
        break;

    case WM_MMPLAY_BREAK:
        MessageBox(hWnd, (LPSTR)lParam, szAppName, MB_OK);
        break;

    case WM_MMPLAY_LOOP:

        // The wLoopState flag indicates the current state of the loop.

        switch(wLoopState)
        {
            // If the flag is LOOP_CLEAR, the movie is just entering
            // the loop. Display the "Continue" button and begin
            // the loop.

            case LOOP_CLEAR:
                CreateWindow(szKeytestName, szKeytestName,
                    WS_CHILD | WS_VISIBLE | WS_DLGFRAME | WS_SYSMENU |
                        WS_CAPTION,
                    10, 10, 100, 60, hWnd, NULL, hInst, 0L);
                wLoopState = LOOP_WAIT;
                mmpGoToFrame(idMovie, wParam, MMP_DRAW_FRAME);
                break;

            // If the flag is LOOP_WAIT, the movie is in the loop.
            // The flag remains LOOP_WAIT until the user presses the
            // Continue button.
```

```
                     case LOOP_WAIT:
                         mmpGoToFrame(idMovie, wParam, MMP_DRAW_FRAME);
                         break;

                     // If the flag is LOOP_CONTINUE, exit the loop.

                     case LOOP_CONTINUE:
                         wLoopState = LOOP_CLEAR;
                         break;
                 }
                 break;

         case WM_MMPLAY_CLOSE:

             MessageBox(hWnd, (LPSTR)lParam, szAppName, MB_OK);
             PostQuitMessage(1);
             break;
     }
     return 0L;
}
```

Hooking and Removing the Callback Function

An application can insert the callback function into the playback after opening
the Movie Player instance. Notice how the following code fragment records the
current callback-function address in a global variable before calling
mmpSetFrameHook:

```
lpfnCallback = mmpGetFrameHook(idMovie);
if(lpfnMyCallback = MakeProcInstance(MyFrameHook, hInst))
    mmpSetFrameHook(idMovie, lpfnMyCallback);
```

The application unhooks its frame function before exiting. The following code
fragment shows the WM_DESTROY block of the main message handler:

```
case WM_DESTROY :
    mmpSetFrameHook(idMovie, lpfnCallback);      // Restore previous callback.
    FreeProcInstance(lpfnMyCallback);

    if(!mmpClose(idMovie, 0))
        PrintError(idMovie, "Failed to stop Movie Player.");

    WriteFlags();
    break;
```

Chapter 8
Special Video Topics

This chapter discusses the display drivers available in the Multimedia extensions. The first part describes what to consider when displaying images prepared for one display format in a different format. Other sections explain how to use specific Multimedia display-driver enhancements. The main topics include:

- Evaluating images for display with the Multimedia display drivers

- Working with color palettes

- Working with the Multimedia display drivers

- Working with images in memory

- Using **DisplayDib** to display 256-color images on VGA displays

About the Multimedia Display Drivers

The 256-color high-resolution display will be the dominant display used by most multimedia computers. The OEM computer market has already selected this display as the preferred display. OEMs producing multimedia upgrade kits are encouraged to recommend the 256-color high-resolution display to their customers and to provide options to their customers so they can easily obtain this hardware. Multimedia application developers should also author for this display to create the most competitive products.

The Multimedia extensions provide enhanced display drivers for the 256-color high-resolution displays as well as new display drivers for standard VGA displays. Our goal is to create an environment for 256-color images by improving the existing 256-color drivers and providing additional drivers that can adequately display these images with standard VGA hardware when necessary. The Multimedia extensions add the following VGA display drivers:

- MMV7VGA.DRV (providing 256 colors with high resolution for the Video 7 VGA display adapter)

- MMWD480.DRV (providing 256 colors with high resolution for the Paradise VGA display adapter or other display adapter based on the Western Digital 90C11 display processor)

- MCGA256.DRV (providing 256 colors with low resolution for standard and high-resolution VGA display adapters)

- VGAGRAY.DRV (providing 16 shades of gray with high resolution for standard VGA display adapters)

- VGAPAL.DRV (providing a changeable with 16 colors for standard VGA display adapter)

The multimedia 256-color high-resolution display drivers are optimized versions of the Windows 3.0 display drivers. The video performance of the Multimedia display drivers has been improved on both 80286- and 80386-equipped systems. Multimedia computers with an 80386 processor will realize additional performance improvements. When these drivers detect an 80386 processor in the system, they use 80386-specific code in place of 80286 code.

The low-resolution MCGA256.DRV display driver provides advantages on standard VGA and high-resolution 256-color displays. Reducing the number of display pixels lets standard VGA displays use 256 colors. The reduced number of pixels also lets games update the full display quickly and be more responsive. Games will benefit from this display driver on both types of VGA displays.

The VGAGRAY.DRV and VGAPAL.DRV display drivers provide the high-resolution needed for multimedia applications with a gray-scale mapping of the image color or a reduced color palette. Both of these drivers can provide an acceptable presentation of 256-color images on standard VGA displays.

Users can select the display driver they want using the Display applet in the Control Panel used for the Multimedia extensions. Your application, along with the user's hardware and other critical applications, can influence a user's selection by its image-display requirements.

Evaluating the Display Requirements of Your Images

The following table summarizes the results of displaying different image formats using the different display drivers. When evaluating images for use with alternate display drivers, look carefully at color, resolution, and scale shifts. For example, displaying a 256-color image with a 16-color driver might produce unsatisfactory results. Changing the display resolution can also produce some startling results. For example, without cropping or scaling an image, the low-resolution driver will display only one-quarter of a full-screen, high-resolution image.

Display Driver	Image Type			
	256-Color High Resolution	16-Color High Resolution	Gray Scale (16-Grays) High Resolution	**256-Color Low Resolution**
640-by-480 256-Color	Appears as created	Appears as created	Appears as created	Appears reduced, aspect ratio changed
640-by-480 16-Color Fixed Palette	Good resolution, poor color representation	Appears as created	Color arbitrarily introduced, might appear as an abstract	Appears reduced, poor color representation
640-by-480 16-Color Palettized	Good resolution, limited colors	Appears as created	Appears as created	Appears reduced, limited colors
640-by-480 Gray Scale	Good resolution, good representation with color loss	Loss of color, might appear as an abstract	Appears as created	Appears reduced, good representation with color loss
320-by-200 256-Color	Appears zoomed, appears grainy, aspect ratio changed	Appears zoomed, appears grainy, aspect ratio changed	Appears zoomed, appears grainy, aspect ratio changed	Appears as created

Appearance of images when displayed using different drivers.

Displaying Images with the 256-Color High-Resolution Driver

A high-resolution 256-color driver (such as MMV7VGA.DRV for Video 7 display adapters, MMWD480.DRV for Paradise display adapters, and the Windows driver V7VGA.DRV) offers a resolution of 640-by-480 pixels with a color palette of 256 colors. By using this fine resolution and a configurable color palette, your applications can reproduce the color of very detailed images.

Low-Resolution Images

Low-resolution images don't necessarily force the user to run the application with the low-resolution driver. Because the application is simply opening a 320-by-200 window with 8-bit color depth, high-resolution displays can display such an application in a 320-by-200 window on a standard 640-by-480 display. An application can also display these images in a larger window using either the **StretchBlt** or **StretchDIBits** functions. Images stretched using these functions can appear to have more grain than an unstretched image.

Gray-Scale and 16-Color Images

Images produced for either a 16-color display or gray-scale display transfer easily to a 256-color display. Of course, there is no enhancement to such an image.

Displaying Images with the 16-Color and Gray-Scale Drivers

The multimedia drivers VGAGRAY.DRV and VGAPAL.DRV, and the Windows driver VGA.DRV produce the high resolution of the MMV7VGA.DRV or MMWD480.DRV driver with a limited range of color or gray-scale. The advantages of these displays include small image files, relatively fast disk transfers, and use of a standard VGA display.

16-Color and Gray-Scale Images

Images produced for a 16-color display might be incompatible with a gray-scale display; conversely, images produced for a gray-scale display might be incompatible with a 16-color display. If your images must appear on both 16-color and gray-scale displays, you might want to check your images for undesirable color or brightness shifts. The changeable palette of the VGAPAL.DRV lets you control the display of both 16-color and gray-scale images on a standard VGA display without the unanticipated color or brightness shifts. You can set the 16 changeable colors in the palette to shades of gray for a gray-scale display, or set it to the 16 colors you want.

256-Color Images

With a 4-bit display driver, the system remaps 256 colors to the existing 16-color palette by default. This is the fastest way to display an 8-bit image on a 4-bit display. Unfortunately, the standard system colors don't usually provide enough color range to adequately display a 256-color image. Selecting the colors in the palette of the VGAPAL.DRV display driver can let you display many color images on a standard VGA display. While this driver limits the number of colors to 16, you can select the exact color shades you need to effectively display your images.

With a gray-scale display driver, the system remaps 256 colors to the gray-scale palette. Instead of attempting to match colors, GDI effectively matches brightness values from the 256-color image into the 16 levels of gray. This approach is as fast as remapping to 16 colors, as it uses the same method to display the image.

Remapping of 256-color images has some performance implications due to the additional time required to load an 8-bit image from disc (compared to a 4-bit image). You can improve performance at the expense of disc space by preparing two versions of images on disc—one in 256-color, and the other already mapped to standard system colors or gray scale. Applying a custom remapping algorithm (for example, one based on brightness for gray-scale) to your images lets you control the final appearance of your images. Remapping using a custom algorithm can also reduce the loss of information due to loss of color or color shifts.

Displaying Images with the Low-Resolution Driver

The low-resolution driver, MCGA256.DRV, uses a 320-by-200 display format with a 256-color palette. Low-resolution images require one-fourth the amount of memory and disc space of a 256-color high-resolution image. As a result, data transfer of a low-resolution image is faster than that of a high-resolution image. Also, because the entire display memory fits in 64K, the driver is simpler and faster.

Displaying high-resolution images using the low-resolution driver has the appearance of zooming in on the image. The aspect ratio also changes when displaying high-resolution images with the low-resolution driver. To use images created for a high-resolution display, you might crop the image or scale the image appropriately.

Another way to display 256-color images on standard VGA displays is to use **DisplayDib**. This function uses a 320-by-200 or 320-by-240 full-screen display format to display images with a 256-color palette. Use this function when you need to switch between a high-resolution display and a 256-color display to effectively show your images. The **DisplayDib** function is described later in this chapter.

Working with Color Palettes

If your application uses multiple windows, you can create a palette common to all images displayed simultaneously. This prevents color shifts by GDI remapping colors when your application displays different images. A common color palette can also reduce frame update time.

The following palette files are included with the Multimedia Development Kit:

Palette File	Description
VGA.PAL	Standard VGA 16 color palette.
STANDARD.PAL	A 196-color palette that conforms to NTSC color standards.
BW.PAL	A 2-color black and white palette useful for dithering images to black and white.
GRAY16.PAL	A 16-color gray-scale palette useful for mapping images to gray-scale for display on VGA displays.
GRAY236.PAL	A 236-color gray-scale palette useful for mapping 16-bit and 24-bit images to gray-scale for display on 256-color displays.
SEPIA236.PAL	A 236-color palette with sepia colors useful for creating images with an antique look.
RGB8.PAL RGB64.PAL RGB216.PAL	A linear *n*-color palette created by traversing the color cube in *n* steps. These palettes are useful for dithering images. The 8, 64, and 216 color sizes are based on the cubes of 2, 4, and 6. The 216-color RGB palette is commonly used on the Macintosh.

You can use PalEdit to edit your color palette. With PalEdit, you can modify any color in the palette to obtain a special color. Alternately, you can use the Windows Clipboard within PalEdit to cut, copy, and paste parts of one palette to another.

Working with the Multimedia Display Drivers

The Multimedia display drivers are enhanced versions of the Windows 3.0 drivers. The VGAPAL.DRV, VGAGRAY.DRV, and MCGA256.DRV display driver enhancements provide your application with capabilities to alter the color characteristics of a standard VGA color display. The MMV7VGA.DRV and MMWD480.DRV display driver enhancements include optimizations to significantly improve video performance.

Using 256-Color High-Resolution Display Drivers

The Multimedia high-resolution 256-color display drivers MMV7VGA.DRV and MMWD480.DRV are enhanced versions of the Windows 3.0 display drivers. These display drivers have the following enhancements:

- **BitBlt** and **StretchBlt** can ignore a background color while moving a bitmap

- **StretchBlt** and **StretchDIBits** operations are handled by the display driver when they expand an 8-bit bitmap or DIB by integer factors

- **SetDIBitsToDevice** is optimized for 8-bit DIBs

- **SetDIBitsToScreen**, **StretchBlt**, **StretchDIBits**, and the new transparent background mode of **BitBlt** and **StretchBlt** use 80386-specific code when they detect 80386 processors

Bitmap Blits with Transparent Backgrounds

The Multimedia display drivers add a transparent mode to the **BitBlt** and **StretchBlt** functions. These functions check the background mode (BkMode) of the destination display context. When they find the background mode set to NEWTRANSPARENT, they don't copy the pixels in the source bitmap matching the current device-context background. As a result, they treat the matching pixels as transparent. Your applications can use this mode to remove the background color from an image and add the image onto another background. The statements in the following example move a bitmap with red designated as the background transparent color:

```
SetBkColor(hdc, RGB (255, 0, 0));
SetBkMode (hdc, NEWTRANSPARENT);
BitBlt (hdc, 0, 0, 100, 100, hdcBits, 0, 0, SRCCOPY);
```

The following fragment uses the new constants CAPS1 and C1_TRANSPARENT defined in MMSYSTEM.H to determine if a display driver supports the transparent mode:

```
if (GetDeviceCaps(hDC, CAPS1) & C1_TRANSPARENT)))
    return TRUE;
```

Using StretchBlt and StretchDIBits

The display driver optimizations for **StretchBlt** and **StretchDIBits** are transparent to your application. The Multimedia display drivers automatically use the optimized versions of these functions under the following conditions:

- Your application is using an 8-bit bitmap or DIB

- Your application expands the image by integer factors

- Your application does not mirror the image

- Your application does not use a clipped destination wider than 1024

Your application can improve the speed of **StretchBlt** and **StretchDIBits** by using a one-to-one mapping between the image palette and the system palette. When these functions detect the one-to-one mapping, they avoid translating the image color palette to the system palette. Refer to the *Data Preparation Tools User's Guide* for information on using PalEdit to create an identity palette which will map directly to the system palette.

The **StretchBlt** and **StretchDIBits** also use 80386-specific code when they detect an 80386 processor. Thus, these functions operate faster on an 80386 processor than on an 80286 processor.

Using SetDIBitsToDevice with 8-bit DIBs

The display driver optimizations for **SetDIBsToDevice** are also transparent to your application. The code for your application will operate with both the multimedia display drivers and the standard display drivers.

Although operation of this function is transparent, your application can do the following to get the best speed improvements from **SetDIBsToDevice** when working with 8-bit DIBs:

- Use the DIB_PAL_COLORS option to prevent color matching by GDI.

- Use a one-to-one mapping for the palette. This function detects the one-to-one mapping and avoids translating the image color palette to the system palette.

While your application cannot select the processor, your application can anticipate a performance improvement from **SetDIBitsToDevice** when used with an 80386 processor. The performance of **SetDIBitsToDevice** approaches **BitBlt** when used with an 8-bit DIB and used with an 80386 processor.

Using the MCGA256.DRV Display Driver

The MCGA256.DRV display driver uses a 320-by-200 display format with a 256-color palette. Your application might require this driver when it needs a full color palette on a standard VGA display. On high-resolution displays, your application might require this driver when the ability to rapidly update a large display area is critical to your application. With the exception of the 320-by-200 display, this display driver has the same operating characteristics of the Windows V7VGA.DRV display driver.

Using the VGAGRAY.DRV Display Driver

The VGAGRAY.DRV display driver maps the color in an image to a gray-scale palette with 16 shades of gray. This display driver provides a good monochrome representation of 256-color images on a standard VGA display. The gray-scale value used is determined from the RGB color based on the following color weights:

$$Gray\_value = (2 \times Red\_value + 5 \times Green\_value + 1 \times Blue\_value) / 8$$

By default, the VGAGRAY.DRV display driver uses a linear palette, but it can be changed by adding a [DISPLAY] section to the WIN.INI file. When Windows is started with VGAGRAY.DRV, VGAGRAY.DRV reads the [DISPLAY] section of the WIN.INI file and substitutes the values listed for the default values. The [DISPLAY] section has the following form:

```
[DISPLAY]
    Gray0 = 0        ;   0
    Gray1 = 31       ;   1F
    Gray2 = 47       ;   2F
    Gray3 = 63       ;   3F
    Gray4 = 79       ;   4F
    Gray5 = 95       ;   5F
    Gray6 = 111      ;   6F
    Gray7 = 127      ;   7F
    Gray8 = 143      ;   8F
    Gray9 = 159      ;   9F
    GrayA = 175      ;   AF
    GrayB = 191      ;   BF
    GrayC = 207      ;   CF
```

```
GrayD = 223    ;    DF
GrayE = 239    ;    EF
GrayF = 255    ;    FF
```

The characters 0 through F appended to the Gray keyword is the index to the
gray-scale value. The integer is the gray-scale value. The gray-scale value can
range from 0 through 255. Values listed represent the internal gray-scale values
VGAGRAY.DRV uses by default. You must add the [DISPLAY] section to the
WIN.INI file only if you want VGAGRAY.DRV to use other gray-scale values.

Using the VGAPAL.DRV Display Driver

The VGAPAL.DRV display driver operates as a standard 16-color VGA driver
with a custom color table defined by an application. VGAPAL.DRV uses the
SETCOLORTABLE escape to define the colors used for the display.

About VGAPAL.DRV Display Modes

For default operation, VGAPAL.DRV operates as a standard VGA driver with the
default 16-color palette. That is, if your application uses palette functions, GDI
matches the color being requested to one of the standard VGA colors. When a
custom color table is used, dithering of colors is disabled. All requested colors are
matched to the nearest color in the custom color table.

When VGAPAL.DRV is used with a custom color table, it provides the best
display when used as a maximized window. When used this way, your application
can change the colors without being concerned about the color shifts introduced in
the Windows environment and in other applications using the display.

Detecting VGAPAL.DRV

To detect VGAPAL.DRV, your application should check for a 16-color driver that
supports the SETCOLORTABLE escape. The following fragment does this:

```
i = SETCOLORTABLE;
fVgaPal = (GetDeviceCaps(hdc, NUMCOLORS)==16) &&
    Escape(hdc, QUERYESCSUPPORT, sizeof(int), (LPVOID)&i, NULL);
```

Your application might also check for a palettized driver. While this check will not
uniquely identify VGAPAL.DRV, you can use the result to determine if you can
use functions for palette operations. VGAPAL.DRV is not a palettized driver so
your application cannot use the palette functions with it. The following frament
interrogates a device driver to determine if it is a palletized driver:

```
fPalette = GetDeviceCaps(hdc, RASTERCAPS) & RC_PALETTE;
```

Setting the Color Table

Your application sets the color table of VGAPAL.DRV by using the SETCOLORTABLE escape code and the **Escape** function. The following fragment shows the structure of the **Escape** function for VGAPAL.DRV:

```
Escape(hdc, SETCOLORTABLE, sizeof(COLORTABLE), lpInData, lpOutData)
```

If you specify NULL for *lpInData*, VGAPAL.DRV uses the default colors. If you want to change colors, set *lpInData* to point to a data structure defining your color table. This structure, which is defined by your application, has the following fields:

```
struct {
    BYTE     ctStart;       //Starting palette index to set
    BYTE     ctLen;         //Number of entries to set
    COLORREF ctColors[];    //Color values
} ct;
```

The **ctStart** field specifies the first color table index that will be set. The **ctLen** field specifies the number of entries that will be set. Set this value to the number of colors in the array used for the **ctColors** field. If **ctLEN** is set to zero, it will be treated as if it were set to one. The **ctColors** field specifies the colors that will be used. For changing single index entries, your application can use the **COLORTABLE_STRUCT** data structure.

The *lpOutData* variable points to a **COLORREF** structure. VGAPAL.DRV returns the color set corresponding to the first color in the array specified by *lpInData*. If you the values of the current color table, use the GETCOLORTABLE escape to interrogate VGAPAL.DRV. If you do not want return data, specify NULL for *lpOutData*.

The following example uses SETCOLORTABLE to set the color table:

```
BOOL SetDevicePalette(HDC hdc,int iStart,int iLen,LPPALETTEENTRY ppe)
{   int i;
    struct {
        BYTE     ctStart;
        BYTE     ctLen;
        COLORREF ctColors[16];
    } ct;
    i = SETCOLORTABLE; //Check if SETCOLORTABLE is supported.
    if (!Escape (hdc, QUERYESCSUPPORT, sizeof(i), (LPVOID)&i, NULL))
        return FALSE;
```

```
         if (ppe)
         {   if (iLen  16) //Limit colors to 16.
                 iLen = 16;
             ct.ctStart = iStart; //Set colors.
             ct.ctLen   = iLen;
             for (i=0; i ; i++)
                 ct.ctColors[i] = RGB(ppe[i].peRed, ppe[i].peGreen,p pe[i].peBlue);
             Escape (hdc,SETCOLORTABLE, sizeof(ct), (LPVOID)&ct,NULL); //Set palette
         } else
         {   Escape (hdc, SETCOLORTABLE, 0, NULL, NULL); //Restore palette
         }
         return TRUE;
}
```

Setting the Color Table for Other Applications

Your application should switch to the custom color table whenever it becomes
active. Conversely, your application should restore the previous colors when
another application becomes active. Your application's window processor receives
the WM_ACTIVATEAPP message when either of these events occur and can use
this message to switch modes.

Your application can use the following example to switch color tables when it
receives the WM_ACTIVATEAPP message. The argument for this example is the
wParam value of WM_ACTIVATEAPP. (A nonzero value in *wParam* for the
message indicates activation of the window.)

```
#define NumSysColors 19
//Define system palette
int SysPalIndex[NumSysColors] = {
        COLOR_ACTIVEBORDER,

    .

    .

    .

        COLOR_WINDOWTEXT
};

//Define monochrome palette
#define rgbBlack RGB(0,0,0)
#define rgbWhite RGB(255,255,255)
COLORREF MonoSysColors[NumSysColors] = {
        rgbBlack,           // ACTIVEBORDER

    .

    .

    .

        rgbBlack            // WINDOWTEXT
};
```

```
COLORREF OldSysColors[NumSysColors];

void VGAPalActivate(BOOL f)
    {HDC hdc;
    int i;
    static  BOOL fPalActive = False;
    hdc = GetDC(NULL);
    if (f && !fPalActive)
        {if (fVgaPal) SetDevicePalette(hdc, 0, 16, AppPalette);
        for (i=0; i<NumSysColors; i++) //Save UI colors and map to black/white
            OldSysColors[i] = GetSysColor(SysPalIndex[i]);
        SetSysColors (NumSysColors, SysPalIndex, MonoSysColors);
        }
    if (!f && fPalActive)
        {if (fVgaPal)
            SetDevicePalette(hdc, 0, 16, NULL);
        SetSysColors (NumSysColors, SysPalIndex, OldSysColors);
        }
    fPalActive = f;
    UnrealizeObject(hpalApp);
    ReleaseDC(NULL,hdc);
    }
```

Working with Images in Memory

Many MS-DOS applications directly manipulate screen memory. To maintain the device independence of Windows, it's not possible to allow an application to directly access screen memory. However, an application using the Multimedia extensions can use the DIB driver DIB.DRV to directly manipulate an image in memory or with GDI.

Creating a DIB Driver Display Context

Your application loads the DIB driver by passing the DIB driver name and a BITMAPINFO structure containing the DIB bits to **CreateDC**. For example, the following statement creates a DIB display context that represents the packed-DIB described by the BITMAPINFO data structure *bi*:

```
hdc = CreateDC ("DIB", NULL, NULL, (LPSTR)&bi);
```

When working with this device context, you must observe the following rules:

- If the last parameter of **CreateDC** is NULL, the display context is associated with a 0-by-0 8-bit DIB. Any attempt to draw with it will fail.

- The BITMAPINFO structure must remain locked for the life of the device context.

- The DIB driver supports 1-bit, 4-bit, or 8-bit DIB bitmaps. The RLE format is not supported.

- The DIB driver supports only Windows 3.0 format DIB headers. The OS/2 BITMAPCOREHEADER format is not supported.

- Multiple DIB driver display contexts can be active.

- DIBs reside in the memory-based image buffer in the CF_DIB (packed-DIB) format.

- The DIB driver expects the RGBQUAD data structure for color matching. (It dos not use palette indexes.)

The following code fragment uses the DIB driver to draw a circle in a DIB copied from the Clipboard:

```
if (IsClipboardFormatAvailable(CF_DIB) && OpenClipboard())
    {
    HANDLE hdib;
    HDC hdc;

    // Get the DIB from the Clipboard
    hdib = GetClipboardData (CF_DIB);

    // Create a DIB driver hdc on the DIB surface
    hdc = CreateDC ("DIB", NULL, NULL,
                    (LPSTR)(LPBITMAPINFO)GlobalLock(hdib));

    // Draw a circle in the DIB
    Ellipse (hdc, 0, 0, 100, 100);

    // Delete the DIB driver HDC now that you are done with it
    DeleteDC (hdc);

    // Unlock the DIB
    GlobalUnlock (hdib);

    // Release the Clipboard
    CloseClipboard ();
    }
```

Color Matching in the DIB Driver

If you use an RGB for drawing, the DIB driver will use the closest match found in the color table of the DIB. If you want to draw with a direct color table index, use the **DIBINDEX** macro in the MMSYSTEM.H file to obtain the index.

Moving DIBs To and From the Display

The DIB driver is a separate driver not associated with the display driver. Because of this, you cannot use **BitBlt** to move bitmaps between a DIB driver device context and a screen-device context. To copy from the screen-device context to a DIB-device context, use **GetDIBits**. To copy a DIB device context to the screen device context, use **StretchDIBits**.

You can maximize the speed of **StretchDIBits** in two ways. First, you might use a one-to-one mapping for the palette. Second, you might use the DIB_PAL_COLORS option to prevent color matching by GDI.

The following code fragment uses **StretchDIBits** to draw a CF_DIB to the physical display:

```
/* Draws a bitmap in CF_DIB format, using SetDIBits to device. Takes the
 * same parameters as BitBlt.
 */

BOOL DibBlt(HDC hdc, int x0, int y0, int dx, int dy, HANDLE hdib,
            int x1, int y1, LONG rop, WORD wUsage)
{
    LPBITMAPINFOHEADER  lpbi;
    LPSTR       pBuf;
    WORD        wNumColors;
    BOOL        f;

    if (!hdib)
        return PatBlt(hdc, x0, y0, dx, dy, rop);

    if (wUsage == 0)
        wUsage = DIB_RGB_COLORS;

    lpbi = (VOID FAR *)GlobalLock (hdib);

    if (!lpbi)
        return FALSE;

    wNumColors  = lpbi->biClrUsed ? lpbi->biClrUsed : 256;
    pBuf = (LPSTR)lpbi + lpbi->biSize + wNumColors * sizeof(RGBQUAD);
```

```
        f = StretchDIBits (hdc, x0, y0, dx, dy, x1, y1, dx, dy,
                           pBuf, (LPBITMAPINFO)lpbi, wUsage, rop);

    GlobalUnlock(hdib);
    return f;
}
```

Using the SELECTDIB Escape

Although the preferred method of associating a DIB with a device context is by using **CreateDC**, you can associate a new DIB with an existing DIB driver display context using the SELECTDIB escape, as shown in the following example:

```
Escape (hdc, SELECTDIB, sizeof(BITMAPINFOHEADER), (LPSTR)lpbi,
        (LPSTR)lpBits)
```

For this example, *hdc* is a handle to a DIB-driver device context, *lpbi* points to a BITMAPINFOHEADER that describes the DIB, and *lpBits* points to the DIB bits. If *lpBits* is NULL, the bits are assumed to follow the DIB color table.

Use the SELECTDIB escape to only change the pointer to the DIB bits. Do not change the size of the DIB or the bit depth in the BITMAPINFOHEADER.

Using DisplayDib to Display 256-color Images

The **DisplayDib** function provides a convenient way to display 256-color bitmaps on a standard VGA display. This function reduces the display resolution to 320-by-200 or 320-by-240 to add the 256-color palette to the display. Bitmaps displayed with **DisplayDib** can use the BI_RGB or BI_RLE8 format.

To use **DisplayDib** in your application, you must use the following header files and libraries in addition to the standard Windows and Multimedia extensions header files and libraries.

File	Description
DISPDIB.H	Header file containing function and data declarations.
DISPDIB.LIB	Import library used to resolve function-call references.

When you call **DisplayDib**, your application must be the active application. All inactive applications are suspended while **DisplayDib** temporarily reconfigures the display. (GDI screen updates are also suspended while the display is reconfigured.) The **DisplayDib** function has the following syntax:

WORD DisplayDib(*lpbi, lpBits, wFlags*)

The *lpbi* parameter is a pointer to BITMAPINFO data structure that describes the DIB bitmap.

The *lpBits* parameter is a pointer to the start of the bitmap. If *lpBits* is NULL, **DisplayDib** assumes that the bitmap starts immediately after the BITMAPINFO data structure.

The *wFlags* parameter contains the flags that specifies the operation of **DisplayDib**. The following flags are defined for *wFlags*:

Flag	Description
DISPLAYDIB_MODE_DEFAULT	Sets display resolution to 320-by-240.
DISPLAYDIB_MODE_320x200x8	Sets display resolution to 320-by-200.
DISPLAYDIB_MODE_320x240x8	Sets display resolution to 320-by-240.
DISPLAYDIB_NOCENTER	Displays the image in the lower-left corner of the display.
DISPLAYDIB_NOPALETTE	Ignores the bitmap palette.
DISPLAYDIB_NOWAIT	Returns from the call without waiting for a key press or mouse click.
DISPLAYDIB_BEGIN	Start of multiple calls to **DisplayDib**.
DISPLAYDIB_END	End of multiple calls to **DisplayDib**.

Without any flags, **DisplayDib** defaults to the 320-by-240 resolution and provides a 1-to-1 aspect ratio. When the function displays the bitmap, it realizes the bitmap palette and centers the image on the display. (The bitmap is clipped as required for the display.) The function does not return to the application until the user presses a key or clicks a mouse button.

Use the DISPLAYDIB_MODE_320x200x8 flag to change the display resolution to 320-by-200. This display resolution matches that of the MCGA256.DRV display driver. You can change the resolution back to the 340-by-240 resolution by Using DISPLAYDIB_MODE_320x240x8 or DISPLAYDIB_MODE_DEFAULT.

Use the DISPLAYDIB_NOCENTER flag if you don't want your images centered on the display. With this flag, **DisplayDib** aligns the lower-left corner of the image with the lower-left corner of the display.

The default conditions of waiting for a key press or mouse button click, and automatically realizing the bitmap palette, are both overridden with the DISPLAYDIB_NOWAIT and DISPLAYDIB_NOPALETTE flags. These flags are most effectively used with the DISPLAYDIB_BEGIN and DISPLAYDIB_END flags. The DISPLAYDIB_BEGIN flag marks the start of a series of calls to **DisplayDib**. This flag keeps **DisplayDib** from switching the low-resolution display back to the standard VGA display. This avoids display flicker if your application is displaying a series of images.

The DISPLAYDIB_NOWAIT flag returns control to your application. During a DISPLAYDIB_BEGIN sequence, this flag lets your application perform any processes it needs while the image is displayed. This can include monitoring Windows keyboard and mouse messages for a particular response, or it might include preparing to display another image in the display sequence.

Use the DISPLAYDIB_NOPALLETTE flag if your image sequence has a common palette to avoid realizing the palette for each new image. Use the DISPLAYDIB_END flag to end a sequence image. If your application must perform processes during the display of the last image, display the last image without the DISPLAYDIB_END flag. When your application competes its processes, you can send this flag with *lpbi* and *lpBits* set to NULL to end the display sequence and restore the display to normal.

When **DisplayDib** switches to a low-resolution display, it disables the current display driver. As a result, your application cannot use GDI to update the display. However, your application can use GDI with the DIB driver to update a bitmap for display with **DisplayDib**. When **DisplayDib** switches back to the normal VGA display, it invalidates all windows to repaint the display.

When it encounters a problem with the DIB format, **DisplayDib** returns DISPLAYDIB_INVALIDDIB or DISPLAYDIB_INVALIDFORMAT. If you encounter one of these error returns, check that your bitmaps are 8-bit bitmaps with the BI_RGB or BI_RLE8 format. Also check the bitmap headers for the Windows 3.0 DIB BITMAPINFOHEADER data structure; **DisplayDib** does not support the OS/2 BITMAPCOREHEADER data structure.

This function returns DISPLAYDIB_INVALIDTASK when it is called by a inactive application. When **DisplayDib** is invoked, it prevents any inactive applications from running. To avoid this error return, make sure your application is the active application before calling **DisplayDib**.

Chapter 9
Timer and Joystick Services

This chapter shows you how to add joystick input capabilities to your application and how to control event timing. Timer interrupt services provide improved timer resolution with up to one-millisecond accuracy. The joystick services can receive control signals from up to two joysticks.

This chapter includes the following main topics:

- Timer interrupt services
- Joystick services

Functions and data structures associated with the joystick and timer-interrupt services are defined in MMSYSTEM.H and MMSYSTEM.LIB.

Function Prefixes

The names of functions discussed in this chapter begin with the following prefixes:

Prefix	Description
time	Timer-interrupt functions
joy	Joystick functions

Timer Services

The timer services provided with the Multimedia extensions let applications schedule timed periodic or one-time interrupt events at a higher resolution than is available through the existing Windows timer services. The timer services are loaded when Windows is booted.

Unlike the Windows timer services, the Multimedia timer services are interrupt-based; rather than post WM_TIMER messages to a message queue, they call a callback function at interrupt time. Because the callback code is accessed at interrupt time, it must adhere to strict programming guidelines. Also, high-resolution, periodic interrupt events require significant processor time. This can drastically affect the performance of your application and any other application running at the same time.

The Multimedia timer services are useful for applications that demand high-resolution timing; for example, a MIDI sequencer requires a high-resolution timer because it must maintain the pace of MIDI events within a one-millisecond accuracy rate. For less-demanding synchronization tasks, use the Windows **SetTimer** function.

Timer Data Types

The MMSYSTEM.H file defines new data types and function prototypes for timer functions. You must include this header file in any source module that uses timer services. MMSYSTEM.H defines the following new data types:

MMTIME
  A data structure for representing time in one of several formats.

TIMECAPS
  A data structure for querying timer capabilities.

Using Timer Services

Timer services let an application request and receive timer messages at application-specified intervals. Real-time multimedia applications can use the following functions to control the pace of data and synchronized presentations:

timeBeginPeriod
Establishes the minimum timer resolution an application will use.

timeEndPeriod
Clears a minimum timer resolution previously set using **timeBeginPeriod**.

timeGetDevCaps
Returns information about the capabilities of the timer services.

timeGetTime
Returns the system time in milliseconds.

timeGetSystemTime
Fills an MMTIME structure with the system time in milliseconds.

timeSetEvent
Creates a timer event that executes a specific action at a specific time or at periodic intervals.

timeKillEvent
Cancels a timer event previously created using **timeSetEvent**.

Getting the System Time

An application can get the current system time using the **timeGetTime** or **timeGetSystemTime** functions. The system time is the count of milliseconds since Windows was started. The **timeGetTime** function returns the system time, and the **timeGetSystemTime** function fills an MMTIME structure with the system time.

The **timeGetTime** function has the following syntax:

DWORD timeGetTime()

The **timeGetSystemTime** function has the following syntax:

WORD timeGetSystemTime(*lpMMTime, wSize*)

The *lpMMTime* parameter is a far pointer to an MMTIME structure. The *wSize* parameter specifies the size of the MMTIME structure.

The **timeGetSystemTime** function returns TIMERR_NOERROR if successful.

Determining Maximum and Minimum Event Periods

You can use the **timeGetDevCaps** function to determine the minimum and maximum timer-event periods provided by the timer services. These values vary across computers and can vary depending on the current Windows mode. The **timeGetDevCaps** function has the following syntax:

WORD timeGetDevCaps(*lpCaps, wSize*)

The *lpCaps* parameter is a far pointer to a TIMECAPS structure. The second parameter, *wSize*, specifies the size of the TIMECAPS structure. The TIMECAPS structure has the following format:

```
typedef struct timecaps_tag {
    WORD    wPeriodMin;
    WORD    wPeriodMax;
} TIMECAPS;
```

The two fields in this structure specify, in milliseconds, the minimum and maximum period (and resolution) supported.

Establishing Minimum Timer Resolution

Before starting timer events, your application must establish the minimum timer resolution that it intends to use. It must clear this value after finishing with the timer-event services.

Use the **timeBeginPeriod** and **timeEndPeriod** functions to set and clear the minimum timer-event resolution for your application. You must match a call to **timeBeginPeriod** with a corresponding call to **timeEndPeriod**, specifying the same minimum resolution in both calls. An application can make multiple **timeBeginPeriod** calls, as long as each call is matched with a call to **timeEndPeriod**.

The **timeBeginPeriod** function has the following syntax:

void timeBeginPeriod(*wMinRes*)

The **timeEndPeriod** function has the following syntax:

void timeEndPeriod(*wMinRes*)

In both functions, the *wMinRes* parameter indicates the minimum timer resolution in milliseconds. You can specify any resolution value within the range of resolution values supported by the timer. The **wPeriodMin** and **wPeriodMax** fields of the TIMECAPS structure (filled by the **timeGetDevCaps** function) specify the minimum and maximum resolution supported by the timer services.

Starting Timer Events

To initialize and start timer events, use the **timeSetEvent** function. This function returns a timer ID that can be used to stop or identify timer events. The **timeSetEvent** function has the following syntax:

WORD timeSetEvent(*wDelay, wResolution, lpFunction, dwUser, wFlags*)

The *wDelay* parameter specifies the period, in milliseconds, for timer events. If this value is less than the minimum timer period or greater than the maximum period, **timeSetEvent** fails.

The *wResolution* value establishes the accuracy of the timer event. The accuracy of the timer event can increase with smaller *wResolution* values. For example, on a one-time event with a *wResolution* value of 5 and a *wDelay* value of 100, the timer services notify your callback function after an interval ranging from 95 to 105 milliseconds. The application must have called **timeBeginPeriod** to specify a minimum resolution of 5 milliseconds.

Larger *wResolution* values provide flexibility to reduce the number of timer interrupts, which can seriously affect system performance. To reduce system overhead, use the maximum *wResolution* value appropriate for your application. To ensure that periodic events occur at specified intervals, use a resolution of zero.

Pass the name of the callback function in the *lpFunction* parameter, and pass any instance data in the *dwUser* parameter. The callback function must reside in a DLL, so you don't need to call **MakeProcInstance** to get the procedure-instance address of the callback function.

The *wFlags* parameter takes one of the following flags:

Flag	Description
TIME_ONESHOT	Event should occur once, after *wPeriod* elapses
TIME_PERIODIC	Event should occur repeatedly, waiting *wPeriod* between each event

The **timeSetEvent** function returns a timer ID if successful or NULL if unsuccessful. Interrupt timers are a scarce resource, and periodic timers with resolution less than 100 milliseconds consume a significant portion of CPU time. For periodic timers, you must pair calls to **timeSetEvent** with calls to **timeKillEvent**. For more information, see the following section, "Canceling a Timer Event."

The *lpFunction* parameter contains the procedure-instance address of the function to be called when the timer event takes place.

Since the callback function is accessed at interrupt time, it must adhere to strict programming guidelines. Timer-callback functions follow the same programming guidelines as callback functions for the low-level audio services. See "Using a Callback Function to Process Driver Messages" in Chapter 5, "Low-Level Audio Services," for information on writing an interrupt callback function.

The timer-event callback function must have the following syntax:

```
void FAR PASCAL TimerCallback(
    WORD idTimer,                   // Timer ID
    WORD msg,                       // Not used
    DWORD dwUser,                   // User-instance data
    DWORD dw1,                      // Not used
    DWORD dw2 )                     // Not used
```

The *idTimer* parameter receives the timer ID, and the *dwUser* parameter receives the user-instance data passed to the **timeSetEvent** function. The *msg*, *dw1*, and *dw2* parameters are not used.

Canceling a Timer Event

You can cancel an active timer event at any time. Be sure to cancel any outstanding timers before freeing the DLL containing the callback function. To cancel a timer event, use the **timeKillEvent** function, which has the following syntax:

WORD timeKillEvent(*wId*)

Pass the timer ID returned by **timeSetEvent** to the *wId* parameter.

Using Timer Callbacks

This section describes how an application might use the timer services. First, the application calls the **timeGetDevCaps** function to determine the minimum and maximum resolution supported by the timer services. Before setting up any timer events, the application uses **timeBeginPeriod** to establish the minimum timer resolution it will use, as shown in the following code fragment:

```
#define TARGET_RESOLUTION 1          // Try for 1-millisecond accuracy

TIMECAPS tc;
WORD     wTimerRes;

if(timeGetDevCaps(&tc, sizeof(TIMECAPS)) != TIMERR_NOERROR)
{
    // Error; application can't continue
}

wTimerRes = min(max(tc.wPeriodMin, TARGET_RESOLUTION), tc.wPeriodMax);
timeBeginPeriod(wTimerRes);
```

To start the timer event, the application specifies the amount of time before the callback occurs, the required resolution, the address of the callback function, and user data to supply with the callback. The application might use a function like the following to start a one-time timer event:

```
WORD SetTimerCallback(NPSEQ npSeq,           // Sequencer data
                      WORD msInterval)       // Event interval
{
    npSeq->wTimerID = timeSetEvent(
        msInterval,                          // Delay
        wTimerRes,                           // Resolution (global variable)
        OneShotCallback,                     // Callback function
        (DWORD)npSeq,                        // User data
        TIME_ONESHOT );                      // Event type (one-time)

    if(! npSeq->wTimerID)
        return ERR_TIMER;
    else
        return ERR_NOERROR;
}
```

The following callback function resides in a fixed code segment in a DLL. It is limited to calling those functions that are interrupt-callable. The TimerIntRoutine procedure it calls also resides in a fixed code segment.

```
void FAR PASCAL
OneShotTimer(WORD wId, WORD msg, DWORD dwUser, DWORD dw1, DWORD dw2)
{
    NPSEQ npSeq;             // Pointer to sequencer data

    npSeq = (NPSEQ)dwUser;
    npSeq->wTimerID = 0;     // Invalidate timer id, since no longer in use

    TimerIntRoutine(npSeq);  // Handle interrupt-time tasks
}
```

Before freeing the DLL that contains the callback function, the application cancels any outstanding timers. To cancel one timer event, it might call the following function:

```
void DestroyTimer(NPSEQ npSeq)
{
    if(npSeq->wTimerID)                      // If timer event is pending
    {
        timeKillEvent(npSeq->wTimerID);      // Cancel the event
        npSeq->wTimerID = 0;
    }
}
```

Finally, to cancel the minimum timer resolution it established, the application calls **timeEndPeriod** as follows:

```
timeEndPeriod(wTimerRes);
```

Joystick Services

The joystick is an input device that provides position information. It is an additional supported input device, not a replacement for the mouse. All absolute-position devices, including touch screens, digitizing tablets, and light pens, can use the joystick services to provide position and button information to applications.

The joystick services are loaded when Windows is started. The joystick services can monitor two joysticks, each with two- or three-axis movement, and up to four buttons. Applications access the joystick services through the set of functions described in this section.

Note The driver for the IBM Game Adapter (IBMJOY.DRV) supports two 2-axis joysticks or one 3-axis joystick.

Joystick Data Types

The MMSYSTEM.H file defines new data types and function prototypes for joystick functions. MMSYSTEM.H defines the following new data types:

JOYCAPS
A data structure that contains joystick capability information.

JOYINFO
A data structure that contains joystick position and button information.

Using Joystick Services

Joystick services include functions to query each joystick for its capabilities, to poll each joystick for position and button information, and to receive messages in response to joystick events. Your application can use the following joystick functions to accept input from one or two joysticks:

joyGetNumDevs
Returns the number of joysticks supported by the joystick services.

joyGetDevCaps
Returns joystick capabilities.

joyGetPos
Returns joystick position and button information.

joySetCapture
Causes joystick input to be sent to a specified window at regular intervals or when the joystick state changes.

joyReleaseCapture
Releases the joystick captured using **joySetCapture**.

joyGetThreshold
Returns the movement threshold of a joystick.

joySetThreshold
Sets the movement threshold of a joystick.

Determining Joystick Capabilities

The various joysticks in use today can support two or three axes and a variety of button configurations. Also, joysticks support different ranges of motion and polling frequencies. Joystick drivers can support either one or two joysticks. Two functions allow you to determine the capabilities of the joystick services and joystick devices installed on a system.

Note The IBMJOY.DRV joystick driver supports either one 3-axis joystick or two 2-axis joysticks. The driver includes a configuration routine (accessed through the Control Panel Drivers applet) that allows a user to specify which type of device is connected.

Getting the Driver Capabilities

You can use the **joyGetNumDevs** function to determine the number of joystick devices supported by the joystick services. This function has the following syntax:

WORD joyGetNumDevs()

This function returns the number of supported joysticks, or zero if there is no joystick support. The value returned is not necessarily the number of joysticks attached to the system. To determine whether a joystick is attached, call the **joyGetPos** function for the device. The **joyGetPos** function, discussed in "Polling the Joystick," later in this chapter, returns JOYERR_UNPLUGGED if the specified device is disconnected.

The following code fragment determines whether the joystick services are available and then determines if a joystick is attached to one of the ports:

```
JOYINFO joyinfo;
WORD wNumDevs, wDeviceID;
BOOL bDev1Attached, bDev2Attached;

    if((wNumDevs = joyGetNumDevs()) == 0)
        return ERR_NODRIVER;

    bDev1Attached = joyGetPos(JOYSTICKID1,&joyinfo) != JOYERR_UNPLUGGED;
    bDev2Attached = wNumDevs == 2 &&
                    joyGetPos(JOYSTICKID2,&joyinfo) != JOYERR_UNPLUGGED;

    if(bDev1Attached || bDev2Attached)      // Decide which joystick to use
        wDeviceID = bDev1Attached ? JOYSTICKID1 : JOYSTICKID2;
    else
        return ERR_NODEVICE;
```

Getting the Joystick Capabilities

You can use the **joyGetDevCaps** function to obtain the specific capabilities of each joystick attached to a given system. The **joyGetDevCaps** function has the following syntax:

WORD joyGetDevCaps(*wID, lpJoyCaps, wSize*)

The *wID* parameter identifies the joystick as either JOYSTICKID1 or JOYSTICKID2. The *lpJoyCaps* parameter points to a JOYCAPS structure to be filled by the function. The *wSize* parameter specifies the size of the JOYCAPS structure.

JOYCAPS Structure   The JOYCAPS structure specifies the range of each axis on the joystick, the number of buttons, and the maximum and minimum polling frequency. This structure has the following fields:

Field	Description
wMid	Manufacturer identification
wPid	Product identification
szPname[MAXPNAMELEN]	Product name in a null-terminated string
wXmin, wXmax	Minimum and maximum *x*-position values
wYmin, wYmax	Minimum and maximum *y*-position values
wZmin, wZmax	Minimum and maximum *z*-position values
wNumButtons	Number of buttons
wPeriodMin	Minimum period between messages
wPeriodMax	Maximum period between messages

Methods for Checking Joystick Status

An application can receive information from the joystick in one of two ways:

- By processing joystick messages from a captured joystick

- By polling the joystick directly

The message-processing method can be simpler to use; your application is sent messages that indicate the position of the stick and the state of the buttons (pressed or released).

Capturing Joystick Messages to a Window Function

You can capture joystick input to a window function; your application then receives joystick messages at specified intervals or when the user manipulates the joystick. The messages are described in "Processing Joystick Messages," following this section.

Only one application can capture joystick messages from a given joystick. Capturing joystick messages does not, however, prevent your application (or other applications) from polling the joystick using **joyGetPos**. If **joyGetPos** is called while joystick input is captured, joystick events occurring close to the time of the **joyGetPos** call might not be accurately reported to the capture window.

Capturing Joystick Input The **joySetCapture** function captures joystick input to a window function you specify. To release the joystick, call the **joyReleaseCapture** function. The **joySetCapture** function has the following syntax:

WORD joySetCapture*(hWnd, wID, wPeriod, bChanged)*

Specify the handle of the window to receive the messages in the *hWnd* parameter. For *wID*, specify which joystick to capture; use the constants JOYSTICKID1 or JOYSTICKID2. The *wPeriod* parameter specifies the frequency, in milliseconds, of the joystick messages, and the *bChanged* parameter specifies whether messages are to be sent only when the stick position or button states change. The joystick messages are described in the next section.

To capture messages from two joysticks attached to the system, you must call **joySetCapture** twice, once for each joystick. Your window then receives separate messages for each device.

You cannot capture an unplugged joystick. The **joySetCapture** function returns zero if successful; it returns JOYERR_UNPLUGGED if the specified device is unplugged.

Note   The joystick services set up a Windows timer event with each call to **joySetCapture**.

Specifying the Resolution and Threshold

Assign the *wPeriod* parameter a value that falls within the minimum and maximum resolution range for the joystick. To determine the minimum and maximum resolution of the joystick, call the **joyGetDevCaps** function, which fills the **wPeriodMin** and **wPeriodMax** fields in the **JOYCAPS** structure.

If the *wPeriod* value is outside the range of valid resolution values for the joystick, the joystick services use the minimum or maximum resolution value, whichever is closer to the *wPeriod* value.

The *bChanged* parameter controls when the window receives joystick movement messages. If *bChanged* is set to FALSE, these messages occur approximately every *wPeriod* milliseconds, regardless of whether the position has changed since the last time the joystick was polled. If *bChanged* is set to TRUE, messages are sent when the position of a joystick axis changes by a value greater than the movement threshold of the device. To change the movement threshold, use the **joySetThreshold** function, discussed in "Setting the Movement Threshold," later in this chapter.

Processing Joystick Messages

The following joystick messages can be sent to a window function. Numerals 1 and 2 in these messages correspond to the joystick initiating the message. MM_JOY1 messages are sent to the window function if your application requests input from the first joystick, and MM_JOY2 messages are sent if your application requests input from the second joystick. All messages report nonexistent buttons as released.

Messages	Description
MM_JOY1MOVE MM_JOY2MOVE	Report a change in the *x*-axis and/or *y*-axis position of the joystick.
	The *wParam* parameter contains a combination of JOY_BUTTON bit flags specifying which buttons were pressed.
	The low-order word of *lParam* contains the *x*-position of the joystick, and the high-order word contains the *y*-position.
MM_JOY1ZMOVE MM_JOY2ZMOVE	Report a change in the *z*-axis position of a 3-axis joystick.
	The *wParam* parameter contains a combination of JOY_BUTTON bit flags specifying which buttons were pressed.
	The low-order word of *lParam* contains the *x*-position of the joystick, and the high-order word contains the *y*-position.
MM_JOY1BUTTONUP MM_JOY2BUTTONUP MM_JOY1BUTTONDOWN MM_JOY2BUTTONDOWN	Report that a joystick button has been pressed or released.
	The *wParam* parameter contains one JOY_BUTTONCHG bit flag specifying which button changed state and a combination of JOY_BUTTON bit flags specifying the current button states.
	The low-order word of *lParam* contains the *x*-position of the joystick, and the high-order word contains the *y*-position.

Using the Button Flags

The joystick services use the following bit flags, passed in the *wParam* parameter of the window function, to report the state of the joystick buttons:

Flag	Description
JOY_BUTTON1	Set when button 1 is pressed.
JOY_BUTTON1CHG	Set when button 1 has changed state.
JOY_BUTTON2	Set when button 2 is pressed.
JOY_BUTTON2CHG	Set when button 2 has changed state.
JOY_BUTTON3	Set when button 3 is pressed.
JOY_BUTTON3CHG	Set when button 3 has changed state.
JOY_BUTTON4	Set when button 4 is pressed.
JOY_BUTTON4CHG	Set when button 4 has changed state.

The MM_JOYMOVE messages use the JOY_BUTTON flags to report the state (pressed or released) of all buttons on the specified joystick.

The MM_JOYBUTTONUP and MM_JOYBUTTONDOWN messages use the JOY_BUTTON flags to report the state (pressed or released) of all buttons on the specified joystick. Also, they use JOY_BUTTONCHG flags to indicate which button changed state, thereby generating the message.

For example, if the user presses and holds buttons 1 and 2 and then moves the stick, a window function might receive the following messages:

Message	wParam Flags
MM_JOY1BUTTONDOWN	JOY_BUTTON1 I JOY_BUTTON1CHG
MM_JOY1BUTTONDOWN	JOY_BUTTON1 I JOY_BUTTON2 I JOY_BUTTON2CHG
MM_JOY1MOVE	JOY_BUTTON1 I JOY_BUTTON2

A window function might receive the following messages when the user presses and releases button 3 without moving the stick:

Message	wParam Flags
MM_JOY1BUTTONDOWN	JOY_BUTTON3 I JOY_BUTTON3CHG
MM_JOY1BUTTONUP	JOY_BUTTON3CHG

Releasing the Joystick

When your application no longer needs to receive periodic joystick messages, it should release the joystick using the **joyReleaseCapture** function. If your application does not release the joystick before ending, the joystick is released shortly after the capture window is destroyed.

The **joyReleaseCapture** function has the following syntax:

WORD joyReleaseCapture(*wID*)

The *wID* parameter is the joystick ID of the captured joystick. You can use the constants JOYSTICKID1 or JOYSTICKID2.

Setting the Movement Threshold

You can change the movement threshold of the joystick by calling the **joySetThreshold** function. The movement threshold is the number of device units that the stick must be moved before an MM_JOYMOVE message is sent to the window that has captured the device. The **joySetThreshold** function has the following syntax:

WORD joySetThreshold(*wID, wThreshold*)

The two parameters, *wID* and *wThreshold*, identify the joystick device and specify the movement threshold. You can get the minimum resolution of the joystick by calling the **joyGetDevCaps** function.

Polling the Joystick

You can poll the joystick for position and button information. For example, an application might poll the joystick to get baseline position values; the Joystick Control Panel applet uses this technique when calibrating the joystick. The **joyGetPos** function allows you to poll the joystick for position and button information. It has the following syntax:

WORD joyGetPos(*wID*, *lpJoyInfo*)

The *wID* parameter identifies the joystick. The *lpJoyInfo* parameter is a far pointer to a JOYINFO structure that is filled by the function.

Note Calling **joyGetPos** while joystick input is captured can prevent the joystick services from accurately reporting joystick events to the capture window.

The JOYINFO Structure

The JOYINFO structure has the following form:

```
typedef struct joyinfo_tag {
    WORD    wXpos;
    WORD    wYpos;
    WORD    wZpos;
    WORD    wButtons;
} JOYINFO;
```

The **wXpos**, **wYpos**, and **wZpos** fields specify the current *x*-, *y*-, and *z*-position of the joystick.

The **wButtons** field specifies the button states. This can be any combination of the JOY_BUTTON bit flags. For example, the following expression evaluates to TRUE if button 1 is pressed:

```
joyinfo.wButtons & JOY_BUTTON1
```

See "Processing Joystick Messages," earlier in this chapter, for an explanation of the JOY_BUTTON flags.

Using Joystick Messages

The remainder of this chapter presents code fragments from a simple joystick game that performs the useful function of shooting holes in the desktop: it gets position and button-state information from the joystick services and, when a user presses the joystick buttons, plays waveform resources and paints bullet holes on the screen.

Most of the joystick-control code is in the main window function. In the following WM_CREATE case of the message handler, the application captures input from joystick 1:

```
case WM_CREATE:
    if(joySetCapture(hWnd, JOYSTICKID1,  NULL, FALSE))
    {
        MessageBeep(MB_ICONEXCLAMATION);
        MessageBox(hWnd, "Couldn't capture the joystick.", NULL,
                      MB_OK | MB_ICONEXCLAMATION);
        PostMessage(hWnd,WM_CLOSE,0,0L);
    }
    break;
```

In response to the MM_JOY1MOVE messages, the application changes the position of the cursor and, if either button is pressed, draws a hole in the desktop:

```
case MM_JOY1MOVE :
    if(wParam & (JOY_BUTTON1 | JOY_BUTTON2))
        DrawFire(hWnd);
    DrawSight(lParam);                          // Calculate new cursor position
    break;
```

In response to the MM_JOY1BUTTONDOWN messages, the application uses **sndPlaySound** to play a waveform audio file:

```
case MM_JOY1BUTTONDOWN :
    if(wParam & JOY_BUTTON1)
    {
        sndPlaySound(lpButton1, SND_LOOP | SND_ASYNC | SND_MEMORY);
        DrawFire(hWnd);
    }
    else if(wParam & JOY_BUTTON2)
    {
        sndPlaySound(lpButton2, SND_ASYNC | SND_MEMORY |  SND_LOOP);
        DrawFire(hWnd);
    }
    break;
```

By specifying the SND_LOOP and SND_ASYNC flags with **sndPlaySound**, the JOYTOY application repeats the waveform playback until the button is released.

When a button is released, the window function receives a MM_JOY1BUTTONUP message, which it handles as follows:

```
case MM_JOY1BUTTONUP :
    sndPlaySound(NULL, 0);
    break;
```

This sequence stops the waveform-audio playback.

Chapter 10
Multimedia File I/O Services

Most multimedia applications require file I/O—the ability to create, read, and write disk files. Multimedia file I/O services provide buffered and unbuffered file I/O, and support for standard IBM/Microsoft Resource Interchange File Format (RIFF) files. The services are extensible with custom I/O procedures that can be shared among applications.

This chapter covers the following topics:

- Using basic file I/O services

- Performing buffered file I/O

- Working with RIFF files

- Directly accessing a file I/O buffer

- Using memory files

- Writing a custom I/O procedure

Note The Multimedia file I/O services will provide support for RIFF compound files in a future release of the Multimedia extensions.

About the Multimedia File I/O Services

The Multimedia file I/O services provide support for the following file I/O operations:

- Basic unbuffered and buffered file I/O

- RIFF file I/O

- Direct access to the file I/O buffer

- Memory files

- Custom storage system I/O using application-supplied I/O procedures

Most applications only need the basic file I/O services and the RIFF file I/O services. Applications sensitive to file I/O performance, such as applications that stream data from a CD-ROM in real time, can optimize performance by using services to directly access the file I/O buffer. Applications that access custom *storage systems* can provide their own I/O procedure that reads and writes elements of the storage system. A storage system is a method of physically storing data in a file, such as a file archival system or a database storage system.

Comparison with MS-DOS, C Run-time, and Windows File I/O

You might ask why you need another set of file I/O services, when you already have the services of MS-DOS, the C run-time libraries, and Windows. The Multimedia file I/O services offer the following advantages over other file I/O services:

- They provide more functionality and are easier to use than the MS-DOS services

- They are a part of the system software, so they don't increase the size of your application, like linking to the C run-time libraries

- They provide more functionality than the Windows services, such as support for buffered I/O, RIFF files, memory files, and custom storage systems

In addition, the Multimedia file I/O services are optimized for performance-intensive applications. The CPU overhead of using these services versus going directly to MS-DOS is very low.

Function Prefixes

All Multimedia file I/O function names begin with the **mmio** prefix. Similarly, all Multimedia file I/O message names begin with the **MMIOM_** prefix.

Data Types

The MMSYSTEM.H header file defines data types and function prototypes for all Multimedia file I/O functions. You must include this header file in any source module that uses these functions. MMSYSTEM.H depends on declarations made in WINDOWS.H, so you must first include the WINDOWS.H header file. MMSYSTEM.H defines the following data types for the Multimedia file I/O functions:

FOURCC
A four-character code identifying an element of a RIFF file.

HMMIO
A handle to an open file.

MMCKINFO
A data structure containing information about a chunk in a RIFF file.

MMIOINFO
A data structure used to maintain the current state of a file accessed using the Multimedia file I/O services.

MMIOPROC
A custom Multimedia file I/O procedure.

Performing Basic File I/O

Using the basic I/O services is similar to using the C run-time file I/O services. Files must be opened before they can be read or written. After reading or writing, the file must be closed. You can change the current read/write location by seeking to a specified position in an open file. The following table lists the basic file I/O functions:

mmioClose
   Closes an open file.

mmioOpen
   Opens a file for reading and/or writing, and returns a handle to the open file.

mmioRead
   Reads a specified number of bytes from an open file.

mmioSeek
   Changes the current position for reading and/or writing in an open file.

mmioWrite
   Writes a specified number of bytes to an open file.

These file I/O functions provide the core of the Multimedia file I/O services—you can use them for buffered and unbuffered I/O, as well as for I/O to RIFF files, memory files, and custom storage systems.

Opening a File

Before doing any I/O operations to a file, you must first open the file using the **mmioOpen** function. The **mmioOpen** function returns a file handle which you use to identify the open file when calling other file I/O functions. The **mmioOpen** function has the following syntax:

HMMIO mmioOpen(*szFileName, lpmmioinfo, dwFlags*)

The *szFileName* parameter points to a null-terminated string containing the pathname of the file to open.

The *lpmmioinfo* parameter is a far pointer to an MMIOINFO structure containing additional parameters. For basic file I/O services, this parameter should be NULL.

The *dwFlags* parameter specifies options for opening the file. The most commonly used flags for basic file I/O are MMIO_READ, MMIO_WRITE, and MMIO_CREATE.

The return value is a file handle of type HMMIO. Use this file handle to identify the open file when calling other file I/O functions. If the file cannot be opened, the return value is NULL.

Warning   An HMMIO file handle is not a MS-DOS file handle. Do not use HMMIO file handles with MS-DOS, Windows, or C run-time file I/O functions.

There are options you can use with the **mmioOpen** function for operations beyond basic file I/O. By specifying an MMIOINFO structure with the *lpmmioinfo* parameter, you can open memory files, specify a custom I/O procedure, or supply a buffer for buffered I/O. These topics are discussed later in this chapter. First, this chapter discusses the most basic use of **mmioOpen**—opening files for basic unbuffered file I/O.

Opening a File   To open a file for basic I/O operations, set the *lpmmioinfo* parameter of **mmioOpen** to NULL. For example, the following code fragment opens a file named "C:\SAMPLES\SAMPLE1.TXT" for reading, and checks the return value for errors:

```
HMMIO hFile;
    .
    .
    .
if ((hFile = mmioOpen("C:\\SAMPLES\\SAMPLE1.TXT", NULL, MMIO_READ)) != NULL)
    /* File opened successfully */

else
    /* File cannot be opened */
```

Options for Opening a File

When you open a file, you must specify whether you are opening the file for reading, writing, or both reading and writing. In addition, you can specify other options, such as to create or delete a new file. Use the *dwFlags* parameter of **mmioOpen** to specify options for opening a file.

Basic Options   The following table lists the basic options for opening a file using **mmioOpen**:

Flag	Description
MMIO_READ	Opens a file for reading only.
MMIO_WRITE	Opens a file for writing only.
MMIO_READWRITE	Opens a file for reading and writing.
MMIO_CREATE	Creates a new file (if the file already exists, it truncates it to zero length).
MMIO_DELETE	Deletes a file.
MMIO_ALLOCBUF	Opens a file for buffered I/O.

The MMIO_READ, MMIO_WRITE, and MMIO_READWRITE flags are read/write privilege flags. These flags are mutually exclusive—specify only one when opening a file. If you don't specify one of these flags, **mmioOpen** opens the file for reading only.

The MMIO_CREATE and MMIO_DELETE flags are also mutually exclusive. You can specify one of the read/write privilege flags with the MMIO_CREATE flag. You can't specify any additional flags with the MMIO_DELETE flag.

See "Performing Buffered File I/O," later in this chapter, for information on using the MMIO_ALLOCBUF flag.

Sharing Options   In addition to the basic options for opening a file, there are sharing options you can use for opening MS-DOS files so they can be opened and accessed by more than one process. The following table lists the sharing options for opening a file using **mmioOpen**.

Flag	Description
MMIO_COMPAT	Opens a file in compatibility mode.
MMIO_EXCLUSIVE	Opens a file in exclusive mode.
MMIO_DENYWRITE	Opens a file and denies other processes write access to the file.
MMIO_DENYREAD	Opens a file and denies other processes read access to the file.
MMIO_DENYNONE	Opens a file without denying other processes read or write access to the file.

The sharing options are rarely used by applications, and are provided only because they are available through MS-DOS. They are not available for memory files or for files opened using custom I/O procedures. For more information on sharing options, see the *Microsoft MS-DOS Programmer's Reference* or the *Microsoft MS-DOS Encyclopedia.*

Note   MS-DOS sharing options only work if the MS-DOS **share** command is used before the file is opened.

Creating and Deleting Files

To create a new file, specify the MMIO_CREATE option with the **mmioOpen** function. For example, the following code fragment creates a new file and opens it for both reading and writing:

```
HMMIO hFile;
.
.
.
hFile = mmioOpen("NEWFILE.TXT", NULL, MMIO_CREATE | MMIO_READWRITE);
if (hFile != NULL)
    /* File created successfully */

else
    /* File could not be created */
```

Note   If the file you are creating already exists, it will be truncated to zero length.

To delete a file, specify the MMIO_DELETE flag with the **mmioOpen** function. Once you delete a file, it can't be recovered (except possibly by using certain MS-DOS based file recovery utilities). If the file deletion is the result of a request from a user, you should always query the user to be sure the user wants to delete the specified file before actually deleting it.

Reading and Writing a File

To read and write to open files, use the **mmioRead** and **mmioWrite** functions. Each of these functions takes an HMMIO file handle, a pointer to a buffer, and a parameter specifying the number of bytes to read or write. The read and write operations are not limited to 64K—the buffer pointers are huge pointers.

See "Example of RIFF File I/O," later in this chapter, for an example using **mmioRead** to read from a file.

Seeking to a New Position in a File

The *current position* or *file pointer* in a file is the location where the next read or write operation will occur. To change the current position in an open file, use the **mmioSeek** function. The **mmioSeek** function has the following syntax:

LONG mmioSeek(*hmmio, lOffset, iOrigin*)

The *hmmio* parameter specifies the file handle for the file.

The *lOffset* parameter specifies an offset for changing the current position in the file.

The *iOrigin* parameter specifies how the offset given by *lOffset* is interpreted. If *iOrigin* is SEEK_SET, the offset is from the beginning of the file. If it is SEEK_CUR, the offset is from the current position. If it is SEEK_END, the offset is from the end of the file.

The return value is the new position, specified in bytes from the beginning of the file. If an error occurs, the return value is −1. If you seek to an invalid location in a file, such as past the end of the file, **mmioSeek** might not return an error, but subsequent I/O operations can fail.

Examples Using mmioSeek

To seek to the beginning of an open file, use the following:

```
mmioSeek(hFile, 0L, SEEK_SET);
```

To seek to the end of an open file, use the following:

```
mmioSeek(hFile, 0L, SEEK_END);
```

To seek to a position ten bytes from the end of an open file, use the following:

```
mmioSeek(hFile, -10L, SEEK_END);
```

Performing Buffered File I/O

Most of the overhead in file I/O involves accessing the media (the physical device). If you are reading or writing many small blocks of information, the media device can spend a lot of time seeking to find the physical location on the media for each read or write operation. In this case, better performance is achieved by using buffered file I/O. With buffered I/O, the file I/O manager maintains an intermediate buffer larger than the blocks of information you are reading or writing. It only accesses the media when the buffer must be filled from or written to the disk.

Deciding When to Use Buffered File I/O

It's difficult to provide exact metrics telling you when you need to use buffered I/O. It depends on how many read and write operations you perform on a file, and on the size of these read and write operations. A general guideline is if you are doing a lot of I/O operations less than 2K each, then use buffered I/O. But this rule isn't absolute—it's best to understand exactly how your program uses file I/O and experiment to optimize file I/O for your program's requirements.

Opening a File for Buffered File I/O

The Multimedia file I/O manager provides several ways to set up and use buffered file I/O. The main distinction between these different approaches is whether the file I/O manager or the application allocates the buffer—either the file I/O manager or the application can allocate the I/O buffer. Unless you want to directly access the I/O buffer or open a memory file, you should let the file I/O manager allocate the buffer. For more information on directly accessing an I/O buffer and using memory files, see "Directly Accessing a File I/O Buffer" and "Performing File I/O on Memory Files," both later in this chapter.

A buffer allocated by the file I/O manager is called an *internal buffer*. To open a file for buffered I/O using an internal buffer, specify the MMIO_ALLOCBUF flag with the **mmioOpen** function when you open the file. Once a file is opened for buffered I/O, the buffer is essentially transparent to the application. You can read, write, and seek the same way as with unbuffered I/O.

I/O Buffer Control Functions

The Multimedia file I/O services also include some functions giving you more control over the file I/O buffer. Using the following functions, you can force the contents of an I/O buffer to be written to disk, enable buffered I/O on a file opened for unbuffered I/O, change the size of an I/O buffer, and supply your own I/O buffer:

mmioFlush
Writes the contents of the I/O buffer to disk.

mmioSetBuffer
Changes the size of the I/O buffer, and allows applications to supply their own buffer.

Flushing an I/O Buffer

Flushing an I/O buffer means writing the contents of the buffer to disk. You don't have to call **mmioFlush** to flush an I/O buffer—the buffer is automatically flushed when you close a file using **mmioClose**. If you don't close a file immediately after writing to it, you should flush the buffer to ensure the information is written to disk.

Note If you run out of disk space, **mmioFlush** might fail, even if the preceding **mmioWrite** calls were successful. Similarly, **mmioClose** might fail when it is flushing its I/O buffer.

Changing the Size of the Internal I/O Buffer

The default size of the internal I/O buffer is 8K. If this size is not adequate, you can use **mmioSetBuffer** to change the size of the buffer. You can also use **mmioSetBuffer** to enable buffering on a file opened for unbuffered I/O. The **mmioSetBuffer** function has the following syntax:

WORD mmioSetBuffer(*hmmio, pchBuffer, cchBuffer, wFlags*)

The *hmmio* parameter specifies the file handle for the file associated with the buffer.

The *pchBuffer* parameter specifies a pointer to a user-supplied buffer. For an internal buffer, set this parameter to NULL.

The *cchBuffer* parameter specifies the size of the buffer.

The *wFlags* parameter is unused and should be zero.

The return value is zero if the function is successful; otherwise, the return value specifies an error code.

Changing the I/O
Buffer Size For example, the following code fragment opens a file named "SAMPLE.TXT" for unbuffered I/O, and then enables buffered I/O with an internal 16K buffer:

```
HMMIO hFile;
.
.
.
if ((hFile = mmioOpen("SAMPLE.TXT", NULL, MMIO_READ)) != NULL) {
    /* File opened successfully; request an I/O buffer */
    if (mmioSetBuffer(hFile, NULL, 16384L, 0))
        /* Buffer cannot be allocated */
    else
        /* Buffer allocated successfully */
}

else
    /* File cannot be opened */
```

Supplying Your Own I/O Buffer

You can also use **mmioSetBuffer** to supply your own buffer for use as a memory file. For details on using memory files, see "Performing File I/O on Memory Files," later in this chapter.

Working with RIFF Files

The preferred format for multimedia files is the Resource Interchange File Format (RIFF). The RIFF format is a tagged-file structure, and is described in detail in the file formats chapter in the *Programmer's Reference*.

The Multimedia file I/O services provide the following functions to support file I/O to RIFF files:

mmioAscend
Ascends out of a RIFF file chunk to the next chunk in the file.

mmioCreateChunk
Creates a new chunk in a RIFF file.

mmioDescend
Descends into a RIFF file chunk beginning at the current file position, or searches for a specified chunk.

mmioFOURCC
Converts four individual characters into a four-character code.

mmioStringToFOURCC
Converts a null-terminated string into a four-character code.

These functions work with the basic buffered and unbuffered file I/O services— you can open, read, and write RIFF files the same as other file types.

About RIFF Files

The basic building block of a RIFF file is called a *chunk*. Each chunk consists of the following fields:

- A four-character code specifying the chunk ID

- A DWORD specifying the size of the data field in the chunk

- A data field

The only chunks allowed to contain other chunks (subchunks) are those with a chunk ID of "RIFF" or "LIST". The first chunk in a RIFF file must be a "RIFF" chunk. All other chunks in the file are subchunks of the "RIFF" chunk.

"RIFF" Chunks

"RIFF" chunks include an additional field in the first four bytes of the data field. This additional field provides the form type of the field. The *form type* is a four-character code identifying the format of the data stored in the file. For example, Microsoft waveform audio files (WAVE files) have a form type of "WAVE". The following illustration shows a "RIFF" chunk containing two subchunks:

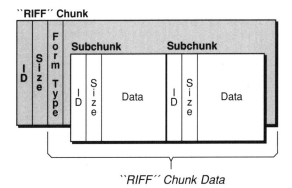

A "RIFF" chunk containing two subchunks.

"LIST" Chunks

"LIST" chunks also include an additional field in the first four bytes of the data field. This additional field contains the list type of the field. The *list type* is a four-character code identifying the contents of the list. For example, a "LIST" chunk with a list type of "INFO" can contain "ICOP" and "ICRD" chunks providing copyright and creation date information. The following illustration shows a "RIFF" chunk containing a "LIST" chunk and one other subchunk (the "LIST" chunk contains two subchunks):

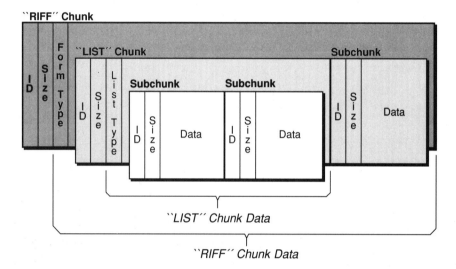

A "RIFF" chunk containing a "LIST" subchunk.

The MMCKINFO Structure

Several Multimedia file I/O functions use the MMCKINFO structure to specify and retrieve information about RIFF chunks. The MMSYSTEM.H header file defines the MMCKINFO structure as follows:

```
typedef struct _MMCKINFO
{
    FOURCC    ckid;           // chunk ID
    DWORD     cksize;         // chunk size
    FOURCC    fccType;        // form type or list type
    DWORD     dwDataOffset;   // offset of data portion of chunk
    DWORD     dwFlags;        // flags
} MMCKINFO;
```

Generating Four-Character Codes

A *four-character code* is a 32-bit quantity representing a sequence of one to four ASCII alphanumeric characters, padded on the right with blank characters. The data type for a four-character code is FOURCC. Use the **mmioFOURCC** function to convert four characters to a four-character code, as shown in the following code fragment, which generates a four-character code for "WAVE":

```
FOURCC fourccID;
  .
  .
  .
fourccID = mmioFOURCC('W', 'A', 'V', 'E');
```

To convert a null-terminated string into a four-character code, use **mmioStringToFOURCC**, as shown in the following code fragment, which also generates a four-character code for "WAVE":

```
FOURCC fourccID;
  .
  .
  .
fourccID = mmioStringToFOURCC("WAVE", 0);
```

The second parameter in **mmioStringToFOURCC** specifies options for converting the string to a four-character code. If you specify the MMIO_TOUPPER flag, **mmioStringToFOURCC** converts all alphabetic characters in the string to uppercase. This is useful when you need to specify a four-character code to identify a custom I/O procedure (four-character codes identifying file-extension names must be all uppercase).

Creating RIFF Chunks

To create a new chunk, use **mmioCreateChunk** to write a chunk header at the current position in an open file. The **mmioCreateChunk** function has the following syntax:

WORD mmioCreateChunk(*hmmio, lpmmckinfo, wFlags*)

The *hmmio* parameter specifies the file handle for an open RIFF file.

The *lpmmckinfo* parameter specifies a far pointer to an MMCKINFO structure containing information about the new chunk.

The *wFlags* parameter specifies option flags for creating the new chunk. To create a "RIFF" chunk, specify the MMIO_CREATERIFF flag. To create a "LIST" chunk, specify the MMIO_CREATELIST flag.

The return value is zero if the chunk is successfully created; otherwise, if there is an error creating the chunk, the return value specifies an error code.

Creating a "RIFF" Chunk The following example creates a new chunk with a chunk ID of "RIFF" and a form type of "RDIB":

```
HMMIO       hmmio;
MMCKINFO    mmckinfo;
 .
 .
 .
mmckinfo.fccType = mmioFOURCC('R', 'D', 'I', 'B');
mmioCreateChunk(hmmio, &mmckinfo, MMIO_CREATERIFF);
```

If you're creating a "RIFF" or "LIST" chunk, you must specify the form type in the **fccType** field of the MMCKINFO structure. In the previous example, the form type is "RDIB".

If you know the size of the data field in a new chunk, you can set the **cksize** field in the MMCKINFO structure when you create the chunk. This value will be written to the data size field in the new chunk. If this value is not correct when you call **mmioAscend** to mark the end of the chunk, it will be automatically rewritten to reflect the correct size of the data field.

After you create a new chunk using **mmioCreateChunk**, the file position is set to the data field of the chunk (8 bytes from the beginning of the chunk). If the chunk is a "RIFF" or "LIST" chunk, the file position is set to the location following the form type or list type (12 bytes from the beginning of the chunk).

Navigating RIFF Files

RIFF files consist of nested chunks of data. Multimedia file I/O services include two functions you can use to navigate between chunks in a RIFF file: **mmioAscend** and **mmioDescend**. You might think of these functions as high-level seek functions. When you *descend* into a chunk, the file position is set to the data field of the chunk (8 bytes from the beginning of the chunk). For "RIFF" and "LIST" chunks, the file position is set to the location following the form type or list type (12 bytes from the beginning of the chunk). When you *ascend* out of a chunk, the file position is set to the location following the end of the chunk.

Descending Into a Chunk

The **mmioDescend** function descends into a chunk or searches for a chunk, beginning at the current file position. The **mmioDescend** function has the following syntax:

WORD mmioDescend(*hmmio, lpck, lpckParent, wFlags*)

The *hmmio* parameter specifies the file handle for an open RIFF file.

The *lpck* parameter specifies a far pointer to an MMCKINFO structure that **mmioDescend** fills with information on the current chunk. The structure can also contain additional parameters, depending on the *wFlags* parameter.

The *lpckParent* parameter specifies a far pointer to an MMCKINFO structure describing the parent or enclosing chunk. If there is no parent chunk, this parameter should be NULL.

The *wFlags* parameter specifies options for searching for a chunk. Valid flags are MMIO_FINDCHUNK, MMIO_FINDRIFF, and MMIO_FINDLIST. If no flags are specified, **mmioDescend** descends into the chunk at the current file position.

The return value is zero if the operation is successful; otherwise, the return value specifies an error code.

The **mmioDescend** function fills an MMCKINFO structure with information on the chunk. This information includes the chunk ID, the size of the data field, and the form type, or list type if the chunk is a "RIFF" or "LIST" chunk.

Searching for a Chunk

To search for a chunk in an open RIFF file, specify the MMIO_FINDCHUNK flag in the *wFlags* parameter of **mmioDescend**. Set the **ckid** field of the MMCKINFO structure referenced by *lpck* to the four-character code of the chunk you want to search for.

If you are searching for a "RIFF" or "LIST" chunk, you don't need to set the **ckid** field of the MMCKINFO structure—**mmioDescend** sets this field for you. Set the **fccType** field to the four-character code of the form type or list type of the chunk.

Searching for a "RIFF" Chunk

The following code fragment searches for a "RIFF" chunk with a form type of "WAVE" to verify that the file that has just been opened is a WAVE waveform audio file.

```
HMMIO       hmmio;
MMCKINFO    mmckinfoParent;
MMCKINFO    mmckinfoSubchunk;
.
.
.
/* Locate a "RIFF" chunk with a "WAVE" form type
 * to make sure the file is a WAVE file
 */
mmckinfoParent.fccType = mmioFOURCC('W', 'A', 'V', 'E');
if (mmioDescend(hmmio, (LPMMCKINFO) &mmckinfoParent, NULL, MMIO_FINDRIFF))
    /* The file is not a WAVE file. */
else
    /* The file is a WAVE file */
```

If the chunk you are searching for is a subchunk enclosed by a parent chunk (as are all chunks other than "RIFF" chunks), you should identify the parent chunk with the *lpckParent* parameter. In this case, **mmioDescend** will only search within the specified parent chunk.

Searching for a Subchunk

The following code fragment searches for the "fmt " chunk in the "RIFF" chunk descended into by the previous example:

```
/* Find the format chunk (form type "fmt "); it should be
 * a subchunk of the "RIFF" parent chunk
 */
mmckinfoSubchunk.ckid = mmioFOURCC('f', 'm', 't', ' ');
if (mmioDescend(hmmio, &mmckinfoSubchunk, &mmckinfoParent, MMIO_FINDCHUNK))
    /* Error, cannot find the "fmt " chunk */
else
    /* "fmt " chunk found */
```

If you do not specify a parent chunk, the current file position should be at the beginning of a chunk before you call **mmioDescend** to search for a chunk. If you do specify a parent chunk, the current file position can be anywhere in the parent chunk.

If the search for a subchunk fails, the current file position is undefined. You can use **mmioSeek** and the **dwDataOffset** field of the MMCKINFO structure for the enclosing parent chunk to seek back to the beginning of the parent chunk, as in the following example:

```
mmioSeek(hmmio, mmckinfoParent.dwDataOffset + 4, SEEK_SET);
```

Since the **dwDataOffset** field specifies the offset to the beginning of the data portion of the chunk, you must seek four bytes past **dwDataOffset** to set the file position to be after the form type.

Ascending Out of a Chunk

After you descend into a chunk and read the data in the chunk, you can move the file position to the beginning of the next chunk by ascending out of the chunk by using the **mmioAscend** function. The **mmioAscend** function has the following syntax:

WORD mmioAscend(*hmmio, lpck, wFlags*)

The *hmmio* parameter specifies the file handle for an open RIFF file.

The *lpck* parameter specifies a far pointer to an MMCKINFO structure identifying a chunk. The function ascends to the location following the end of this chunk.

The *wFlags* parameter is not used and should be set to zero.

The return value is zero if the operation is successful; otherwise, the return value specifies an error code.

Ascending Out of a Subchunk   For example, the following statement ascends out of the "fmt " subchunk descended into by the previous example, illustrating searching for a subchunk:

```
/* Ascend out of the "fmt " subchunk
 */
mmioAscend(hmmio, &mmckinfoSubchunk, 0);
```

Example of RIFF File I/O

The following code fragment shows how to open a RIFF file for buffered I/O, as well as how to descend, ascend, and read RIFF chunks.

```c
/* ReversePlay--Plays a WAVE waveform audio file backwards
 */
void ReversePlay()
{
    char        szFileName[128];        // filename of file to open
    HMMIO       hmmio;                   // file handle for open file
    MMCKINFO    mmckinfoParent;          // parent chunk information structure
    MMCKINFO    mmckinfoSubchunk;        // subchunk information structure
    DWORD       dwFmtSize;               // size of "fmt " chunk
    DWORD       dwDataSize;              // size of "data" chunk
    WAVEFORMAT  *pFormat;                // pointer to memory for "fmt " chunk
    HPSTR       lpData;                  // pointer to memory for "data" chunk
    ...

    /* Get the filename from the edit control
     */
    ...

    /* Open the given file for reading with buffered I/O
     * using the default internal buffer
     */
    if(!(hmmio = mmioOpen(szFileName, NULL, MMIO_READ | MMIO_ALLOCBUF))){
        Error("Failed to open file.");
        return;
    }

    /* Locate a "RIFF" chunk with a "WAVE" form type
     * to make sure the file is a WAVE file
     */
    mmckinfoParent.fccType = mmioFOURCC('W', 'A', 'V', 'E');
    if (mmioDescend(hmmio, (LPMMCKINFO) &mmckinfoParent, NULL,
                MMIO_FINDRIFF)){
        Error("This is not a WAVE file.");
        mmioClose(hmmio, 0);
        return;
    }
```

```
/* Find the "fmt " chunk (form type "fmt "); it must be
 * a subchunk of the "RIFF" parent chunk
 */
mmckinfoSubchunk.ckid = mmioFOURCC('f', 'm', 't', ' ');
if (mmioDescend(hmmio, &mmckinfoSubchunk, &mmckinfoParent,
                MMIO_FINDCHUNK)){
    Error("WAVE file has no "fmt " chunk.");
    mmioClose(hmmio, 0);
    return;
}

/* Get the size of the "fmt " chunk--allocate and lock memory for it
 */
dwFmtSize = mmckinfoSubchunk.cksize;
...

/* Read the "fmt " chunk
 */
if (mmioRead(hmmio, (HPSTR) pFormat, dwFmtSize) != dwFmtSize){
    Error("Failed to read format chunk.");
    ...
    mmioClose(hmmio, 0);
    return;
}

/* Ascend out of the "fmt " subchunk
 */
mmioAscend(hmmio, &mmckinfoSubchunk 0);

/* Find the data subchunk. The current file position should be at the
 * beginning of the data chunk, however, you should not make this
 * assumption--use mmioDescend to locate the data chunk.
 */
mmckinfoSubchunk.ckid = mmioFOURCC('d', 'a', 't', 'a');
if (mmioDescend(hmmio, &mmckinfoSubchunk, &mmckinfoParent,
                MMIO_FINDCHUNK)){
    Error("WAVE file has no data chunk.");
    ...
    mmioClose(hmmio, 0);
    return;
}
```

```
/* Get the size of the data subchunk
 */
dwDataSize = mmckinfoSubchunk.cksize;
if (dwDataSize == 0L){
    Error("The data chunk contains no data.");
    ...
    mmioClose(hmmio, 0);
    return;
}

/* Open a waveform output device
 */
...

/* Allocate and lock memory for the waveform data
 */
...

/* Read the waveform data subchunk
 */
if(mmioRead(hmmio, (HPSTR) lpData, dwDataSize) != dwDataSize){
    Error("Failed to read data chunk.");
    ...
    mmioClose(hmmio, 0);
    return;
}

/* Close the file
 */
mmioClose(hmmio, 0);

/* Reverse the sound and play it
 */
...

}
```

The MMIOINFO Structure

The Multimedia file I/O manager uses the MMIOINFO data structure to maintain state information on an open file. The MMIOINFO data structure is defined in the MMSYSTEM.H header file as follows:

```
typedef struct _MMIOINFO
{
    /* general fields */
    DWORD       dwFlags;        // general status flags
    FOURCC      fccIOProc;      // ptr. to I/O procedure
    LPMMIOPROC  pIOProc;        // ptr. to I/O procedure
    WORD        wErrorRet;      // location for error to be returned
    WORD        wReserved;      // reserved for structure alignment

    /* fields maintained by MMIO functions during buffered I/O */
    LONG        cchBuffer;      // size of I/O buffer (or 0L)
    HPSTR       pchBuffer;      // start of I/O buffer (or NULL)
    HPSTR       pchNext;        // ptr. to next byte to read/write
    HPSTR       pchEndRead;     // ptr. to last valid byte to read
    HPSTR       pchEndWrite;    // ptr. to last available byte to write
    LONG        lBufOffset;     // disk offset of start of buffer

    /* fields maintained by I/O procedure */
    LONG        lDiskOffset;    // disk offset of next read/write
    DWORD       adwInfo[3];     // data specific to MMIOPROC type

    /* other fields maintained by MMIO */
    DWORD       dwReserved1;    // reserved for internal use
    DWORD       dwReserved2;    // reserved for internal use
    HMMIO       hmmio;          // handle to open file
} MMIOINFO;
```

For more information and examples using the MMIOINFO structure, see "Directly Accessing a File I/O Buffer," "Performing I/O on Memory Files," and "Using Custom I/O Procedures," all later in this chapter.

Directly Accessing a File I/O Buffer

Applications that are performance sensitive, such as applications that must stream data in real time from a CD-ROM, can optimize file I/O performance by directly accessing the file I/O buffer. Care should be exercised if you choose to do this—by accessing the file I/O buffer directly, you bypass some of the safeguards and error checking provided by the file I/O manager.

The Multimedia file I/O services provide the following functions to support direct I/O buffer access:

mmioAdvance
Fills and/or flushes the I/O buffer of a file set up for direct I/O buffer access.

mmioGetInfo
Retrieves information on the file I/O buffer of a file opened for buffered I/O.

mmioSetInfo
Changes information on the file I/O buffer of a file opened for buffered I/O.

To directly access a file I/O buffer, open the file for buffered I/O, as described in "Performing Buffered File I/O," earlier in this chapter. You can use the internal file I/O buffer or supply your own buffer with **mmioSetBuffer**.

Getting Information on the File I/O Buffer

Use the **mmioGetInfo** function to get information on a file I/O buffer, such as the buffer size and address. The **mmioGetInfo** function has the following syntax:

WORD mmioGetInfo(*hmmio, lpmmioinfo, wFlags*)

The *hmmio* parameter specifies the file handle for an open file.

The *lpmmioinfo* parameter specifies a far pointer to a MMIOINFO structure that **mmioGetInfo** fills with information on the file I/O buffer.

The *wFlags* parameter specifies options for the operation. Currently, there are no options for **mmioGetInfo**.

The return value is zero if the operation is successful; otherwise, the return value specifies an error code.

Reading and Writing the File I/O Buffer

There are three fields in the MMIOINFO structure used for reading and writing the file I/O buffer: **pchNext**, **pchEndRead**, and **pchEndWrite**. The **pchNext** field points to the next location in the buffer to read or write. You must increment **pchNext** as you read and write the buffer. The **pchEndRead** field identifies the last valid character you can read from the buffer. Likewise, **pchEndWrite** identifies the last location in the buffer you can write. To be precise, both **pchEndRead** and **pchEndWrite** point to the memory location *following* the last valid data in the buffer.

Advancing the File I/O Buffer

When you reach the end of the file I/O buffer, you must *advance* the buffer to fill it from the disk (if you are reading), and flush it to the disk (if you are writing). Use the **mmioAdvance** function to advance a file I/O buffer. The **mmioAdvance** function has the following syntax:

WORD mmioAdvance(*hmmio, lpmmioinfo, wFlags*)

The *hmmio* parameter specifies the file handle for a file opened for buffered I/O.

The *lpmmioinfo* parameter specifies a far pointer to an MMIOINFO structure containing information on the I/O buffer for the file.

The *wFlags* parameter specifies options for the operation. To fill an I/O buffer, use the MMIO_READ flag. To flush an I/O buffer, use the MMIO_WRITE flag. To flush the current buffer and fill it with more data from the file, use both flags.

The return value is zero if the operation is successful; otherwise, the return value specifies an error code.

The following illustrations show how the file I/O buffer is advanced as a file is read or written.

The application opens the file for buffered I/O. The buffer is initially empty, so **mmioOpen** sets **pchNext** and **pchEndRead** to point to the beginning of the file I/O buffer.

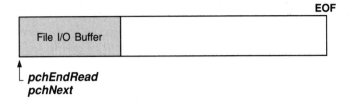

The application calls **mmioAdvance** to fill the I/O buffer. **mmioAdvance** fills the buffer and sets **pchEndRead** to point to the end of the buffer.

The application reads from the I/O buffer and increments **pchNext**.

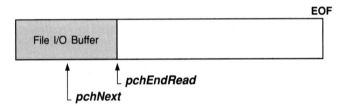

The application continues to read the buffer and call **mmioAdvance** to refill the buffer when it's empty. When **mmioAdvance** reaches the end of the file, there is not enough information to fill the buffer. **mmioAdvance** sets **pchEndRead** to point to the end of valid data in the buffer.

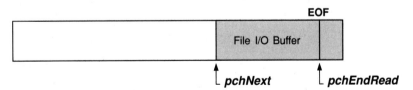

Advancing a file I/O buffer for reading.

The application opens the file for buffered I/O. **mmioOpen** sets **pchNext** to point to the beginning of the file I/O buffer and **pchEndWrite** to point to the end of the buffer.

The application writes to the I/O buffer and increments **pchNext**.

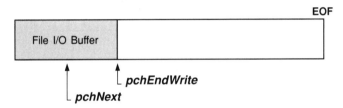

Once the application fills the buffer, it calls **mmioAdvance** to flush the buffer to disk. **mmioAdvance** resets **pchNext** to point to the beginning of the buffer.

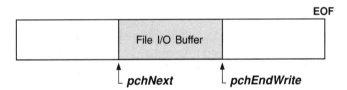

The application continues to write to the buffer and call **mmioAdvance** to flush the buffer when it's full. At the end of the file, there is not enough information to fill the buffer. When the application calls **mmioAdvance** to flush the buffer, **pchNext** points to the end of valid data in the buffer.

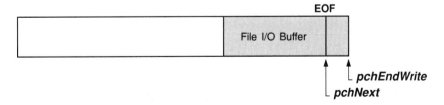

Advancing a file I/O buffer for writing.

Using the mmioAdvance Function

To fill a file I/O buffer from disk, call **mmioAdvance** with the MMIO_READ flag. If there is not enough data remaining in the file to fill the buffer, the **pchEndRead** field in the MMIOINFO structure points to the location following the last valid byte in the buffer.

To flush a buffer to disk, first set the MMIO_DIRTY flag in the **dwFlags** field of the MMIOINFO structure. Then call **mmioAdvance** with the MMIO_WRITE flag.

Example of Accessing a File I/O Buffer

The following code fragment is based on the ReversePlay example function discussed in "Example of RIFF File I/O," earlier in this chapter. In this example, direct-buffer access is used to read waveform data from a file.

```
HMMIO        hmmio;
MMIOINFO     mmioinfo;
DWORD        dwDataSize;
DWORD        dwCount;
HPSTR        hptr;
    .
    .
    .


/* Get information on the file I/O buffer.
 */
if (mmioGetInfo(hmmio, &mmioinfo, 0))
{
    Error("Failed to get I/O buffer info.");
    ...
    mmioClose(hmmio, 0);
    return;
}

/* Read the entire file by directly reading the file I/O buffer.
 * When the end of the I/O buffer is reached, advance the buffer.
 */
for (dwCount = dwDataSize, hptr = lpData; dwCount  0; dwCount--)
{
    /* Check to see if the I/O buffer must be advanced.
     */
    if (mmioinfo.pchNext == mmioinfo.pchEndRead){
        if(mmioAdvance(hmmio, &mmioinfo, MMIO_READ)){
            Error("Failed to advance buffer.");
            ...
            mmioClose(hmmio, 0);
```

```
            return;
        }
    }

    /* Get a character from the buffer.
     */
    *hptr++ = *mmioinfo.pchNext++;
}

/* End direct buffer access and close the file.
 */
mmioSetInfo(hmmio, &mmioinfo, 0);
mmioClose(hmmio, 0);
```

Ending Direct Access of a File I/O Buffer

When you finish accessing a file I/O buffer, pass the MMIOINFO structure filled
by **mmioGetInfo** to **mmioSetInfo** to terminate direct-buffer access. If you wrote
to the buffer, set the MMIO_DIRTY flag in the **dwFlags** field of the MMIOINFO
structure before calling **mmioSetInfo**. Otherwise, the buffer will not be flushed
to disk.

Performing File I/O on Memory Files

The Multimedia file I/O services let you to treat a block of memory as a file.
This can be useful if you already have a file image in memory. Memory files
let you reduce the number of special-case conditions in your code because, for
I/O purposes, you can treat file memory images as if they were disk-based files.
You can also use memory files with the Clipboard.

Opening Memory Files

Like I/O buffers, memory files can use memory allocated by the application or by
the file I/O manager. In addition, memory files can be either expandable or
non-expandable. When the file I/O manager reaches the end of an expandable
memory file, it expands the memory file by a predefined increment.

To open a memory file, use **mmioOpen** with the *szFileName* parameter set to
NULL and the MMIO_READWRITE flag set in the *dwOpenFlags* parameter. Set
the *lpmmioinfo* parameter to point to an MMIOINFO structure as follows:

- Set the **pIOProc** field to NULL.

- Set the **fccIOProc** field to FOURCC_MEM.

- Set the **pchBuffer** field to point to the memory block. To request that the file I/O manager allocate the memory block, set **pchBuffer** to NULL.

- Set the **cchBuffer** field to the initial size of the memory block.

- Set the **adwInfo[0]** field to the minimum expansion size of the memory block. For a non-expandable memory file, set **adwInfo[0]** to NULL.

- Set all other fields to zero.

Allocating Memory for Memory Files

There are no restrictions on allocating memory for use as a non-expandable memory file. You can use static memory or stack memory, or you can use locally allocated or globally allocated memory. For expandable memory files, you must use memory allocated using **GlobalAlloc** and locked using **GlobalLock**.

Using Custom I/O Procedures

Multimedia file I/O services use I/O procedures to handle the physical input and output associated with reading and writing to different types of storage systems, such as file-archival systems and database-storage systems. There are predefined I/O procedures for standard MS-DOS files and for memory files. In the future, there will be a predefined I/O procedure for accessing elements of *compound files*. Compound files consist of a number of individual files, called *file elements*, bound together in one physical file.

You can supply a custom I/O procedure for accessing a unique storage system such as a database or file archive. This I/O procedure can be private to your application or it can be shared with other applications.

The Multimedia file I/O services provide the following functions to support custom I/O procedures:

mmioInstallIOProc
  Installs, removes, or locates an I/O procedure.

mmioSendMessage
  Sends a custom message to the I/O procedure associated with a file.

Opening a File Using a Custom I/O Procedure

Before learning about how to write an I/O procedure, it's helpful to understand how to use one. To open a file using a custom I/O procedure, use **mmioOpen** as you would to open any other file. Use a plus sign (+) in the filename to separate the name of the physical file from the name of the element of the file you want to open. For example, the following statement opens a file element named "element" from a file named "filename.arc":

```
mmioOpen("filename.arc+element", NULL, MMIO_READ);
```

When the file I/O manager encounters an plus sign in a filename, it looks at the preceding filename extension to determine which I/O procedure to associate with the file. In the previous example, the file I/O manager will attempt to use the I/O procedure associated with the .ARC filename extension. If no I/O procedure is installed, the **mmioOpen** function returns an error.

Writing an I/O Procedure

An I/O procedure is a message-processing function supplied by an application. An I/O procedure function has the following syntax:

LONG FAR PASCAL IOProc(*lpmmioinfo, wMsg, lParam1, lParam2*)

The *lpmmioinfo* parameter specifies a pointer to an MMIOINFO structure associated with the file being accessed.

The *wMsg* parameter specifies the message being sent by the file I/O manager to the I/O procedure.

The *lParam1* parameter specifies 32 bits of message-dependent information.

The *lParam2* parameter specifies 32 bits of message-dependent information.

The return value is message-dependent. If the I/O procedure does not recognize a message, it should return zero.

I/O Procedure Messages

I/O procedures must respond to the MMIOM_CLOSE, MMIOM_OPEN, MMIOM_READ, MMIOM_WRITE, and MMIOM_SEEK messages. Each of these messages has two parameters. For details about these messages and their parameters, see the *Programmer's Reference*.

You can also create custom messages and send them to your I/O procedure using the **mmioSendMessage** function. If you define your own messages, be sure they are defined at or above the MMIOM_USER message. For example, the following code fragment defines a message named MMIOM_MYMESSAGE:

```
#define MMIOM_MYMESSAGE    MMIOM_USER + 0
```

Using the MMIOINFO Structure

In addition to processing messages, an I/O procedure must maintain the **lDiskOffset** field in the MMIOINFO structure referenced by the *lpmmioinfo* parameter. The **lDiskOffset** field must always contain the file offset to the location that the next MMIOM_READ or MMIOM_WRITE message will access. The offset is specified in bytes and is relative to the beginning of the file. The I/O procedure can use the **adwInfo[]** field to maintain any required state information. The I/O procedure should not modify any other fields in the MMIOINFO structure.

Installing an I/O Procedure

Use **mmioInstallIOProc** to install, remove, or locate an I/O procedure. The **mmioInstallIOProc** function has the following syntax:

LPMMIOPROC mmioInstallIOProc(*fccIOProc*, *pIOProc*, *dwFlags*)

The *fccIOProc* parameter specifies the filename extension associated with the I/O procedure. Use a four-character code to specify the extension. All characters in the four-character code must be uppercase characters.

The *pIOProc* parameter specifies a far pointer to the I/O procedure being installed. If the I/O procedure resides in the application (rather than being in a DLL), use **MakeProcInstance** to get a procedure-instance address and specify this address for *pIOProc*. If you are removing or locating an I/O procedure, *pIOProc* should be NULL.

The *dwFlags* parameter specifies whether to install, remove, or locate the specified I/O procedure. Specify one of the following flags for *dwFlags*: MMIO_INSTALLPROC, MMIO_REMOVEPROC, or MMIO_FINDPROC.

The return value is the address of the I/O procedure installed, removed, or located. If there is an error, the return value is NULL.

For example, to install an I/O procedure associated with the filename extension "ARC", use the following statement:

```
mmioInstallIOProc (mmioFOURCC('A', 'R', 'C', ' '),
                   (LPMMIOPROC)lpmmioproc, MMIO_INSTALLPROC);
```

Note Be sure to remove any I/O procedures you've installed before exiting your application.

Installing an I/O Procedure Using mmioOpen

When you install an I/O procedure using **mmioInstallIOProc**, the procedure remains installed until you remove it. The I/O procedure will be used for any file you open if the file has the appropriate filename extension. You can also temporarily install an I/O procedure using **mmioOpen**. In this case, the I/O procedure is only used with a file opened by **mmioOpen** and is removed when the file is closed using **mmioClose**.

To specify an I/O procedure when you open a file using **mmioOpen**, use the *lpmmioinfo* parameter to reference an MMIOINFO structure as follows:

- Set the **fccIOProc** field to NULL.

- Set the **pIOProc** field to the procedure-instance address of the I/O procedure.

- Set all other fields to zero (unless you are opening a memory file, or directly reading or writing to the file I/O buffer).

Sharing an I/O Procedure with Other Applications

To share an I/O procedure with other applications, follow these guidelines:

- Put the code for the I/O procedure in a dynamic-link library (DLL).

- Create a function in the DLL that calls **mmioInstallIOProc** to install the I/O procedure.

- Export this function in the module-definitions file of the DLL.

To use the shared I/O procedure, an application must first call the function in the DLL to install the I/O procedure.

A p p e n d i x
Writing Screen Savers

Windows with Multimedia provides special applications called *screen savers* that start when the mouse and keyboard have been idle for a period of time. Screen savers exist for two main reasons:

- To avoid phosphor burn on a display caused by static images.

- To conceal sensitive information left on a display.

Clearing a display addresses both goals, but screen savers are not restricted to this simple use. They can also display animated sequences such as a fish tank or fireworks. For animated sequences, there's just one rule of thumb: to avoid phosphor burn, keep changing the image.

Windows with Multimedia provides a program that monitors the mouse and keyboard and starts the screen saver after a period of inactivity. Also, the Control Panel includes a Screen Saver applet that allows you to select from a series of screen savers, as well as allowing you to enable or disable the screen-saver feature and specify the time period before which the screen saver is started. The applet also allows you to configure and preview screen savers.

The screen-saver feature is extensible. This chapter describes how to create a custom screen saver and add it to the library of screen savers you can select through the Screen Saver applet.

About Screen Savers

Screen savers are Windows applications that contain specific variable declarations, exported functions and resource definitions. The MDK provides a static-link library, SCRNSAVE.LIB, that contains the **WinMain** function and other startup code required for a screen saver. To create a screen saver, you create a source module containing specific function and variable definitions and link it with SCRNSAVE.LIB. Your screen saver module is responsible only for configuring itself and for providing the visual and/or audio effects that comprise the screen-saving activity.

A Windows application, SCRNSVR.EXE, is loaded automatically when Windows is started or when the user activates the screen-saver feature using the Screen Saver applet. Using a Windows hook, SCRNSVR.EXE monitors keystrokes and mouse movements and starts the screen saver after a period of inactivity or when the user double-clicks the desktop using the right mouse button.

SCRNSVR.EXE does not start the screen saver if any of the following conditions are present:

- The currently active application is a non-Windows (MS-DOS) application.

- A computer-based training (CBT) window is present.

- The currently active application returns a non-zero value in response to the WM_SYSCOMMAND message sent with the SC_SCREENSAVE identifier.

Window Class Registration
When your screen saver starts, the startup code in SCRNSAVE.LIB creates a full-screen window. The window class for the screen-saver window is declared as follows:

```
WNDCLASS cls;

    cls.lpfnWndProc   = ScreenSaverProc;                        // You supply
    cls.hIcon         = LoadIcon(hInst,MAKEINTATOM(ID_APP));    // You supply
    cls.lpszClassName = szAppName;                              // You supply

    cls.style         = CS_VREDRAW | CS_HREDRAW | CS_SAVEBITS | CS_DBLCLKS;
    cls.hInstance     = hInst;
    cls.cbWndExtra    = 0;
    cls.cbClsExtra    = 0;
    cls.hCursor       = NULL;
    cls.lpszMenuName  = NULL;
    cls.hbrBackground = GetStockObject(BLACK_BRUSH);
```

Your source-code module provides the **ScreenSaverProc** window procedure, as well as the **szAppName** string variable, used as the class name for the screen-saver window. Your resource-script file supplies the **ID_APP** icon.

Creating a Screen Saver

The SCRNSAVE.H header file, included on your MDK disc, defines the function prototypes for the screen-saver functions in SCRNSAVE.LIB. You must include this header file in your source module.

You must also define a global character array, **szAppName**, in your source module. The **szAppName** array should contain a screen-saver name of form **ScreenSaver.**_Name_, where _Name_ is a unique name for your screen saver. For example, the Bouncer screen saver described at the end of this appendix includes the following declaration:

```
char szAppName[] = "ScreenSaver.Bouncer";
```

The **WinMain** function in SCRNSAVE.LIB uses this variable as the class name for the screen-saver window class. If your screen saver stores configuration information, it should use the **szAppName** variable as the application heading for the configuration block in the CONTROL.INI file. For complete guidelines for storing screen-saver configuration information, see "Providing a Configuration Routine," later in this appendix.

External Handle Variables
Your application can declare the following global variables, which are defined in SCRNSAVE.LIB:

```
extern HANDLE hMainInstance;
extern HWND   hMainWindow;
```

The **hMainInstance** variable contains the instance handle for your application. The **hMainWindow** variable contains the window handle for the screen-saver window.

Processing Screen Saver Messages

Your screen-saver module must include a **ScreenSaverProc** window function to receive and process messages for the screen-saver window. Declare the **ScreenSaverProc** function as you would any window function:

```
LONG FAR PASCAL ScreenSaverProc(HWND hWnd, WORD msg, WORD wParam, LONG
lParam)
```

Your **ScreenSaverProc** function can process messages, but it must pass unprocessed messages to the **DefScreenSaverProc** function rather than to the **DefWindowProc** function.

Be sure to export the **ScreenSaverProc** function by including it in the EXPORTS section of your module definition (.DEF) file.

The following code fragment shows the **ScreenSaverProc** function for a screen saver that substitutes a gray screen for the default black screen:

```
LONG FAR PASCAL ScreenSaverProc(HWND hWnd, WORD wMsg, WORD wParam,
LONG lParam)
{
    RECT rc;

    switch(wMsg)
    {
        case WM_ERASEBKGND:
            GetClientRect(hWnd,&rc);
            FillRect(wParam,&rc,GetStockObject(GRAY_BRUSH));
            return 01;                              // Avoid default action
    }
    return DefScreenSaverProc (hWnd, wMsg, wParam, lParam);
}
```

Handling
WM_CREATE and
WM_DESTROY

The preceding screen saver does not perform any actions in response to the WM_CREATE and WM_DESTROY messages. However, you can use these messages as a cue to initialize variables and then clean up before termination.

If your window procedure traps the WM_DESTROY message, it must do one of the following to properly end the screen saver:

- After processing the message, pass it to **DefScreenSaverProc**

- In the WM_DESTROY case of the message handler, call **PostQuitMessage** to properly end the screen saver.

Your **ScreenSaverProc** function can substitute its own actions for the messages handled by **DefScreenSaverProc**. The **DefScreenSaverProc** function responds as follows to key window messages:

Message	Response
WM_ACTIVATE WM_ACTIVATEAPP	If *wParam* is FALSE, terminates the screen saver. A *wParam* value of FALSE indicates that the screen saver is losing focus.
WM_ERASEBKGND	Paints the screen background black.
WM_SETCURSOR	Removes the cursor from the screen by setting the cursor to NULL.
WM_KEYDOWN WM_MOUSEMOVE WM_LBUTTONDOWN WM_MBUTTONDOWN WM_RBUTTONDOWN	Posts a WM_CLOSE message to close the screen-saver window.
WM_DESTROY	Calls **PostQuitMessage** to terminate the screen saver.

Providing a Configuration Routine

The Screen Savers applet has a Setup button that is enabled for screen savers that support user configuration. The Screen Savers applet uses the DESCRIPTION line in your module-definition file to determine whether your screen saver supports configuration. "Creating Module-Definition and Resource Script Files," later in this chapter, describes the required format of the DESCRPTION line.

When the user chooses the Setup button, the applet starts the screen saver with a special command-line switch. There are two ways that the screen saver is started; the command-line switches for these modes are as follows:

Switch	Description
-s or **/s**	Activates the screen saver.
-c or **/c**	Displays the screen-saver configuration dialog box. The currently active dialog box is the parent for the configuration dialog box.

When the screen saver is started with the **-c** command-line switch, the **WinMain** function in SCRNSAVE.LIB displays the screen-saver configuration dialog box. For example, a screen saver called BOUNCER.EXE, started with the following command line, displays its configuration dialog box:

```
bouncer -c
```

If your screen saver supports user configuration, your source module must provide the following functions and dialog-box resource to handle configuration:

Name	Description
ScreenSaverConfigureDialog	Dialog-box function for a configuration dialog box.
RegisterDialogClasses	Function that registers any special or nonstandard window classes needed for a configuration dialog box.
SCREENSAVERCONFIGURE	Dialog-box template for a configuration dialog box, included in the resource-script file for the screen-saver application.

When the Screen Savers applet starts your screen saver with the configuration switch, the **WinMain** function in SCRNSAVE.LIB calls **RegisterDialogClasses** and then displays the configuration dialog box.

Defining Configuration Functions

Define the **ScreenSaverConfigureDialog** function as you would any dialog-box function. The Bouncer sample screen saver, included on the MDK disc, has a **ScreenSaverConfigureDialog** function that you can examine.

Your screen saver should save its configuration settings in the CONTROL.INI file. Use the **WritePrivateProfileString** and **WritePrivateProfileInt** functions to store your configuration information. Use the **szAppName** variable as your CONTROL.INI application heading.

Define the **RegisterDialogClasses** function as follows:

```
BOOL RegisterDialogClasses(HANDLE hInst)
```

The *hInst* parameter contains the instance handle for the screen saver. This is the same value contained in the **hMainInstance** global variable.

The following code fragment shows a **RegisterDialogClasses** function that registers a window class for a screen saver:

```
BOOL RegisterDialogClasses (HANDLE hInst)
{
    WNDCLASS wc;

    wc.hInstance = hInst;
        .
        .
        .
    return (RegisterClass(&wc));
}
```

If your configuration routine does not require any special window classes, your **RegisterDialogClasses** function can simply return TRUE.

Creating Module-Definition and Resource-Script Files

Be sure to export the **ScreenSaverProc** function and, if present, the **ScreenSaverConfigureDialog** function. The **RegisterDialogClasses** function is called by routines in the SCRNSAVE.LIB file, so you should *not* export it.

The DESCRIPTION line in your module-definition line must use the following format:

DESCRIPTION 'SCRNSAVE *<config-info>***:***<description>***'**

Replace *<config-info>* with a lowercase x if your screen saver does *not* support configuration; otherwise, leave *<config-info>* blank. You can replace *<description>* with a short description of your screen saver; the *<description>* text appears in the Method box of the Screen Savers dialog box.

For example, a screen saver that paints the screen gray and does not support configuration might use the following DESCRIPTION line:

```
DESCRIPTION 'SCRNSAVE x:Paint the screen gray'
```

Your resource-script (.RC) file must contain an icon resource with the **ID_APP** identifier. This icon is displayed in the Screen Savers applet window when the screen saver is selected.

Also, if your screen saver includes a configuration routine, include a dialog-box template with the **SCREENSAVERCONFIGURE** identifier.

Installing New Screen Savers

Screen savers must have a .SCR filename extension. They must reside in the Windows SYSTEM directory or in the directory where the Screen Saver applet (SSDLG.CPL) resides. The Screen Saver applet searches these two directories for files with the .SCR extension when compiling the list of available screen savers.

Using the Bouncer Sample Application

The MDK disc contains a sample screen saver called Bouncer. Bouncer bounces a small bitmap across the screen, accompanying each bounce with a sound from a waveform audio file. The NMAKE file for Bouncer allows you to build Bouncer into one of two forms:

- A screen saver applet, with .SCR extension

- A standard Windows .EXE file that includes CodeView debugging information. You can run this version from CodeView or from Program Manager.

You can use the Bouncer sample application as a template for your screen saver. Just remove the code that bounces the bitmap and substitute your own screen-saver effects. The declarations and code specific to bouncing the bitmap are clearly labeled in the source files. "Using Bouncer as a Screen Saver Template," later in this appendix, lists the specific changes you must make when converting Bouncer.

General-Purpose Declarations

Bouncer defines one variable, **szAppName**, used by routines in SCRNSAVE.LIB, as follows:

```
char szAppName[] = "ScreenSaver.Bouncer";        // Substitute your own name
```

The **szAppName** variable identifies the name of the screen saver. The name to the right of the period is a unique name for the screen saver.

Bouncer also declares the following external variables.

```
extern HANDLE    hMainInstance;
extern HWND      hMainWindow;
```

These external variables are defined in SCRNSAVE.LIB. They contain handles
to the application instance and main window.

Message Handling

The **ScreenSaverProc** for Bouncer performs the following tasks in response
to messages:

Message	Response
WM_CREATE	Loads user settings from the CONTROL.INI file; loads the bouncing bitmap resource and the waveform-audio resource that contains the bounce sound; starts a timer used to trigger the bitmap movements.
WM_TIMER	Moves the bitmap.
WM_DESTROY	Deletes the bitmap from memory; kills the timer; unlocks and frees the waveform-audio resource.

After performing these actions, Bouncer passes these messages, as well as all
unprocessed messages, to **DefScreenSaverProc**.

Configuration Dialog Box

The Bouncer screen saver includes a configuration dialog box that allows a user
to specify the following:

- Bitmap starting position

- Gravity and horizontal velocity

- Add or remove sound

- Add or remove a pause at the bottom of the screen

The Bouncer screen saver implements the configuration dialog using the
ScreenSaverConfigureDialog function. The resource-script (.RC) file for
Bouncer includes the **ScreenSaverConfigure** dialog-box template. The
configuration dialog box is displayed when the user selects the Setup button
from the Screen Saver applet.

The **ScreenSaverConfigureDialog** function saves its configuration information in CONTROL.INI. The following is a sample configuration section created by Bouncer:

```
[ScreenSaver.Bouncer]
Speed=100
xPosition=65426
yPosition=0
xVelocity=10
Gravity=3
Sound=1
Pause at bottom=1
```

The Bouncer screen saver doesn't register any special window classes for the configuration dialog box, so the **RegisterDialogClasses** function just returns TRUE.

Using Bouncer as a Screen Saver Template

To prepare Bouncer as a base for your own screen saver, make the following changes:

File	Change
BOUNCER.C	Replace code specific to displaying and moving the bitmap across the screen. All Bouncer-specific code is marked with comments.
	Change the **szAppName** string to your screen-saver name.
BOUNCER.H	Replace this file with your own header file.
BOUNCER.DEF	Change the NAME and DESCRIPTION lines to reflect the name and description of your screen saver. If your screen saver does not support configuration, put a lowercase x in front of the first colon in the DESCRIPTION line.
BOUNCER.DLG	Change the SCREENSAVERCONFIGURE dialog-box definition to match your configuration routine.
BOUNCER.RC	Change the ID_APP filename to match your icon filename.
	Remove the bitmap and waveform resource statements.

File	Change
MAIN.C	No changes required. This module is required only for the debugging (.EXE) version of your screen saver.
MAKEFILE	Change the NAME macro to the name assigned to your screen-saver source files.
	Change the windir macro to the name of the directory in which Windows is installed.

Using the NMAKE Build Options The NMAKE file for the Bouncer screen saver allows you to build a debugging .EXE file or a .SCR file for inclusion in the list of screen savers. It builds a debug version automatically; to build the finished .SCR file, use the following NMAKE command:

```
C:\MWINDEV\MMSAMPLE\BOUNCER> nmake DEBUG=NO
```

Note   Be sure to define the DEBUG macro exactly as shown above, with "NO" in all capitals.

When the DEBUG macro is undefined, your screen-saver module is linked with the MAIN.OBJ module rather than with SCRNSAVE.LIB. MAIN.C contains a **WinMain** function that replaces the **WinMain** function in SCRNSAVE.LIB. You can run this version of your screen saver under CodeView, simplifying the debugging process.

The **WinMain** function defined in MAIN.C works similarly to the **WinMain** defined in SCRNSAVE.LIB. It performs the following actions, depending on the command-line switch you use to start the program:

Switch	Action
-s or **/s**	Activates the screen saver.
-c or **/c**	Displays the screen-saver configuration dialog box.
None	Displays the screen-saver configuration dialog box and then activates the screen saver. This action differs from the standard screen-saver behavior.

The screen saver runs until you press a key or click a mouse button.

Glossary

A

ADPCM (Adaptive Differential Pulse Code Modulation)   An audio-compression technique.

animation   The display of a series of graphic images, simulating motion. Animation can be frame-based or cast-based. The Movie Player included with the Multimedia extensions uses cast-based animation.

applet   An application started from the Control Panel. Control Panel applets each configure a particular system feature; for example, printers, video drivers, or system sounds.

auxiliary audio device   Audio devices whose output is mixed with the MIDI and waveform output devices in a multimedia computer. An example of an auxiliary audio device is the compact disc audio output from a CD-ROM drive.

B

background   Images displayed behind other images in a movie. In the Movie Player, objects that appear behind other objects and objects located in lower-numbered channels in scores are all part of the background.

BitBlt (Bit Block Transfer)   The **BitBlt** function, which is part of the Windows API, copies a bitmap from a source to a destination device context.

blitting   Process of transferring a bit map from a source device context to a window client area.

break key   In MCI, a keystroke that interrupts a wait operation. By default, MCI defines this key as CTRL+BREAK. An application can redefine this key by using the MCI_BREAK command message.

C

cast   A collection of bitmaps, graphical objects, and text displayed during playback of a multimedia movie.

cast-based animation   A form of animation, also known as *object animation*, where each object involved in the presentation is an individual element with its own movement pattern, color, size, shape, and speed. A script controls the placement and movement of objects at each frame.

cast member   A single visual object drawn on a multimedia movie frame for display. A cast member can be a bitmap, text string with supporting font characteristics, or a graphical object like a line or rectangle.

CD-DA (Compact Disc-Digital Audio)   An optical data-storage format that provides for the storage of up to 73 minutes of high-quality digital-audio data on a compact disc. Also known as Red Book audio.

CD-ROM (Compact Disc-Read Only Memory)   An optical data-storage technology that allows large quantities of data to be stored on a compact disc.

CD-XA (CD-ROM Extended Architecture)   An extension of the CD-ROM standard that provides for storage of compressed audio data along with other data on a CD-ROM disc. This standard also defines the way data is read from a disc. Audio signals are combined with text and graphic data on a single track so they can be read at virtually the same time.

channel   MIDI provides a way to send messages to an individual device within a MIDI setup. There are 16 MIDI channel numbers. Devices in a MIDI setup can be directed to respond only to messages marked with a channel number specific to the device.

In the Movie Player, the score, which controls the cast members used in the animation, consists of a series of channels. Each channel can hold a cast member, a special effect such as a transition or change-tempo command, or a script command. The score is like a grid; columns represent frames, while rows represent channels. Each cell defines the behavior of one aspect of the animation for a single frame.

channel map   The MIDI Mapper provides a channel map that can redirect MIDI messages from one channel to another.

chunk   The basic building block of a RIFF file, consisting of an identifier (called a *chunk ID*), a chunk-size variable, and a chunk data area of variable size.

CLUT (Color Look-Up Table)   A palette.

command message   In MCI, a command message is a symbolic constant that represents a unique command for an MCI device. Command messages have associated data structures that provide information a device requires to carry out a request.

command string   In MCI, a command string is a null-terminated character string that represents a command for an MCI device. The text string contains all the information that an MCI device needs to carry out a request. MCI parses the text string and translates it into an equivalent command message and data structure that it then sends to a MCI device driver.

compound device   An MCI device that requires a *device element*, usually a data file. An example of a compound device is the MCI waveform-audio driver.

compound file   A number of individual files bound together in one physical file. Each individual file in a compound file can be accessed as if it were a single physical file.

control change   See MIDI control-change message.

D

default palette   See system colors.

device element   Data required for operation of MCI compound devices. The device element is generally an input or output data file.

DIB (Device-Independent Bitmap)   A Windows bitmap data structure consisting of header fields, an optional color table (palette), and bitmap data. Depending on the number of colors represented in a given bitmap, the bitmap bits can be represented in 1, 4, 8, or 24 bits, with or without a palette.

F

file element   An complete file contained in a RIFF compound file.

FM (Frequency Modulation) synthesizer
Asynthesizer that creates sounds by combining the output of digital oscillators using a frequency modulation technique.

foreground   Images displayed in front of other images in a movie. In the Movie Player, visual objects in higher-numbered score channels appear in front of objects in lower-numbered channels.

form type   A four-character code (FOURCC) identifying the type of data contained in a RIFF chunk. For example, a RIFF chunk with a form type of WAVE contains waveform audio data.

FOURCC (Four-Character Code)   A code used to identify RIFF chunks. A FOURCC is a 32-bit quantity represented as a sequence of one to four ASCII alphanumeric characters, padded on the right with blank characters.

frame   A segment of time in an animated movie.

In frame-based animation, the frame is an actual picture shown on a screen for a specified time period. Traditional motion pictures and animated cartoons, as well as old-fashioned animated flip books, use frame animation.

In cast-based animation, the frame is a time slice that defines the usage and position of cast members. There is no picture, only a collection of information defining the position and behavior of objects at a particular moment. The Movie Player uses cast-based animation.

frame-based animation   A series of screens displayed in quick succession. The changing appearance of the screens from frame to frame produces the animation.

frame hook   An application-supplied callback function that the Movie Player executes with each frame advance. The frame-hook function is passed frame and subframe numbers with one message and script-channel text with another message.

frame index   A Movie Player variable that tracks the current movie frame. The current movie frame is the one imaged in the off-screen buffer.

G

General MIDI   A synthesizer specification created by the MIDI Manufacturers Association (MMA) defining a common configuration and set of capabilities for consumer MIDI synthesizers.

H

HMS time format   A time format used by MCI to express time in hours, minutes, and seconds. The HMS time format is used primarily by videodisc devices.

I

identity palette   A 256-color palette in which the first and last 10 colors make up the system colors. The identity palette speeds up the loading of bitmaps.

IMA (International MIDI Association)
The non-profit organization that circulates information about the MIDI specification.

IMA (Interactive Multimedia Association)
A professional trade association of companies, institutions, and individuals involved in producing and using interactive multimedia technology.

ink effect   In Movie Player files, ink effects modify the way the Movie Player draws cast members to the stage. Ink effects also modify the appearance of cast members already on the stage. For example, the Transparent ink effect makes the background pixels of the cast member transparent (the background shows through the transparent pixels).

L

LIST chunk   A RIFF chunk with a chunk ID of LIST. LIST chunks contain a series of subchunks.

list type   A four-character code (FOURCC) identifying the type of data contained in a RIFF chunk with a chunk ID of LIST. For example, a LIST chunk with a list type of INFO contains a list of information about a file, such as the creation date and author.

logical palette   A Windows GDI data object that contains a list of colors needed by an application. An application can request that Windows use the colors in its logical palette (a process called *realizing the palette*).

M

Media Control Interface (MCI)   High-level control software that provides a device-independent interface to multimedia devices and media files. MCI includes a command-message interface and a command-string interface.

MIDI (Musical Instrument Digital Interface)   A standard protocol for communication between musical instruments and computers.

MIDI control-change message   A MIDI message sent to a synthesizer to change different synthesizer control settings. An example of a control-change message is the volume controller message, which changes the volume of a specific MIDI channel.

MIDI file   A file format for storing MIDI songs. In Windows with Multimedia, MIDI files have a .MID filename extension. RIFF MIDI files have a .RMI filename extension.

MIDI Mapper   Multimedia extensions software that modifies MIDI output messages and redirects them to a MIDI output device using values stored in a MIDI setup map. The MIDI Mapper can change the destination channel and output device for a message, as well as modify program-change messages, volume values, and key values.

The Control Panel includes a MIDI Mapper applet that allows a user to create and edit MIDI setup maps.

MIDI mapping   The process of translating and redirecting MIDI messages according to data defined in a MIDI map setup.

MIDI program-change message   A MIDI message sent to a synthesizer to change the patch on a specific MIDI channel.

MIDI sequence   Time-stamped MIDI data that can be played by a MIDI sequencer.

MIDI sequencer   A program that creates or plays songs stored as MIDI files. When a sequencer plays MIDI files, it sends MIDI data from the file to a MIDI synthesizer, which produces the sounds. The Multimedia extensions provide a MIDI sequencer, accessible through MCI, that plays MIDI files.

MIDI setup map   A complete set of data for the MIDI Mapper to use when redirecting MIDI messages. Only one setup map can be in effect at a given time, but the user can have several setup maps available and can choose between them using the MIDI Mapper Control Panel applet.

MIDI time code (MTC)   MIDI messages used for synchronizing MIDI sequences with external devices. The MCI MIDI sequencer does not support any type of synchronization.

MMA (MIDI Manufacturers Association)   A collective organization composed of MIDI instrument manufacturers and MIDI software companies. The MMA works with the MIDI Standard Committee to maintain the MIDI specification.

MSF time format   A time format used by MCI to express time in minutes, seconds, and frames. The number of frames in a second depends on the device type being used. Compact disc audio devices use 75 frames per second. The MSF time format is used primarily by compact disc audio devices.

movie file   A Multimedia Movie Player data file with a .MMM filename extension. The movie file contains animation objects called *cast members* and control information called the *score*. The RIFF-based file format for movie files is called the *RMMP format*.

Movie files can be created using MacroMind Director. Director files written on the Macintosh can be converted to the Movie Player format using the Multimedia Movie Convertor utility.

movie ID   A Movie Player instance identifier. When an application opens a Movie Player instance, it receives an identifier called a *movie ID*. Most Movie Player functions require the movie ID as a means of identifying the Movie Player instance.

Movie Player instance   An invocation, or copy, of the Movie Player. Each Movie Player instance can play one movie file at any given time.

MSCDEX (Microsoft Compact Disc Extensions)
A terminate-and-stay-resident (TSR) program that makes CD-ROM drives appear to MS-DOS as network drives. MSCDEX uses hardware-dependent drivers to communicate with a CD-ROM drive.

O

object animation   See cast-based animation.

off-screen buffer   A memory area that the Movie Player uses to prepare movie frames off screen before displaying them in the stage window. Preparing movie frames off screen improves animation performance.

P

palette   In Windows, a palette is a data structure defining the colors used in a bitmap image. The palette consists of a palette header and a color table consisting of a series of RGB (red, green, blue) values. Bitmap data consists of indexes into the palette table, indicating which color to use for each pixel.

patch   A particular setup of a MIDI synthesizer that results in a particular sound, usually a sound simulating a specific musical instrument. Patches are also called *programs*. A MIDI program-change message changes the patch setting in a synthesizer. Patch also refers to the connection or connections between MIDI devices.

patch caching   Some internal MIDI synthesizer device drivers can preload, or cache, their patch data. Patch caching reduces the delay between the moment that the synthesizer receives a MIDI program-change message and when it plays a note using the new patch. Patch caching also ensures that required patches are available (the synthesizer might load only a subset of its patches).

pitch scale factor   An application can request that a waveform audio driver scale the pitch by a specified factor. A scale factor of two results in a one-octave increase in pitch. Pitch scaling requires specialized hardware. The playback rate and sample rate are not changed.

playback rate scale factor   In waveform audio, an application can request that the waveform audio driver scale the playback rate by a specified factor. Playback scaling is accomplished through software; the sample rate is not changed, but the driver interpolates by skipping or synthesizing samples. For example, if the playback rate is changed by a factor of two, the driver skips every other sample.

PPQN (Parts Per Quarter Note)   A time format used for MIDI sequences. PPQN is the most common time format used with standard MIDI files.

preimaging   The process of building a movie frame in a memory buffer before it is displayed.

Q

QuickDraw objects   Macintosh graphical objects used as cast members in MacroMind Director movie files. The Movie Player supports the use of most QuickDraw objects.

R

realizing the palette   The process of mapping colors in a logical palette into the system palette. An application requests that Windows provide it the colors in a logical palette. Windows provides exact matches for as many logical-palette colors as is possible given the capabilities of the display driver. Any logical-palette colors that Windows cannot provide are mapped to colors already available in the system palette.

Red Book audio   See CD-DA.

Resolution   For bitmaps, resolution depends on the size of the pixels that make up the image. Higher-resolution bitmaps are composed of smaller pixels than lower-resolution bitmaps. The video drivers included with the Multimedia extensions support two resolution levels: 640 by 480 pixels and 320 by 240 pixels.

For joysticks, resolution refers to the minimum and maximum intervals between joystick messages sent for a captured joystick.

For timers, resolution refers to the accuracy of the timer event. A resolution value of zero means that the event must occur at the exact time requested, while a resolution value of ten means that the event must occur within ten milliseconds of the requested time.

RIFF (Resource Interchange File Format)

A tagged-file specification used to define standard formats for multimedia files. Tagged-file structure helps prevent compatibility problems that often occur when file-format definitions change over time. Because each piece of data in the file is identified by a standard header, an application that does not recognize a given data element can skip over the unknown information.

RIFF chunk   A chunk with chunk ID RIFF that includes an identifying code and zero or more sub-chunks, the contents of which depend on the form type.

RIFF file   A file whose format complies with one of the published RIFF forms.

Examples of RIFF files include WAVE files for waveform audio data, RMID files for MIDI sequences, RDIB files for bitmaps, and RMMP files for multimedia Movie Player movies.

RIFF form   A file-format specification based on the RIFF standard.

S

sample   A discrete piece of waveform data represented by a single numerical value. Sampling is the process of converting analog data to digital data by taking samples of the analog waveform at regular intervals.

sampling rate   The rate at which a waveform audio driver performs audio-to-digital or digital-to-audio conversion. For CD-DA, the sampling rate is 44.1 kHz.

score   A script that controls the activities of cast members in a movie. In MacroMind Director, the score appears as a grid into which an author can place animation commands. Grid rows are channels; columns of the grid are movie frames.

script channel   In Movie Player movies, one of the channels in the score can contain script commands. On the Macintosh, the script channel is used for Lingo script statements. Under Windows with Multimedia, the script channel can contain MCI commands, as well as user-defined commands to be interpreted by specific applications using the Movie Player.

seek   With file I/O, seek means to change the current position in the file. The current position is the location where the next read or write operation will take place. With a media device (such as a hard disk), seek means to position the media so a certain sector can be accessed. The seek involves a physical movement of the device, so the time it takes can often be perceived by the user.

sequence   See MIDI sequence.

sequencer   See MIDI sequencer.

simple device   An MCI device that does not require a device element (data file) for playback. The MCI compact-disc audio driver is an example of a simple device.

SMPTE (Society of Motion Picture and Television Engineers)   An association of engineers involved in movie, television, and video production. SMPTE also refers to SMPTE time, the timing standard that this group adopted.

SMPTE division type   One of four SMPTE timing formats. SMPTE time is expressed in hours, minutes, seconds, and frames. The SMPTE division type specifies the frames-per-second value corresponding to a given SMPTE time. For example, a SMPTE time of one hour, 30 minutes, 24 seconds, and 15 frames is useful only if the frames-per-second value, or SMPTE division type, is known.

SMPTE offset   A MIDI event that designates the SMPTE time at which playback of a MIDI file is to start. SMPTE offsets are used only with MIDI files using SMPTE division type.

SMPTE time   A standard representation of time developed for the video and film industries. SMPTE time is used with MIDI audio because many people use MIDI to score films and video. SMPTE time is an absolute time format expressed in hours, minutes, seconds, and frames. Standard SMPTE division types are 24, 25, and 30 frames per second.

square-wave synthesizer   A synthesizer that produces sound by adding square waves of various frequencies. A square wave is a rectangular waveform.

stage window   The window in which the Movie Player plays a movie. Each MMP instance can have an associated stage window.

static colors   See system colors.

streaming   The process of transferring information from a storage device, such as a hard disk or CD-ROM, to a device driver. Rather than transferring all the information in a single data copy, the information is transferred in smaller parts over a period of time, typically while the application is performing other tasks.

system colors   A collection of 20 colors that Windows sets aside for use in coloring window components (such as borders, captions, and buttons). Also known as the *static colors*.

system-exclusive data   In MIDI, messages understood only by MIDI devices from a specific manufacturer. System-exclusive data provides a way for MIDI-device manufacturers to define custom messages that can be exchanged between their MIDI devices. The standard MIDI specification defines only a framework for system-exclusive messages.

system palette   The collection of colors available on a system. These colors are shared by all Windows applications. The size of the system palette depends on the capabilities of the display driver; a 256-color device can have a system palette with up to 256 colors.

T

tagged file format   A file format in which data is tagged using standard headers that identify information type and length.

tempo   In Movie Player animation, the amount of time a frame remains on screen before being replaced by the next frame. Each movie frame can have its own tempo setting, so the playback speed can change during the movie.

With the MIDI sequencer, tempo is the speed that a MIDI file is played. It is measured in beats per minute (BPM). A typical MIDI tempo is 120 BPM.

threshold   For the joystick interface, the movement threshold is the distance in device units that the coordinates must change before the application is notified of the movement. Setting a high threshold reduces the number of joystick messages sent to your application, however, it also reduces the sensitivity of the joystick.

time stamp   With recorded MIDI data (such as MIDI files), MIDI messages are tagged with a time stamp so that a MIDI sequencer can replay the data at the proper moment.

TMSF time format   A time format used by MCI to express time in tracks, minutes, seconds, and frames. The number of frames in a second depends on the device type being used. Compact disc audio devices use 75 frames per second. The TMSF time format is used primarily by compact disc audio devices.

track   A sequence of sound on a CD-DA disc. A CD-DA track usually corresponds to a song.

With a MIDI file, information can be separated into tracks, which are defined by the creator of the MIDI file. MIDI file tracks can correspond to MIDI channels, or they can correspond to parts of a song (such as melody or chorus).

transition   In Movie Player files, the method by which one frame changes to the next. MacroMind Director provides a variety of transition effects. The author can specify the time period over which the transition occurs, as well as the number of pixels changed in each transition movement.

V

volume scalar   A component of a MIDI Mapper patch map that adjusts the volume of a patch on a synthesizer. For example, if the bass patch on a synthesizer is too loud compared to its piano patch, the volume scalar can reduce the volume for the bass or increase the volume for the piano.

Applications playing waveform audio can also adjust the output volume.

W

WAVE file   A Microsoft standard file format for storing waveform audio data. WAVE files have a .WAV filename extension.

waveform audio   A technique of recreating an audio waveform from digital samples of the waveform.

Index

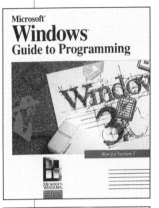

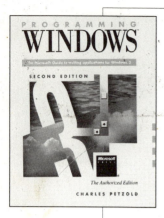

PROGRAMMING WINDOWS,™ 2nd ed.

Charles Petzold

This is *the* Microsoft-authorized guide to writing applications for Windows 3 for both new and seasoned Windows programmers. Now completely updated and revised, this thorough resource is packed with tested programming advice, scores of new sample programs, and straightforward explanations of the Microsoft Windows programming environment. New chapters detail virtual memory, multitasking, Dynamic Data Exchange (DDE), Multiple Document Interface (MDI), and Dynamic Link Library (DLL).

950 pages, softcover 7 ³/₈ x 9 ¹/₄ $29.95
Order Code: PRWI2

Contents:

Section One: A Windows backgrounder.

Section Two: Working with input from the keyboard; using the timer; using the mouse; using child window controls.

Section Three: Understanding memory management; working with icons, cursors, bitmaps, and strings; working with menus, accelerators, and dialog boxes.

Section Four: Introduction to GDI; drawing graphics; manipulating graphical information with bits and metafiles; working with text and fonts; using printers.

Section V: Dynamic Data Exchange (DDE); Multiple Document Interface (MDI); Dynamic Link Library (DLL).

Index.

Microsoft® Windows™ Multimedia Programmer's Library

(See back cover for more information)

MICROSOFT® WINDOWS™ MULTIMEDIA PROGRAMMER'S REFERENCE	MICROSOFT® WINDOWS™ MULTIMEDIA PROGRAMMER'S WORKBOOK	MICROSOFT® WINDOWS™ MULTIMEDIA AUTHORING AND TOOLS GUIDE

To order, call 1-800-MSPRESS or mail this order form:*

Quantity	Order Code	Title	Price	Total Price
_____	WIGUPR	Microsoft Windows Guide to Programming	$29.95	$_____
_____	WIPRRE	Microsoft Windows Programmer's Reference	$39.95	$_____
_____	WIPRTO	Microsoft Windows Programming Tools	$24.95	$_____
_____	PRWI2	Programming Windows, 2nd ed.	$29.95	$_____
_____	MMPRRE	Microsoft Windows Multimedia Programmer's Ref.	$27.95	$_____
_____	MMPRWO	Microsoft Windows Multimedia Programmer's Workbook	$22.95	$_____
_____	MMAUGU	Microsoft Windows Multimedia Authoring and Tools Guide	$24.95	$_____

SUBTOTAL	$_____
Sales Tax	$_____
Shipping	$_____
TOTAL	$_____

SALES TAX CHART	SHIPPING
Add the applicable sales tax for the following states: AZ, CA, CO, CT, DC, FL, GA, HI, ID, IL, IN, IA, KS, KY, ME, MD, MA, MI, MN, MO, NE, NV, NJ, NM, NY, NC, PA, OH, OK, RI, SC, TN, TX, VA, WA, WV, WI.	One book .... $2.50 Two books .... $3.25 Each additional book .... $.75

BHE

NAME _____

COMPANY (if applicable) _____

STREET (No P.O. Boxes) _____

CITY _____ STATE ___ ZIP _____

DAYTIME PHONE _____

CREDIT CARD NUMBER _____ EXP. DATE _____

CARDHOLDER SIGNATURE _____

PAYMENT:

☐ Check/Money Order (U.S. funds)

☐ **VISA** VISA (13 or 16 digits)

☐ **MasterCard** MasterCard (16 digits)

☐ **American Express** American Express (15 digits)

FOR FASTER SERVICE CALL
1-800-MSPRESS
(8AM to 5PM Central Time)
and place your credit card order. Refer to campaign **BHE**.
All orders shipped RPS or UPS.
No P.O. Boxes please. Allow 2–3 weeks for delivery.

*In Canada, contact Macmillan Canada, Attn: Microsoft Press Dept., 164 Commander Blvd., Agincourt, Ontario, Canada M1S 3C7   416-293-8141

In the U.K., contact Microsoft Press, 27 Wrights Lane, London W8 5TZ